AFRICA
CONTINENT OF CHANGE

AFRICA
CONTINENT OF CHANGE

PETER R. GOULD

WADSWORTH PUBLISHING COMPANY
BELMONT, CALIFORNIA

L.C. Cat. Card No.: 61–15839
Printed in the United States of America

That tree down there
Splendidly alone among white faded flowers
Is Africa your Africa which sprouts again
Which resprouts patiently obstinately
Whose fruits little by little acquire
The bitter savor of liberty.

  David Diop

From "Africa—To My Mother," in *Coups de Pilon,* published by Présence Africaine Publications, Paris.

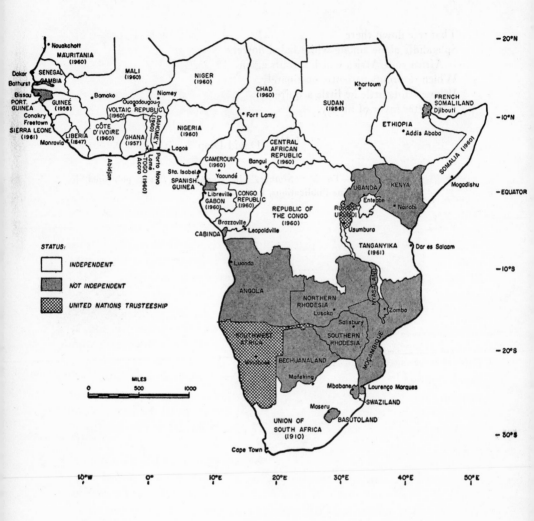

STATUS:

INDEPENDENT

NOT INDEPENDENT

UNITED NATIONS TRUSTEESHIP

MILES
0   500   1000

- 20°N
- 10°N
- EQUATOR
- 10°S
- 20°S
- 30°S

10°W   0°   10°E   20°E   30°E   40°E   50°E

Nouakchott
MAURITANIA
(1960)
Dakar
SENEGAL
Bathurst
GAMBIA
MALI
(1960)
Bamako
NIGER
(1960)
Niamey
CHAD
(1960)
Khartoum
FRENCH
SOMALILAND
Djibouti
Bissau
PORT.
GUINEA
GUINEÉ
(1958)
Ouagadougou
VOLTAIC REPUBLIC
(1960)
Fort Lamy
SUDAN
(1956)
ETHIOPIA
Addis Ababa
Conakry
Freetown
SIERRA LEONE
(1961)
Monrovia
LIBERIA
(1847)
CÔTE
D'IVOIRE
(1960)
GHANA
(1957)
NIGERIA
(1960)
SOMALIA (1960)
Abidjan
Accra
Lomé
TOGO (1960)
DAHOMEY
(1960)
Porto Novo
Lagos
CAMEROUN
(1960)
Bangui
CENTRAL
AFRICAN
REPUBLIC
(1960)
Sta. Isabel
SPANISH
GUINEA
Yaoundé
UGANDA
KENYA
Mogadishu
Libreville
GABON
(1960)
CONGO
REPUBLIC
(1960)
REPUBLIC OF
THE CONGO
(1960)
RUANDA
URUNDI
Entebbe
Nairobi
CABINDA
Brazzaville
Leopoldville
Usumbura
TANGANYIKA
(1961)
Dar es Salaam
Luanda
ANGOLA
NORTHERN
RHODESIA
NYASALAND
Lusaka
Zomba
SOUTHWEST
AFRICA
Windhoek
SOUTHERN
RHODESIA
Salisbury
MOZAMBIQUE
BECHUANALAND
Mafeking
Mbabane
Lourenço Marques
SWAZILAND
Maseru
BASUTOLAND
UNION OF
SOUTH AFRICA
(1910)
Cape Town

PREFACE

The emergence of independent African states and the spread of the cold war to the continent have forced Americans to think deeply about Africa for the first time. Until quite recently, most Americans were barely conscious of Africa—a large continent of colonial territories where little happened—and few had any idea of the ferment under the quiet surface. All that has changed. Today, Africa is seldom off the front pages of the newspapers, and all Americans are now realizing that a giant, albeit an undernourished giant, has emerged since the Second World War.

This collection of readings, selected and edited with the intelligent inquirer in mind, has been designed to give insight into *some* of the major problems facing Africa as it shrugs off its past colonial ties and faces an exciting future of political independence and grave responsibilities. The movement toward independence is yet incomplete, but few who have been watching the spark of nationalism burst into a roaring flame can doubt that a completely noncolonial Africa is not far away. But the old problems—those of cultural conflict, economic development and political stability—will remain, and the decisions that we, as Americans, are going to make concerning our relationship to the new Africa must be based upon an awareness and understanding of the difficulties the continent faces.

The book has been divided into three sections simply as a matter of convenience, for all aspects—political, economic and social—are often so closely intertwined that each molds and affects the others. We are, in a sense, looking at many of the same problems from different angles. Most of the readings are not from professional journals, although such names as Melville Herskovits, James Coleman, Kofi Busia, Pius Okigbo and Margaret Read will be familiar to all African specialists, and an attempt has been made to keep highly particular vocabulary to a minimum.

Finally, I would like to thank all the authors, publishers and editorial boards who have allowed me the privilege of including their work in this volume. Since, for reasons of space alone, some of the readings have been reduced and footnotes omitted, the reader is strongly urged to refer to the original articles, and to have the additional rewarding experience of browsing through the journals from which the articles have been taken.

Peter Gould

CONTENTS

ix

PART THREE   ✸   SOCIAL CHANGE

Part One

POLITICAL CHANGE

1   INTRODUCTION

Of all the developments taking place in Africa today, it is probably the political changes that the average person thinks about first. Almost daily, it seems, new names emerge to replace the old familiar ones on the map as colonial areas arrive at the threshold of nationhood with varying degrees of dignity or chaos. It is appropriate, therefore, to begin by taking note of some of the political problems that Africa faces, as well as the often closely related problems of our own rapidly changing relationship to these proud new countries.

The rapidity with which political developments are taking place was dramatically highlighted in 1960 by Prime Minister Harold Macmillan in a speech before the Union of South Africa Parliament. For a man versed in the ways of courtly diplomatic exchange, and for an official guest of the South African government, it is a statement honest to the point of bluntness. It is important not simply because it points out the political facts of life in the middle of the twentieth century, but because in this speech a statesman of classical education with vast experience in international affairs gives these momentous happenings a perspective that is so often lost in the day-to-day crises of modern Africa. He affirms something so obvious that it is all too easy to nod one's head in assent without thinking through the implications; namely, that nationalism is nothing new, that since Roman times new nations have been emerging, and that what is happening today in Africa is but a continuation of the growth of nationalistic feeling rooted essentially in Western civilization and its ideals.

There are many voices speaking in Africa today, and one of the strongest is that of Kwame Nkrumah, President of Ghana, the first African nation to achieve independence after the Second World War. In a fervent, emotional speech of understandable exaggeration, he voices his deep concern for Africa's future course and place in the world. That an African leader can command the respectful attention of the world at the United Nations, and suggest a permanent seat for Africa on the Security Council, is but one indica-

3

tion of the great changes that have taken place in the past decade.

One of the many questions raised by Ghana's President is the problem of *apartheid,* the deliberate policy of the South African government to separate the different races, even to the extent of creating separate areas (Bantustans) for Africans. What is apartheid, this extraordinary idea of "apartness" and separation? What are its roots, aims, and methods? The answer is given by two South Africans, Professors Rhoodie and Venter, "the apartheid idea evolved mainly from . . . fear." Just how far the idea has evolved, and what the cost has been in terms of human misery, is lucidly stated by the historian Dr. de Kiewiet, President of Rochester University. There is no end to the misery in sight, and the increasingly harsh measures applied by the police, from the Sharpeville shootings down to the petty shameful regulations that slowly eat away a man's self-respect, simply emphasize the inability of the Afrikaner to come to grips with the realities of twentieth-century Africa.

Part of the fear and frustration of the Afrikaner comes today from the very growth of nationalistic feeling outlined by Prime Minister Macmillan and epitomized by the strident call to action by Ghana's President Nkrumah. It is worthwhile, therefore, to step back from the picture for a moment and examine African nationalism with the cool, detached attitude of the political scientist. In an article that has become a classic in its field, Dr. James Coleman, Professor of Political Science and Director of the Program of African Studies at UCLA, focuses upon nationalism in an African context. He tells what nationalism means, what forces impinge upon and mold nationalist political movements, what the roots are in traditional ways, what the roles are of the tiny educated elite, and how the new and the old blend to give nationalistic movements in Africa a flavor of their own—their own "African Personality."

The blending of the new and the old, the modern and the traditional ways, can be seen in all aspects of life in Africa today. Nowhere is this blending process clearer than in many of the constitutions of newly emerged African nations—particularly those constitutions written by Africans themselves. Article 14 of Ghana's new republican constitution shows how the threads of political ideals from the East, the West and Africa itself are woven into a fabric as striking and original as the multi-hued kente cloth of the West African weavers.

One outstanding characteristic of almost all new African governments is the overwhelming dominance of one political party. Many people have viewed this development with alarm, fearing that democracy itself is placed in jeopardy where the members of the Government party outnumber the Opposition, if it exists at all, by a ratio as high as twenty to one. Julius Nyerere, Chief Minister of Tanganyika, gives a pertinent reply to critics by posing several questions: Can we expect a country that has recently channelled all its energy into the fight for independence to come up with a democratic form of government described essentially in Western terms that have themselves taken centuries to define? Or again, is democracy defined in terms of a Government and Opposition bench, in terms of Western parliamentary institutions that have been molded by the peculiar needs of the West, or is democracy essentially "government of the people" even (or especially) when nearly all the people vote for the party that has led them to independence? We should remember these questions when we read about day-to-day political developments in Africa. We should remember them not to blind ourselves to the injustices and undemocratic procedures that are virtually inevitable in a new and vigorous country, but to give us that vital perspective and understanding that is so necessary if we are going to make rational decisions about our relationship to those countries.

All too often we of the West take for granted the basic assumption upon which democratic government rests, specifically, that there is a well-informed electorate willing and able to make its will known by casting ballots. This is so obvious to us that it hardly seems worth mentioning; after all, yesterday we saw our parents vote, we vote ourselves today, and take it for granted that our children will vote tomorrow. The very notion of casting a ballot in secret seems to us the obvious and natural way of making our individual decisions felt. It is not always thus. Over much of Africa, for all its traditionally open discussion at the village level, the secret ballot, the very basis of democracy, is a new and alien thing. Some of the problems of holding an election by secret ballot in an area that has never experienced it before are brought out in a small case study of the Bo District of Sierra Leone. But remember, this sort of thing is going on all over Africa, and is a vital part of the democratic revolution sweeping the continent.

The question of our own relationship to the new countries of Africa is not an easy one to answer, and in our groping for a positive, rational policy towards Africa we have, through our Committee on Foreign Relations, called upon men with a lifetime of experience to report and recommend. There are only a few of these, and it was natural that the Committee turned to Professor Melville Herskovits, Chairman of the Program of African Studies at Northwestern University. The "Northwestern Report," as it has come to be known, is a critical review and summary of the changes and developments in Africa south of the Sahara with sound conclusions and recommendations. The latter have been criticized by some as being very broad and general rather than specific guides to policy. It should be remembered, however, that these recommendations were submitted to members of a committee whose ignorance of African affairs was admitted and some of whose views, as expressed in verbal testimony at a later date, make one wonder if we are really living in the twentieth century. The recommendations are, in fact, concrete guides to policy when compared to the apparent lack of policy we have had to put up with until quite recently. Fortunately, more and more people are becoming concerned with U.S. policy towards Africa, and it is fitting, therefore, to let the African League, a group of younger scholars deeply concerned with America's relationship to the rapidly changing continent, summarize past policy and suggest new lines of action. For as they point out:

> If our nation will have the foresight . . . to take hold of the advantages naturally ours: the echoes in Africa of the words of our own flight for independence, the vitality of an egalitarian country, our true and often misunderstood generosity, the vast humanitarian effects made possible by a technical society—we will be in a frame of mind to weigh individual decisions. So often the outcome of policy decisions depends on *when* they are made. Things change very fast in Africa, and there ought to be in our policy a steady course through caution to a willingness to make use of opportunities quickly.

2   THE WIND OF CHANGE*

Harold Macmillan

It is a great privilege to be invited to address the members of both Houses of Parliament in the Union of South Africa. It is a unique privilege to do so in 1960 just half a century after the Parlia-

* Excerpts from a speech by the Prime Minister, the Right Honourable Harold Macmillan, P.C., M.P., to both houses of the Parliament of the Union of South Africa, in Cape Town on February 3, 1960.

ment of the Union came to birth. I am most grateful to you all for giving me this opportunity and I am especially grateful to your Prime Minister who invited me to visit this country and arranged for me to address you here today. My tour of Africa, parts of Africa, the first ever made by a British Prime Minister in office is now alas nearing its end but it is fitting that it should culminate in the Union Parliament here in Cape Town, in this historic city so long Europe's gateway to the Indian Ocean, and to the East in the Union.

In the fifty years of their nationhood the people of South Africa have built a strong economy founded upon a healthy agriculture and thriving and resilient industries. During my visit I have been able to see something of your mining industry, on which the prosperity of the country is so firmly based. I have seen your Iron and Steel Corporation and visited your Council of Scientific and Industrial Research at Pretoria. These two bodies, in their different ways, are symbols of a lively, forward looking and expanding economy. I have seen the great city of Durban, with its wonderful port, and the skyscrapers of Johannesburg, standing where seventy years ago there was nothing but the open veldt. I have seen, too, the fine cities of Pretoria and Bloemfontein. This afternoon I hope to see something of your wine-growing industry, which so far I have only admired as a consumer.

Sir, as I have travelled round the Union I have found everywhere, as I expected, a deep preoccupation with what is happening in the rest of the African continent. I understand and sympathize with your interest in these events, and your anxiety about them. Ever since the break-up of the Roman Empire one of the constant facts of political life in Europe has been the emergence of independent nations. They have come into existence over the centuries in different forms, with different kinds of government, but all have been inspired by a deep, keen feeling of nationalism which has grown as the nations have grown.

In the twentieth century and especially since the end of the war the processes which gave birth to the nation states of Europe have been repeated all over the world. We have seen the awakening of national consciousness in peoples who have for centuries lived in dependence upon some other power. Fifteen years ago this movement spread through Asia. Many countries there of different races and civilizations pressed their claim to an independent national life. Today the same thing is happening in Africa and the most striking of all the impressions I have formed since I left London a month ago is of the strength of this African national consciousness. In different places it takes different forms, but it is happening every-where. *The wind of change is blowing through this continent,* and whether we like it or not this growth of national consciousness is a political fact. We must all accept it as a fact, and our national poli-cies must take account of it.

Of course you understand this better than anyone. You are sprung from Europe, the home of nationalism, and here in Africa you have yourselves created a new nation. Indeed in the history of our times yours will also be recorded as the first of the African nationalisms, and this tide of national consciousness which is now rising in Africa is a fact for which you and we and the other nations of the western world are ultimately responsible. For its causes are to be found in the achievements of western civilization, in the push-ing forward of the frontiers of knowledge, in the applying of science, in the service of human needs, in the expanding of food pro-duction, in the speeding and multiplying of the means of communi-cation, and perhaps, above all more than anything else, the spread of education.

Let me be very frank with you, my friends. What Governments and Parliaments in the United Kingdom have done since the war in according independence to India, Pakistan, Ceylon, Malaya and Ghana, and what they will do for Nigeria and other countries now nearing independence, all this though we take full and sole responsi-bility for it, we do in the belief that it is the only way to establish the future of the Commonwealth and of the Free World on sound foundations. All this of course is also of deep and close concern to you for nothing we do in this small world can be done in a corner or remain hidden. What we do today in West, Central and East Africa becomes known tomorrow to everyone in the Union what-ever his language, color or traditions. Let me assure you, in all friendliness, that we are well aware of this and that we have acted and will act with full knowledge of the responsibility we have to all our friends. Nevertheless I am sure you will agree that in our own areas of responsibility we must each do what we think right. What we think right derives from a long experience both of failure and success in the management of our own affairs.

We have tried to learn and apply the lessons of both our judg-ment of right and wrong, and our justice is rooted in the same soil as yours—in Christianity and in the rule of law as the basis of a free society. This experience of our own explains why it has been our aim in the countries for which we have borne responsibility, not only to raise the material standards of living but to create a society which respects the rights of individuals, a society in which men are given the opportunity to grow to their full stature, and that must in our view include the opportunity to have an increasing share in political power and responsibility, a society in which individual merit and individual merit alone is the criterion for a man's advancement, whether political or economic.

I have thought you would wish me to state plainly and with full candour the policy for which we in Britain stand. It may well be that in trying to do our duty as we see it we shall sometimes make difficulties for you. If this proves to be so we shall regret it. But I know that even so you would not ask us to flinch from doing our duty. You too will do your duty as you see it. I am well aware of the peculiar nature of the problems with which you are faced here in the Union of South Africa. I know the differences between your situation and that of most of the other states in Africa. You have here some three million people of European origin. This country is their home. It has been their home for many generations. They have no other.

As a fellow member of the Commonwealth it is our earnest desire to give South Africa our support and encouragement, but I hope you won't mind my saying frankly that there are some aspects of your policies which make it impossible for us to do this without being false to our own deep convictions about the political destinies of free men to which in our own territories we are trying to give effect. I think we ought as friends to face together, without seeking to apportion credit or blame, the fact that in the world of today this difference of outlook lies between us.

The fact is that in this modern world no country, not even the greatest, can live for itself alone.[1] Nearly 2000 years ago when the whole of the civilized world was comprised within the confines of the Roman Empire, St. Paul proclaimed one of the great truths of history—we are members one of another. During this twentieth century that eternal truth has taken on a new and exciting significance. It has always been impossible for the individual man to live in isolation from his fellows, in the home, the tribe, the village, or the city; today it is impossible for nations to live in isolation from one another. What Dr. John Donne said of individual men three hundred years ago is true today of my country, your country and

---

[1] What follows is particularly interesting in view of the South African decision to leave the Commonwealth on May the 31st, 1961. One is reminded very strongly of the old Boer wagon trains forming a tight *laager* (a circle of wagons for defense) and daring the world to approach another step further. Private reports from the Union would seem to indicate that the Afrikaner is more relieved than anything else at the decision to "go it alone."

all the countries of the world. "Any man's death diminishes me because I am involved in Mankind; And therefore never send to know for whom the bell tolls. It tolls for thee." All nations now are interdependent one upon another and this is generally realized throughout the western world. I hope in due course the countries of Communism will recognize it too.

I said I was speaking of the interdependence of nations. The members of the Commonwealth feel particularly strongly the value of interdependence. They are independent as any nation in this shrinking world can be, but they have voluntarily agreed to work together.

The independent members of the Commonwealth do not always agree on every subject. It is not a condition of their association that they should do so. On the contrary the strength of our Commonwealth lies largely in the fact that it is a free association of independent sovereign states, each responsible for ordering its own affairs but co-operating in the pursuit of common aims and purposes in world affairs. Moreover these differences may be transitory. In time they may be resolved. Our duty is to see them in perspective against the background of our long association. Of this at any rate I am certain, those of us who by grace of the electorate are temporarily in charge of affairs in your country and in mine, we fleeting transient phantoms in the great stage of history, we have no right to sweep aside on this account the friendship that exists between our countries, for that is the legacy of history. It is not ours alone to deal with as we wish. To adapt a famous phrase, it belongs to those who are living, but it also belongs to those who are dead and to those who are yet unborn. We must face the differences, but let us try to see beyond them down the long vista of the future.

I hope, indeed I am confident, that in another 50 years we shall look back on the differences that exist between us now as matters of historical interest, for as time passes and one generation yields to another, human problems change and fade. Let us remember these truths. Let us resolve to build, not to destroy, and let us remember always that weakness comes from division, strength from unity.

3 AFRICA IN THE WORLD FORUM*

Kwame Nkrumah

Mr. President, Distinguished Delegates:

The great tide of history flows and as it flows it carries to the shores of reality the stubborn facts of life and man's relations, one with another. One cardinal fact of our time is the momentous impact of Africa's awakening upon the modern world. The flowing tide of African nationalism sweeps everything before it and constitutes a challenge to the colonial powers to make a just restitution for the years of injustice and crime committed against our continent.

But Africa does not seek vengeance. It is against her very nature to harbour malice. Over two hundred millions of our people cry out with one voice of tremendous power—and what do we say? We do not ask for death for our oppressors; we do not pronounce wishes of ill-fate for our slave-masters; we make an assertion of a just and positive demand; our voice booms across the oceans and mountains, over the hills and valleys, in the desert places and through the vast expanse of mankind's habitation, and calls out for the freedom of Africa; Africa wants her freedom; Africa must be free. It is a simple call, but it is also a signal lighting a red warning to those who would tend to ignore it.

For years and years Africa has been the foot-stool of colonialism and imperialism, exploitation and degradation. From the North to the South, from the East to the West, her sons languished in the chains of slavery and humiliation, and Africa's exploiters and self-appointed controllers of her destiny strode across our land with incredible inhumanity without mercy, without shame, and without honour. Those days are gone and gone for ever, and now I, an African, stand before this august assembly of the United Nations

* Excerpts from a speech by the President of Ghana, Osgayefo Dr. Kwame Nkrumah, P.C., to the fifteenth session of the General Assembly of the United Nations, New York, Friday, 23rd September 1960.

and speak with a voice of peace and freedom, proclaiming to the world the dawn of a new era.

I look upon the United Nations as the only organization that holds out any hope for the future of mankind. Mr. President, Distinguished Delegates, cast your eyes across Africa: the colonialists and imperialists are still there. In this twentieth century of enlightenment, some nations still extol the vainglories of colonialism and imperialism. As long as a single foot of African soil remains under foreign domination, the world shall know no peace. The United Nations must therefore face up to its responsibilities, and ask those who would bury their heads like the proverbial ostrich in their imperialist sands, to pull their heads out and look at the blazing African sun now traveling across the sky of Africa's redemption. The United Nations must call upon all nations that have colonies in Africa to grant complete independence to the territories still under their control. In my view possession of colonies is now quite incompatible with membership in the United Nations. This is a new day in Africa and as I speak now, thirteen new African nations have taken their seats this year in this august assembly as independent sovereign states. The readiness of any people to assume responsibility for governing themselves can be determined only by themselves. I and the Government of Ghana, and I am sure the Governments and peoples of independent African states share the joy of welcoming our sister states into the family of the United Nations. There are now twenty-two of us in this Assembly and there are yet more to come.

I would suggest that when the Charter of the United Nations comes to be revised, a permanent seat should be created for Africa on the Security Council in view not only of the growing number of African members of the United Nations, but also of the increasing importance of the African continent in world affairs. This suggestion applies equally to Asia and to the Middle East.

Many questions come to my mind at the moment all seeking to be dealt with at once: questions concerning the Congo, disarmament, peace, South Africa, South West Africa, China and Algeria. However, I would like to start with the question of the Congo and to take the others in their turn.

The Congo, as we all know, has been a Belgian colony for nearly a century. In all those years Belgium applied a system of calculated political castration in the hope that it would be completely impossible for African nationalists to fight for emancipation. But to the dismay of Belgium, and to the surprise of everyone outside the

African continent, this dreaded nationalism appeared and within a lightning space of time, secured the independence of the Congo.

The policy of political frustration by the Belgian colonial regime created a situation in which the Belgian administration was unable to continue while at the same time no Congolese had been trained to take over and run the state. The struggle for independence in the Congo is the shortest so far recorded, and the Belgians were so overtaken by events that they pulled out but fully expected to return in one way or another. The high positions in the army, the police and the public services have been the exclusive preserves of the Belgians. No African could hope to rise to the lowest commissioned rank in the army. The whole of the Force Publique was subject to extremely harsh discipline and had very low rates of pay. This situation made it impossible to build up a cadre of indigenous personnel to man the services. As soon as an African became Minister of Defence, the incongruous position of the African in the Force Publique became evident.

The Congo Government called for aid. Congo asked Ghana for help and also wisely called in the United Nations. From this point, Distinguished Delegates, you are more than conversant with the story and there is no need for me to dwell in detail on the facts.

It is only necessary to say that something has happened in the Congo which has justified my constant warning to the African countries to be on their guard against what I call clientele-sovereignty, or fake independence, namely, the practice of granting a sort of independence by the metropolitan power, with the concealed intention of making the liberated country a client-state and controlling it effectively by means other than political ones. What has happened in the Congo has more than justified my daily condemnation of neo-colonialism, the process of handing independence over to the African people with one hand only to take it away with the other hand.

The Congo question is a test case for Africa. What is happening in the Congo today may happen in any other part of Africa tomorrow, and what the United Nations does today must set a precedent for what it may have to do tomorrow. The United Nations will be judged by the success or failure of its handling of this Congo situation.

Having dwelt . . . on the Congo situation, which is only natural in view of its gravity, I now wish, Mr. President and Distinguished Delegates, to turn to other matters . . . to the question of South West Africa. Although opinions delivered by the International Court show that South West Africa is strictly not a

Trust Territory, there can be no doubt whatever that the United Nations, as the successor of the League of Nations, has a particular responsibility towards South West Africa.

In a report made to the General Assembly last year by the Committee on South West Africa, and approved by the General Assembly, the Committee stated that the policy of Apartheid as practised in South West Africa "is a flagrant violation of the sacred trust which permeates the mandate and the Charter of the United Nations and the universal Declaration of Human Rights."

For thirteen years now the Union of South Africa has consistently disregarded the requests of the United Nations in regard to South West Africa. The Union imposes the most harsh and degrading regime upon the inhabitants which is not in any way in accord with the provisions of the Mandate. There is a duty on the United Nations to enforce the Mandate and the United Nations must not fail in this duty.

Mr. President, in this connection, I wish to make the following positive proposal. The Union of South Africa should be asked to surrender the mandate to the United Nations and a Committee of all the Independent African States should be set up to administer the territory on behalf of the United Nations. If the Union of South Africa is unable to accept this, then the next General Assembly of the United Nations should take steps to terminate the mandate, make the territory a trusteeship area, and appoint the Independent African States to undertake the trusteeship.

I now turn to the Union of South Africa itself. The Union Government, against all moral considerations and against every concept of human dignity, self-respect and decency has established a policy of racial discrimination and persecution which in its essential inhumanity surpasses even the brutality of the Nazis against the Jews.

The interest of humanity compels every nation to take steps against such inhuman policy and barbarity and to act in concert to eliminate it from the world.

To this end Ghana has taken the following action. We have as from the 1st August this year [1960] caused a total boycott of South African goods, closed all Ghanaian ports—sea as well as air —to South African shipping and aircraft, except in cases of distress, and have required South African citizens entering Ghana to have in their possession travel documents issued by the Ghana Government or passports with valid Ghanaian transit visas.

This action is in implementation of the unanimous resolution adopted by the Independent African States in Addis Ababa last June. Indeed, the hollow social basis of apartheid and the grievous practical harm it causes, can be judged by the gruesome massacre of defenceless men, women and children at Sharpeville in March this year by the Union police. The untenable claim of a minority in South Africa is steadily building a wall of intense hate which will result in the most violent and regrettable consequences in the future unless this minority abandons the iniquitous racial policy which it pursues.

I now turn to the question of the Portuguese Colonies in Africa. Portugal, a member of the North Atlantic Treaty Organization, has by her metropolitan law claimed the territories she has colonised in Africa as an integral part of Portugal. I have always emphasised that Africa is not, and can never be, an extension of Europe, and this Portuguese arrangement is repugnant to any concept of African freedom.

The NATO treaty states in the preamble the member states "are determined to safeguard the freedom, common heritage and civilizations of their peoples founded on the principles of democracy, individual liberty and the rule of law."

May I ask all members of NATO who are members of the United Nations to point out, when they come to speak in this debate, any single instance where Portugal has observed the NATO principles in regard to her colonies in Africa?

In Portuguese Africa there exists forced labour which is akin to slavery, all political freedom is denied and, though this is difficult to believe, the condition of the ordinary African is worse even than it is in the Union of South Africa. If the situation in the Portuguese territories has not yet become, as has the situation in South Africa, a threat to world peace, this is merely because the inevitable explosion has not as yet taken place.

In regard to Portugal, my view is that a particular responsibility rests on the North Atlantic Treaty Members who are also Members of the United Nations. They can bring pressure to bear on Portugal to accord the same independence to her colonies in Africa as other North Atlantic Treaty Powers have granted to their former colonial possessions.

As I have said elsewhere, the wind blowing in Africa is not an ordinary wind. It is a raging hurricane and it is impossible for Portugal or, for that matter, any other colonial power, to prevent the raging hurricane of African nationalism from blowing through oppressed and down-trodden colonies.

The problem of Africa, looked at as a whole, is a wide and diversified one. But its true solution lies in the application of one principle, namely, the right of a people to rule themselves. No compromise can affect this cardinal and fundamental principle, and the idea that when a handful of settlers acquire a living space on our continent the indigenes must lose this right is not only a serious travesty of justice, but also a woeful contradiction of the very dictates of history.

Out of a total African population of over two hundred and thirty million people, some three per cent are of non-African origin. To suppose that such a small minority could in any other continent produce acute political difficulties would be unthinkable. Yet such is the subconscious feeling of certain European settlers in Africa that to them the paramount issue in Africa is not the welfare of the ninety-seven per cent but rather the entrenchment of the rights of the three per cent of the European settler minorities in Africa.

To these minority settlers a solution seems impossible unless what they describe as "justice" is done to the foreign three per cent. Justice, they say, must be done to this group irrespective of whether it means that injustice continues to be done to the remaining inhabitants. I believe that reasonable solution can be found to the African problem which would not prejudice the minorities on the continent. No effective solution, however, can be found, if political thinking in regard to a solution begins with the rights of the three per cent and only considers the rights of the ninety-seven per cent within the framework which is acceptable to the rest.

The world must begin at last to look at African problems in the light of the needs of the African people and not only of the needs of minority settlers. Colonialism, imperialism and racialism are doomed in Africa, and the sooner the colonial powers recognise this fact the better it will be for them and the world.

4   ꙮ   WHAT IS APARTHEID?*

N. J. Rhoodie and H. J. Venter

The apartheid idea embodies not only relatively immediate and practical steps for the solution of the native question, but also an ultimate aim. In other words, idealism is an integral part of the

* From N. J. Rhoodie and H. J. Venter, *Apartheid: A Socio-Historical Exposition of the Origin and Development of the Apartheid Idea* (Capetown and Pretoria: Haum, 1960), pp. 22–37 with editorial cuts. Reprinted by permission.

apartheid idea or philosophy. As one writer correctly remarks: "To the philosophers of the movement it means the eventual separation of the races. . . . They defend their views in terms of the highest idealism."

In concrete terms this ideal means the comparatively permanent and complete separation of White and Black in South Africa. The Government, the Afrikaans churches, and most Afrikaner intellectuals who are interested in apartheid have identified themselves with this ultimate aim on numerous occasions. Shortly before the National Party came into power in 1948, it formulated its proposed policy for the solution of the native question as follows: "In their own areas the non-White racial groups will receive every opportunity to develop and they will be able to develop their own institutions and social services. . . . The policy of the country must be so formulated *that it will promote the ideal of eventual total apartheid in a natural way."*

Comparatively complete racial separation between White and Black at all points of contact is held as the ultimate aim. This can include the cultural, economic, social, political, biological and territorial spheres of contact.

The fact that the Bantu have become integrated in the country's economic structure to a significant degree, cannot simply be rejected as a political smokescreen. During the Second World War the number of Bantu in the Union's urban areas already exceeded the number of Whites.

The most important reason for this increase was the economic integration of the Bantu in the economy of the Whites—a process which started more than a hundred years ago and was given tremendous impetus by the Second World War. Supporters of apartheid are well aware of this reality, particularly of the fact that this type of integration can eventually lead to total assimilation. One of the main aims of apartheid is to prevent such a catastrophe from overtaking the Whites in this country.

Apartheid presupposes the gradual removal of the Bantu worker as an indispensable factor in the country's economy. This steady process of economic purification does not imply complete and immediate physical elimination now or at a given moment; it is a gradual process of elimination which will not affect the Union's economic balance adversely.

Supporters of apartheid all admit that the Whites will make use of Bantu labour for the foreseeable future—although to a gradually lessening degree.

The Afrikaner's aim is that those Bantu workers who are integrated in the White's economic structure should remain so only temporarily. Dr. W. W. M. Eiselen, the Secretary of the Department of Bantu Administration and Development, sums up the situation as follows: "All the Bantu have their permanent homes in the reserves and their entry into other areas . . . is merely of a temporary nature and for economic reasons. In other words, they are admitted as work-seekers, not as settlers." There must be, however, no question of complete and lasting dependence on a Black proletariat. The development of the Bantu areas is also therefore a logical result of this particular national attitude.

The ultimate configuration in the political and constructional spheres was not as clearly defined during the first decade after 1948 as it is to-day. As far as the *immediate foreseeable future* was concerned, however, there was unmistakable agreement as to the political position of the Bantu in this country. In April, 1950, Dr. E. G. Jansen—the then Minister of Native Affairs—expressed the basic attitude of the Afrikaner very strongly in Parliament: ". . . it is explicitly stated that they (the Bantu) should have no political or equal social or other rights with Europeans."

In due course the Afrikaner began to formulate his political and constitutional aims for the Bantu into a definite policy. The instinct of national self-preservation and political integrity were the fundamental motives behind this development. Assimilation will mean the constitutional and national suicide of the Whites; thence the necessity for effective measures to prevent the Bantu from being taken up in the Union's political structure. The following comment by Professor Olivier describes, more or less, the thoughts behind this sentiment: "No White community in Southern Africa would be willing to commit suicide by following a policy which would lead to their political . . . and ultimate virtual extinction, either by force or by assimilation." This stark fact probably has more meaning for the Afrikaner than for any other White group in Africa as South Africa is the Afrikaner's only home. The Bantu may, in other words, not deny the Whites their right to political autonomy on the grounds that they (the Whites) are supposedly alien to Africa. Today the Union can, with complete justification, lay claim to the status of an African state. Present socio-political developments in Africa have literally forced the Union to commit herself as far as the political and constitutional pattern planned for the Bantu is concerned.

Since the beginning of 1959 the present Afrikaner Government has readily accepted the challenge thrown at it by a world facing new racial situations and problems, by implementing a practical programme for the progressive political emancipation of the various Bantu groups. "South Africa to-day stands at the crossroads," Dr. Verwoerd said in Parliament in January, 1959. "She must decide whether she is going in the direction of a multi-racial community with a common political life, or in the direction of total political separation."

The fact that the Bantu national units—which will be developed into homelands for the various ethnic groups—will eventually become sovereign national states is a prospect which cannot be rejected summarily as speculation. For the foreseeable future however, the Whites will for practical purposes continue to act as guardians in these areas.

Contact in the social, cultural and biological spheres includes the more intimate and personal contact that necessarily occurs in a society. In a multi-racial society such as is found in South Africa these contacts will therefore differ quantitatively and qualitatively from the contacts which normally occur in an homogeneous society. Of all the attitudes the Afrikaner reveals towards the Bantu, that concerned in this sphere of contact has been most clearly defined and, until now, most rigorously applied in practice. The apartheid idea does not make itself felt as strongly in any other sphere. There may still be uncertainty, amongst the Afrikaners, as to the economic, political and territorial implications of the idea but there is no doubt whatsoever as far as the social and biological separation of White and Black is concerned.

Due to the perfectly comprehensible fear that his culture, way of life and bio-genetical identity will be undermined by the numerically superior Bantu, the Afrikaner will do everything in his power to maintain the separation which already exists in the social and cultural spheres, as well as to limit further dangerous contact.

Because the Afrikaner wishes to safeguard his particular way of life the apartheid principle is maintained especially strictly in the wider social sphere. Written or unwritten laws which prohibit racial mixing in marriages, trade unions, organisations, sports meetings, residential areas, etc. have therefore become an integral part of his attitude toward the non-Whites—particularly the Bantu. The fact that this approach is based on colour differences is not without a deeper meaning. A few years ago Dr. Malan wrote in a letter to the Rev. John Piersma of Grand Rapids, U.S.A.: "The difference in colour is merely the physical manifestation of the contrast between two irreconcilable ways of life." As long as the Whites continue to associate this symbol with the more primitive civilisation and culture of the Bantu they will continue to protect their own way of life against Black domination by attaching value to this symbol.

The three foundation stones of apartheid are Western culture, Christian morality and a specific racial identity. In the case of the Afrikaner there is a powerful connecting link between these three elements. His own particular bio-genetic character is, for example, associated with a particular socio-cultural way-of-life and to give up either through amalgamation with a more primitive culture or race must necessarily result in the destruction of the other. To the Afrikaner cultural assimilation is synonymous with racial assimilation—there can be no *laissez-faire* middle path. He believes that his socio-cultural and racial identity is something which must be entrenched—thence his comprehensive apartheid programme. The first entrenchment concerns the daily contact between White and Black. Practices such as miscegenation and mixed residential areas are regarded as dangerous in the extreme and must therefore be eliminated by means of racial separation.

Sustained cultural assimilation generally results in social and eventually biological assimilation. It is for this reason that apartheid is not limited only to the prohibition of miscegenation, but also regulates cultural and social contacts in such a way that the above-mentioned chain reaction cannot be set in motion.

An aspect of apartheid about which there is least agreement, most individual difference of opinion and which produces most difficulties in practice, is undoubtedly the final territorial pattern proposed for the various Bantu groups.

Territorial apartheid presupposes the physical separation of White and Black with a view to the parallel development of each racial group within a particular geo-political unit. Comparatively complete geo-physical separation of White and Bantu is the last step in the realisation of the ideal of apartheid. Without this essential pattern, apartheid is doomed to be a mere theoretical dream.

The Afrikaner people as a whole believe firmly in the *ideal* of comparatively complete geo-physical separation. But, as Dr. Malan once put it, "government is the art of the possible." The *final* territorial pattern which the Bantu homelands will assume must therefore be left to the future.

In the meantime, active steps are being taken not only to limit physical friction between White and Bantu to an absolute minimum but also to develop the potential Bantu homelands at a balanced rate. Local territorial separation is applied systematically in accordance with a purposeful statutory pattern; especially where the incidence of daily contact is greatest, viz. in the urban areas. The consolidation of six Bantu national units for the most important ethnic groups has also been initiated on a statutory basis.

The Whites are certainly not trying haphazardly to force a number of Bantustans on the Bantu, they are merely laying the foundations for the realisation of their ideal.

The Afrikaner has already achieved much in his attempt to create a homeland for each of the different ethnic groups. The Promotion of Bantu Self-government Act thus far embodies the most important measures for the final delimitation of the Bantu homelands. The "systematic linking of each Bantu group to his own homeland" and the "opportunity for full development in all walks of life within the national unit and homeland" are two basic aims of the Act, while the proposed result will be "the creation of homogeneous administrative areas for the Bantu by uniting the members of each Bantu national group in one national unit, concentrated in one coherent homeland where possible." The ideal is that each Bantu should have an ethnic identity and a homeland in which this identity can be expressed fully.

In his address to the Rotary Club in London in 1953, Dr. Geyer stressed the fact that South Africa was the *only* independent country in the world in which a White minority ruled a Black majority. This fact has important sociological, political and psychological implications.

The instinct of self-preservation is undoubtedly the most powerful instinct in any normal individual, man or beast. Sometimes man tries because of his idealism, worship of the heroic, his moral codes of behaviour, romantic sentimentality, even religious principles to convince himself—as well as the society in which he lives—that this cardinal psychological reality is false and is part of the philosophy of life of the arch-materialist or cynic. The truth is that each day of his life every individual asserts his instinct of self-preservation. Seen as a whole this phenomenon is found in a sociological context too—since time immemorial individual cultural, national and biogenetic groups have tried to protect their identity and guarantee their survival against threats from without or within.

If this were not so words like war, atom bomb, defence, etc. would have become mere anachronisms, and the freedom struggles of, for example, the Hungarians and Tibetans would have been meaningless. The psychological and emotional bases of the apartheid idea are therefore extremely important. The fact that in time the Afrikaner, as a result of his instinct of self-preservation, has developed a specific emotional attitude towards the numerically superior Bantu cannot be denied. His emotional attitude towards

illusion that white man and black man could live in separate spheres whose margins usefully touched one another, but only in a secondary manner. Race and colour were the visible signs of differences that were primary and permanent. It was this interpretation of race and colour which caused generations of Europeans throughout Africa to accept the view that the only proper environment for the African was the rural tribe. By inference his entry into the social and economic environment created by European enterprise was incidental, impermanent, and even unnatural.

If it is wise to speak of error in the policies of the principal metropolitan powers, incomparably their greatest error was the illusion that it was possible to protect and preserve a social order which their own economic activities were destroying. That their beliefs were genuine and often deeply humanitarian does not alter the fact that great populations endured the dislocating pressure of western economic forces while their European rulers failed to bring succour to the growing ruin and chaos in their lives. For all but the discerning few, it was for long generations difficult to see the truth of Arnold Toynbee's description of the entry of the west into the life of the rest of the colonial and backward world. "Future historians will say, I think, that the peak event of the twentieth century was the impact of the western world upon all of the other living societies of the world of that day. They will say of the impact that it was so powerful and so pervasive that it turned the lives of its victims upside down and inside out—affecting the behaviour, outlook, feelings and beliefs of individual men, women and children in an intimate way, touching chords in human souls that are not touched by more external forces, however ponderous and terrifying." It was only after the second World War that it became impossible to ignore the truth that Africa had passed into the stage of crisis, and that men must give earnest thought to the nature of the crisis, and the ways of meeting it.

The forces of modern economic development affect all men no matter what the colour of their skin. The development of Africa in modern times can be more easily understood if it is seen as the result of two movements of migration. The first is the migration of European traders, officials and settlers into Africa together with their skills, investments, equipment and governmental organization. The second is the migration of the African tribesman into the new world created by European enterprise. The chords of human compassion are touched by this record of collapse and renewed struggle, of demoralization and readjustment. The native population did not fall into stagnancy or allow their bodies and

spirits to follow the decline of their institutions. While still cling-
ing to the forms of their tribal life they learned the ways of the
white man's commerce and industry. Incomparably the outstanding
phenomenon of South African history is the struggle of its native
population to rise above the atrophy of the tribe, by slowly, pain-
fully and clumsily adapting itself to the functions and activities
which western society made available. In South Africa gold and
diamonds, trade and manufacture called for the services of black
men and white men. At the middle of the twentieth century one-
half of the total native population belonged to the working force
of the white man's economy. In 1921 there were 500,000 natives in
urban areas. In 1936 this number had risen to 1,000,000. A characteristic of all developing modern economies is a radical adjustment
of the proportions between rural and urban populations. That manufacture and mining brought 2,000,000 natives to the towns of
South Africa is just as natural and inevitable a phenomenon as the
urban concentration of 80 per cent of the white population.

In the application of science and technology, in capital investment, mining, industry and commerce there is a power that directs
the flow of social events for all men. The degeneration of the
tribe was an emancipation of its individuals to become members
of the western economic and social system. The breakdown of the
tribe was also the genesis of a new society. To the observer standing in a Johannesburg slum it is hard to see emancipation and
progress in such a mean and ignoble environment, harder still to
see that its inhabitants are not a transient and auxiliary throng
whose discomforts and suffering are temporary since their true
home is elsewhere in the country with the tribe.

South Africa's urban slums must be regarded as an untidy phenomenon of transition, as a painful stage in the incorporation of a
new but indispensable population in the economy of a rapidly growing industrial society. Slums in Johannesburg, Durban and Cape
Town are the unsightly camping grounds of men who are laboriously migrating into a new environment in which their rags and
filthy shacks are not signs of decline but evidence of their escape
from the hopelessness of their collapsed tribal systems. The truest
optimism in South Africa is in the crowded, disease-ridden and
crime-infested urban locations. They represent the black man's
acceptance of the new life of the western world, his willingness to
endure a harsh schooling and an unequal apprenticeship in its ways.
The dingiest slum is yet a place of learning. The ragged, underfed
inhabitants are learning many things. Some are adept in evading
the law and defeating the police. Others learn to read and write, to

tend machines, to use money, to submit to the difficult discipline of punctuality. The sordidness of their environment hides the great sum of positive and beneficial achievement, including a share, however inadequate and disproportionate, in the rising prosperity and productivity of the country. It hides also the grim struggle to carry forward the decency and dignity of the tribe in an unsanitary wilderness where men build homes out of the industrial rubbish of mine and factory. They may be likened to the medieval peasant who settled under the walls of Paris or Augsburg, and endured for generations the pains of living in towns that took little thought how to receive them, and long delayed the recognition of their citizenship. The medieval years of great plagues were but spectacular events in long generations of vileness and overcrowding, of sickness and hunger. But all the while their residence was an education in the things which the towns represented, so that the day came when the descendants of peasants served in the counting houses of the wealthy, went forth in great trading ships, rose to high office in armies, or led their fellows in the conquest of new freedom.

White man and black man have not lived together long enough in the new environment which they are creating together to see that the sum of their similarity and co-operation is each year growing greater than the sum of their differences. Nor have the white communities had time to learn to accept similarity and co-operation lest differences swell and multiply and afflict their society with a sickness that will not heal or that can be cleansed only by tragedy.

That more than three-fourths of the white population of South Africa to-day live in urban areas, and that during a full generation the total natural increase of the rural white population has moved to the towns, are facts that have a convincing meaning. The resources of South Africa can be properly exploited only by concentrating labour and skill in the towns. Conversely, rural South Africa is incapable of building modern prosperity on the soil. The greatest continuous area of sand in the world is South Africa's Kalahari Desert. When experts say that 85 per cent of the country is unfit for cultivation, it is plain that the conventions and laws which inhibit the flow of men and their families to the towns can only become a sentence of poverty and deprivation. Urbanization is the road to progress and prosperity, as incurable rural poverty is the whip that drives South Africa towards ever greater industrialization.

South Africa's racial policies are based on the perverse conviction that the sum of differences between whites and non-whites will always be greater than the sum of their similarities. They do not accept the historical truth that towns in all generations have been centres where culture slowly becomes the common property of all residents, nor do they recognize that in South Africa as in Ancient Greece, the Renaissance or modern America, the growth of new communities proceeds in an atmosphere of long-enduring tension. Meanwhile, life in most urban native locations is precarious, sordid and distressful. One can stand back and let a few phrases and words from the quiet language of the Native Laws Commission of 1948 describe the pains of urbanization for the native population. "The majority of such locations are a menace to the health of the inhabitants . . . disgrace . . . quite unfit for human habitation . . . mere shanties, often nothing more than hovels . . . dark and dirty . . . encumbered with unclean and useless rubbish . . . one could hardly imagine more suitable conditions for the spread of tuberculosis." Indeed, tuberculosis rates in the greater South African towns are amongst the worst in the world. Life expectancy in the non-white population is low, as it was in the slums of most European towns before the great modern improvements in sanitation, medicine and nutrition. Even in salubrious Cape Town amongst the relatively more advanced coloured people the life expectancy of a coloured man is full twenty years less than that of his white neighbour. Undernourishment and malnutrition afflict a high proportion of the non-European population. They are a major cause of the inertia, laziness and fecklessness which inexperienced observers regard as inborn racial characteristics. South Africa's genial sun and healthy climate are a subsidy which partially hides the neglect of its municipalities, and a mercifulness without which the slums of Cape Town and Johannesburg would go beyond the worst suffering of the most distressful period of the Middle Ages. By the side of filth, disease and poverty there is also criminality and immorality. Elements of the population who are unmannerly and unsightly by day, criminal and dangerous by night, explain why there is each year a significant increase in crime. The defects of the native urban population are more obvious than their aptitudes. It requires experience and impartiality to see that there is also a great sum of courage, enlightenment and decency. When men are uninformed or unsympathetic they naturally analyse the native urban populations by a catalogue of their defects and by the unpleasant manifestations of their disorganized entry into the European economy. They are also easily led to the view that the correction of abuse is essentially a task for the police, and that the natives are an alien population living in an environment that is unnatural and unfitting for them. Most significant is the persuasion that the proper reforms of the evils of native urban life must be found in restraint, separation and even exclusion. Crime and turbulence seem to be the mark of the native who attempts to take on the alien culture of the white man's world. Twentieth-century South Africa has not exactly rediscovered the noble savage of the eighteenth century. But it has come to the conclusion that goodness is more easily found in the natives who cling to their own culture and live in their own separate environment.

There is already a considerable body of writing which exposes the discriminatory and oppressive character of the racial policies of South Africa. An image has been created of a harsh and vindictive generation of men who are engaged in fastening a selfish and dictatorial regime upon their fellow men. The unfriendly analysis of *apartheid* has become good sport, and is an easy road to editorial popularity. *Apartheid* is no subject for mockery or facile comment. It is very grim, very important, very difficult. Of the men in South Africa who support it some are uninformed and deeply prejudiced; still others are angry or frightened; many feel helpless or bewildered; selfishness and indifference are common. These attitudes are easily discernible amongst both English and Afrikaans-speaking sections of the population. There is, however, a gross and dangerous error in not recognizing that the best of the advocates of *apartheid* are men of personal worthiness, with genuinely conscientious and moral spirits. This concession is not in conflict with the opposite admission that there exists in the present government an ugly and sinister self-righteousness which seems prepared to sacrifice the liberty and comity of a democratic society in order to attain the harsh ends of an imperious racial nationalism. Yet it is still wrong to believe that a body of ungenerous and selfish motives is all that sustains the doctrines of *apartheid*.

The major pronouncements on racial policy are often remarkable for their frank avowal of the inequities and deficiencies from which the native population suffers. The best of them are free of the traditional dismissal of the natives as incorrigibly backward. Scholarship in this field is often objective and undistorted. The more scholarly proponents of *apartheid* are emphatically not ignorant or ruthless men. Their work shows a penetrating and detailed awareness of facts and figures. It is important to know indeed how much earlier ignorance and indifference have been replaced by knowledge and awareness. It is possible to gather together out of their writings much of the evidence on which the opposition to *apartheid* is founded. *Apartheid* has within it the basis for re-education and a new recognition of the realities of South African life.

It is easy to cull the literature of *apartheid* and bring forth passages which proclaim, not exclusion and denial, but the creation of fuller opportunities and liberties for the natives. It is with real sincerity that many men feel that new and worthy horizons can be opened for the natives. These attitudes explain the pain and indignation which South Africans sometimes show when their policies are assailed in the foreign press or the United Nations. There is no deliberate hypocrisy in the frequent statement that *apartheid* is first of all a movement of emancipation and reform. Even as the Afrikaner has struggled to maintain his language and culture, and win freedom and dignity in his own land, so it surely is a Christian and honourable purpose to lead the native to a condition where he can maintain his own language and develop his own culture, build his own institutions, and above all escape from his unhappy and unequal position in an alien society. In his own homeland, separate from the world of the white man, there will be no passes or curfew, no social indignity, no nightly routine of police raids and arrests. *Apartheid* thus becomes a glowing picture of release and advancement, which are both of them the fruit of the white man's wisdom and self-sacrifice.

Once it is assumed that the white and non-white populations are racially and culturally incompatible it is logical and statesmanlike to express this fact in a separation of the races. To the few extreme theoreticians of the political science of *apartheid* this disengagement of white and non-white should be complete in every way, however great the cost and discomfort to the white population. The white population must place the purity of its race and culture above material self-interest, and endure great sacrifices to preserve its separate identity. Such statements give an apparent sense of freshness and excitement. That they contrast with the often muffled, ambiguous and evasive pronouncements of the political opponents of the Nationalist Party is one explanation of the electoral success of the Nationalist Party. They draw a picture of a proud people facing a difficult future with boldness and enterprise and justice. As long as white and black live together in their present unnatural intimacy the white man is forced to take unchristian steps to protect his race and culture. Therefore, it is moral and Christian and statesmanlike for the races to be separated so that each may enjoy his own. To deny the rights of civilization to the African would indeed be oppressive and lead to hatred and strife. The decision that the black man be excluded from the life of the white man is balanced and justified by another decision which permits the black man to develop a life of his own along the freest and most generous lines.

In the solemn and conscientious atmosphere of pulpit and library the legislation of *apartheid* represents a difficult period of transition and adjustment which all men must courageously endure before the new order can be established. Thus the laws of *apartheid* are transformed into sacrifice and deprivation which the European community inflicts upon itself in order to yield the rights of civilization to all men, black and white. What seems in Delhi or London to be oppression becomes an act of emancipation; what seems rejection is a gateway to opportunity.

Because *apartheid* has diverse origins it means different things to different people. Hypocrisy and selfishness combine with idealism to give it purchase on the minds of men. It is easy to criticize the racial laws of South Africa on humanitarian or historical grounds. It is not difficult to show that those whose advocacy is truly high-minded have simply abolished the real world about them, and have created a paradise without history and in defiance of economics. For the thoughtful man it is still important to understand how men who are sincere in their Christian beliefs and staunch defenders of their own liberties can become identified with policies of discrimination and restriction.

White South Africans feel insecure and are afraid. In this they are akin to Frenchmen in Algeria or Jews in Israel. To borrow a term from nuclear physics, the problem is partly one of critical mass. If the whites of South Africa were a small and scattered community, such as the British were in India, or the Gold Coast, their lack of numbers and compactness would have a compelling influence on political development, however great their reluctance. If on the other hand they enjoyed the numerical preponderance of white Americans, concessions would be easier because security would be greater. The decision of the United States Supreme Court against racial discrimination in education was more than a statement of principle. It was also a manifestation of security. Tolerance does not flourish easily in an atmosphere of fear and insecurity. White South Africa, with a total population of nearly 2,500,000 is large enough and compact enough to have a strong feeling of corporateness. Their status as a self-governing state is as meaningful to South Africans as it is to Canadians or New Zealanders. They know that in a modern state citizenship is more than suffrage, and cannot be conferred merely by document or decree. Citizenship has little real meaning unless it is supported by a foundation of education and skills, by respect for law and the knowledge that the moral

principles of integrity and incorruptibility are practical requirements for orderly and civilized government. These are some of the
reasons why the white community is proud and jealous of its political and cultural achievements, and why also it is afraid of the numbers, the inexperience, and the disorderliness of the natives. It is
true that the historical and inescapable challenge of every plural or
multi-racial society is to develop a larger patriotism in which differences of race, language and creed are subordinated to the major
purpose of social harmony, political stability, economic progress,
and human dignity. It is also true that it is supremely difficult, and
for most ordinary men impossible, to see how such orderliness
and coherence can be built out of such a wilderness of broken tribes,
superstition, ignorance and sloth as they see about them. In their
society, with its towns and factories and schools and government,
white South Africans have a possession which they feel they have
won with their blood and their courage, with their money and their
labour. Modern South Africa is their creation, and only they can
ensure its survival and progress.

In its various forms *apartheid* is a transfer of the responsibilities
of the living world to a dream world of solved problems. It is the
substitution of a wishful simplicity for a real complexity. The basic
premise of *apartheid* is that the natives can seek no remedies and
gain no citizenship within white society, but only within their own
segregated society.

There is no awareness in the architects of *apartheid* that out of
fact and fancy they have ingeniously contrived a mental toy, operating outside history and economics. They do indeed invoke economic and political principles, but they are the principles of a non-
existent world, so that their scholarship becomes spurious and their
logic a deception. Yet these solemn treatises on race politics, properly construed, are an excellent measure of the bafflement and
complexity of South African life. By inversion they are avowals of
pessimism, frustration and even guilt. Under the guise of hope and
deliverance the formula of *apartheid* is a creed of despair and a
flight from the fearfulness of the real problem. In the old days of
native wars Voortrekkers drew their wagons into a circle or laager.
Within its protection men defended themselves against the impis
of the Zulus or the Matabele. To-day their descendants seek to
retreat within a new laager made up of laws and restraints as if
they could thereby be protected against the turmoil of a multi-
racial society. In their statements when they mean them most sin-
cerely, there is both confession and absolution. There is the confession that the natives cannot be indefinitely denied the privileges

of modern life. There is a self-administered absolution of guilt in the promise that these privileges can be theirs. They cannot gain them at the expense of the white man by swamping him with the vote or depressing his standard of living by their competition. But they can achieve them in their own separate areas. This is the higher purpose of *apartheid*.

Such generosity is illusion, and such liberality is fantasy. It is a vision of a false and unattainable utopia imposed upon a native population that does not aspire to it.

The moment will certainly come when a competent study of the policy of developing separate native economic and industrial systems will reveal the shocking balance sheet of impossible expense, inefficiency and social waste which must be the result of trying to herd men into separate areas of life and labour.

The real lines that are drawn by *apartheid* are not drawn between two acceptable spheres of settlement and opportunity. Unhappily they are lines drawn in the mind and the heart, cut deeply by the hatred of the black man for the police, by the resentment of parents who cannot educate their children, by the frustration of men who move daily to and fro between squalor at home and meniality at work, by the dangerous anger of native leaders whose westernized minds can fully measure the indignity and deprivation which are inflicted upon them, by the slow mounting of a conviction that *apartheid* is a frontier of conflict where differences can be resolved only through resistance, violence and sabotage. In the concrete language of economics and politics *apartheid* is actually a system in which the power of the state is used to maintain the economic and political supremacy of the white community over a population of approximately ten million Africans, Indians and coloured men. The segregation laws are an embargo upon the development of the non-European population. In its extreme form *apartheid* punishes the native for his past by robbing him of the future. These laws seek to imprison the population within its own backwardness, and set up blockades against the flow of experience, skills, and amenities on which modern progress is based. In South Africa there is the most marked trend towards what Thomas Jefferson called an elective despotism. The European population lives under a liberal constitution and within a democratic framework which are the equivalent of those in Canada or Australia. But the rest of the population lives largely outside the constitution and under a growing body of laws and administrative decisions designed to impose upon them a separate status and a separate function in the life of the State.

South Africa is a democracy built upon subject peoples. It is a system of free enterprise built upon the labour of unfree and subordinate men. South Africa's critics have sometimes been intemperate in using epithets taken from totalitarian societies. It is easy to forget that some of the unfreedom and inequality has deep and obstinate roots in long centuries of history. The proper words to use of a society which contains the opposites of freedom and unfreedom, of equality and inequality, are difficult to find.

In the United States the amendments to the Constitution and the judicial interpretations by the Supreme Court have gradually removed or diminished special economic or political limitations upon individuals or groups of individuals. In law, if not always in practice, the results are binding upon legislatures, administrations and courts. In South Africa the tendency for many years has been to develop a special system of laws applicable only to the native population. The Ministry of Native Affairs can rule by proclamation against which no appeal to any court of law is possible. Different statutes specifically define a large number of offences of which only a native can be guilty. The Native Administration Act and the much amended Riotous Assemblies Act give the police very wide powers to control the activities of individuals and organizations. The principle of courts that administer the same law equally to all men is fully applicable only to the European community.

To a Zulu or Basuto labourer in an industrial community like Johannesburg the term police state has an added meaning. The laws often lead to harsh police action and summary court procedures which would produce a major scandal if applied to even the worst elements of the European population. Between four and five per cent of the total native population is arrested each year for statutory offences such as failing to show a pass or breaking the strict curfew laws. There is evidence to indicate that between fifteen and twenty per cent of the adult male population in the urban areas is arrested by the police each year.

The catalogue is long of laws which divide race from race and confine men in separate compartments. To explain and analyse them fully is a lengthy and complicated task. The Nationalist Party has declared a war of the laws of Parliament against the laws of economics and against the new rules which the modern world is struggling to apply to its racial affairs. The Prohibition of Mixed Marriages Act makes a crime of marriage between a white man and a person of colour. The Population Registration Act enjoins the compilation of a national register according to race with the intention of confining the present population and its descendants within fixed racial compartments. The Native Labour Act and the Industrial Conciliation Amendment Act undertake to separate natives from Europeans in the trade union movement, and to confine native labour to categories of less skill and lower pay. The prohibition of strikes by natives, the ban upon direct collective bargaining, and the provision that any breach of contract is a criminal offence shackle and confine native workers in a fashion for which parallels can be found only in the earliest stages of the European industrial revolution.

The Bantu Education Act is presented as a notable widening of opportunity for the natives. In the language of the Minister for Native Affairs "all doors are open," and the native can be educated "to serve his community in all respects." In the much less tidy world of racial commingling and interdependence the Bantu Education Act is a more sinister instrument. Its real intention is to arrest the rise of the native population in the western world, and to confine him to a lowly and menial position within it. The late Principal Davie of the University of Cape Town was a sturdy man, and a South African amongst South Africans. In his words, the intention of the Bantu Education Act is to "establish and perpetuate an inferior status in relation to the European." Education aims to prepare the native child for a service "which is primarily that of servant of the Europeans and secondly one which carries with it no promise of advancement towards the eventual social and political status which he covets . . ." Since a great and growing proportion of the native population must live and work in the European areas the Act sets up a total contradiction between what is promised in the native community and denied in the European community, as if the same men can be both bound and unbound according to where they happen to be. Despite its promises the Act reaffirms the white man's monopoly of the technical knowledge and managerial experience through which he controls the economy. It revives the familiar argument of the first generation of the industrial revolution in Great Britain that the education of the poor illiterate masses makes them less fitted for their tasks and less content with their appointed station. Education along western lines is a disservice to the natives and to the nation.

A deeper contradiction reveals the doctrinaire and unrealistic nature of much of the thought and legislation of *apartheid*. To live and work in a European community is to grow in understanding and competence. Almost every service the natives perform, even the act of buying shoes or stealing automobile tyres, becomes obscurely and infinitesimally a step in western education. As science

and technology are further invoked to increase the nation's productivity, no part of the nation's labour force, not even the lowliest,
can be artificially segregated in a special area of ignorance and in-
competence.

The whole myth of a separate native culture collapses when it is
recognized that, for the African, progress and emancipation depend
upon an escape from the tribe and a deeper entry into the life of
the West. At its best and strongest, native leadership aspires to
abandon the past and seek a future in the western world. Its goals
are education, opportunity and advancement in the environment
created by European enterprise. In far-off East Africa the Mau
Mau tragedy shows that the African has nothing to resuscitate in
protest against the white man except tribalism, no tradition to invoke higher or more dignified than the cruel sanctions of witchcraft
and barbarism. On the face of the earth there are few non-western
peoples who depend more than the African upon the west for everything that can be called advancement and progress.

The sum of segregation laws are an effort to prevent failure in a
white man and success in a black man. The horizontal and vertical
separation of white and non-white is carried forward by the controversial Group Areas Act and the Native Resettlement Act. The
first Act aims to create separate zones of habitation in the urban
areas for coloured men, natives, Indians and Europeans. The second seeks to remove all natives from the western areas of Johannesburg and relocate them in separate areas on the far outskirts of
Africa's greatest industrial community. Provided the basic assumptions of racial and cultural separateness are accepted, these acts
once again have admirable qualities of orderliness and reform.
They disengage communities whose commingling causes provocation and discord. They will flush out the sordid slums from the
major urban centres, and aid the work of the police in the more
compact and homogeneous racial communities. These facts, which
must not lightly be dismissed, explain the tacit consent with which
these laws are received throughout much of the European population of South Africa. Even a brief residence in Johannesburg
makes men hungry for something to be done to end the shame and
disorder and danger of its slums. But genuine reform is more than
the removal of human bodies and arbitrarily making them wards of
the police. The truth about these acts is that they are an attack
upon the assimilative tendencies of urban life. They strike at the
hope for which the meanest hovel stood, and block the daily effort
of men to find some lodgement in the only environment in which
they could earn their nourishment. They are a confiscation of the

tiny worlds of little freedoms and opportunities which humble folk were nurturing for themselves and their children. More fundamentally these acts are major restraints upon individualism and the acquisition and use of private property. Johannesburg's new distant locations are an enforced assemblage of men and women into groups to which coercion and control can be swiftly applied. They are an arbitrary creation of communities for purposes of supervision and discipline. The concept of urban locations as a dormitory for a cheap labour force imposes severe disabilities on both industry and labour. It puts a premium on inefficiency, and instability. It depresses earnings and production. This in turn continues the cycle of malnutrition, insecurity and crime. It is even an endorsement of the prostitution, drunkenness, juvenile delinquency and viciousness which persuade even thoughtful white men that a harsh police regime is the only governance the natives can understand.

In a generation less confused by some of the economic and social analysis of the nineteenth century, it is becoming plainer that democratic freedoms are fuller and more meaningful where men are free to improve their economic status and spend their earnings on the goods of their choice. Far more significant at this moment than the laws which restrict rights of political representation and suffrage are the laws and restraints which limit the power of the non-European to earn and his right to acquire and use property. In the free market economy of the western world, earning power and property in the broadest sense are indispensable to individual prestige and influence. To be able to earn more and to buy a widening range of goods and services is in itself an important extension of freedom. At the core of a healthy western democracy there is an area, relatively free of political control, where skills and shillings, industriousness and spending power are the ballots which the man who works and consumes casts in a daily plebiscite where his influence is not limited by his race or the colour of his skin. At its best this is a wide area, "detoxicated" of organized political and statutory control, in which men and groups have considerable initiative in working out the conditions of their economic and social co-operation. The economic progress of the African is a process which enlarges his liberty, tempers the impact of racial discrimination and political arbitrariness. To the extent that the African cannot enter this area of free action he becomes a bondsman, herded into labour camps and condemned to a stagnant and hopeless meniality.

Unusual confidence in the democratic process is required to see that such a zone of freedom for all can exist in a multi-racial society composed of groups on uneven levels of culture. It is the strongest proof of the pessimistic and the authoritarian political philosophy of *apartheid* that it runs rigid and statutory frontiers through the very area which in Great Britain, the United States and Canada are generously open for private initiative, voluntary association, or local government.

Long ago Alexis de Tocqueville noticed the rôle played by private, spontaneous and voluntary effort on the raw and formative American frontier. On the frontier, men experimented with the methods and institutions which would enable them to achieve the co-operativeness and stability of settled communities. The new communities were an area in which men grew in knowledge of one another in their daily association and by methods that were spontaneous, experimental and expedient. They worked out the techniques and institutions of which the fruit was political harmony, social improvement and economic co-operation. In South Africa, however, where the relations between different groups are totally governed by a body of imperative laws passed by a central authority, democracy is weakened in a most vital area. It is the area in which tolerant men explain their minds, and where new ideas and institutions are born. It is an area of incubation. It is not merely a zone of material contact and commercial exchange, but also of spiritual creativeness and intellectual fertility. These are fruitful areas where impulses and discoveries are possible that are unattainable by legislatures and courts. One function of the laws of a democratic society is to protect the vitality and freedom of these areas of personal initiative and of voluntary and spontaneous effort. Otherwise they become barren, and the healthy self-governance of the many is surrendered to political parties, government departments and statutes. One of the indispensable conditions of a thriving and resourceful democracy is that there must be activities and relationships for which the state and organized political power do not lay down the rules of conduct or define the canons of success. Where legislatures and courts encroach too severely upon the realm where ideas like individualism, personal initiative, voluntary association acquire their full meaning and stature, by maintaining privileges of race, imposing restrictions on education and employment, or entrenching the few at the expense of the many, they create a desert of economic frustration, political sterility and social disruption. The guardians of the desert are the police. Of all the causes for fear in modern South Africa this desert is the greatest.

6 ✺ NATIONALISM IN TROPICAL AFRICA*

James S. Coleman

On the level of abstraction at which the political scientist is accustomed to roam, a nation is not a loose catch-all term denoting a larger grouping of tribes (e.g., Zulus, Basutos, Mende, Buganda, or Hausa); rather it is a post-tribal, post-feudal terminal *community* which has emerged from the shattering forces of disintegration that characterize modernity. This does not mean that the Hausa peoples of Northern Nigeria cannot become a nation, nor does it mean that the "national" consciousness of the ordinary Hausaman must reach the level of intensity of the average Frenchman before there is a nation. It does suggest, however, that there must be a much greater awareness of a closeness of contact with "national" compatriots as well as with the "national" government. This closeness of contact on the horizontal and vertical levels has been a distinctly Western phenomenon, for the obvious reason that it is the result of modern technology.

> [The author points up the difficulty of using the term "nationalism" for all forms of discontent and development in Africa, and makes the distinction between Traditionalist movements (initial resistance to European control and nativistic movements often of a religious nature), Syncretistic movements (separatist religious groups, kinship associations, tribal associations), and Modernistic movements (labour unions, cooperative societies, nationalist movements led by a Westernized elite, and Pan-African movements).]

Once these very arbitrary analytical distinctions are drawn it should be stressed that none of the categories can be treated in isolation. Each of the movements is in one way or another a response to the challenge of alien rule, or of the intrusion of the disintegrating forces—and consequently the insecurity—of modernity.

* Excerpts from James S. Coleman, "Nationalism in Tropical Africa," *The American Political Science Review*, Vol. XLVIII, No. 2, June 1954, pp. 404-426. Reprinted by permission.

The recent so-called nationalism in Central Africa has been a mixture of "primary resistance" by the chiefs and traditionalists of Northern Rhodesia and Nyasaland and the nationalist agitation of the Westernized elite. Until the project of Federation became an active issue, African movements in this area were confined principally to religious separatist groups, tribal associations, or, in the case of Northern Rhodesia, labor unions. On the West Coast, where nationalism is far more advanced, traditionalist and syncretistic movements have not been and are not absent. In some instances, kinship associations and separatist religious groups have been the antecedents of nationalist organizations; in others they have provided the principal organizational bases of the latter (e.g., the National Council of Nigeria and the Cameroons was first inaugurated as a federation mainly of kinship associations, and the Africa National Congress of the Rhodesias and Nyasaland was the product of fusion of several African welfare societies). In certain cases unrest or protest of a nativistic flavor has been instigated by nationalists for their modernist ends; in others nationalists have claimed such uncoordinated uprisings, as well as purely economic protest movements, to be manifestations of "nationalism," when in reality the participants were unaware of such implications.

One of the interesting differences between prewar and postwar nationalism on the West Coast of Africa is that in the former period nationalism tended to be—as Lord Lugard insisted—the esoteric pastime of the tiny educated minorities of Lagos, Accra, Freetown, and Dakar; whereas in the latter period these minorities—greatly expanded and dispersed in new urban centers throughout the interior—have made positive efforts to popularize and energize the nationalist crusade in two ways. The first has been to preach education, welfare, progress, and the ideal of self-government among the masses, largely through the nationalist press, independent African schools, and kinship and tribal associations. The aim here has been, in the words of one of their leading prophets, Dr. Nnamdi Azikiwe of Nigeria, to bring about "mental emancipation" from a servile colonial mentality. The second method has been to tap all existing nativistic and religious tensions and economic grievances among the tradition-bound masses, as well as the grievances and aspirations of the urbanized clerks and artisans, and channel the energies thus unleashed into support of the nationalist drive. The technique here has been (1) to make nationalism, and in particular its objective of self-government, an integrating symbol in which even the most disparate goals could find identification, and (2) to politicize—one would like to say nationalize—all existing thought and associations. Until recently, many observers—including colonial administrators—tended to live in the prewar climate of opinion and therefore underestimated the power which had thus been harnessed to the nationalist machine.

In the case of the Mau Mau movement in Kenya we are confronted with a complex mixture of nationalism, with a strong traditional bias on the part of the Westernized leaders, and nativism, manipulated by the leaders, on the part of the masses. Both have been generated to an especially high level of intensity as a consequence of the acute and largely unassuaged sense of frustration on the part of the Westernized elite, growing out of the very bleak outlook arising from the almost total absence, until recently, of meaningful career and prestige opportunities within either the old or the new systems, and of the masses, resulting from the land shortage and the overcrowding on the reservations. The presence of a sizable Asian "third force," which virtually monopolizes the middle-class sector, and which has been and is politically conscious, provides a new variable of no little significance in the total situation.

A particularly striking feature of African nationalism has been the literary and cultural revival which has attended it. In some cases this cultural renaissance has had a purely tribal emphasis; in others it has taken a "neo-African" form, such as the African dress of Dr. Nnamdi Azikiwe, nationalist leader in Nigeria. It has usually been accompanied by a quest for an African history which would in general reflect glory and dignity upon the African race and in particular instill self-confidence in the Western-educated African sensitive to the prejudiced charge that he has no history or culture. In short, there has emerged a new pride in being African. In French areas, the accent until recently has been upon French culture and literature, but there are increasing signs of a shift to African themes amongst the French African literati. The important point is that African nationalism has this cultural content, which renders more difficult any effort to separate rigidly the cultural nationalism of the urban politician from the nativism of the bush peasant.

Yet the differences are important to the student of African nationalism. Primary resistance and nativism tend to be negative and spontaneous revolts or assertions of the unacculturated masses against the disruptive and disorganizing stranger-invader. They are a reflection of a persistent desire of the masses to preserve or re-create the old by protesting against the new. Syncretism is different in that it contains an element of rationality—an urge to recapture those aspects of the old which are compatible with the new, which it recognizes as inevitable and in some respects desirable. Whereas all forms of protest are politically consequential—at least to colonial administrators—only nationalism is primarily political in that it is irrevocably committed to a positive and radical alteration of the power structure. In brief, nationalism is the terminal form of colonial protest.

It is far easier to define and describe nationalism than it is to generalize about the factors which have contributed to its manifestation. Put most briefly, it is the end product of the profound and complex transformation which has occurred in Africa since the European intrusion. It is a commonplace that the imposition of Western technology, socio-political institutions, and ideology upon African societies has been violently disruptive of the old familistic order in that they have created new values and symbols, new techniques for the acquisition of wealth, status, and prestige, and new groups for which the old system had no place. The crucial point here is not that nationalism as a matter of fact happened to appear at a certain point in time after the "Western impact," but rather that the transformation the latter brought about has been an indispensable precondition for the rise of nationalism. Nationalism, as distinguished from primary resistance or nativism, requires considerable gestation. A few of the constituent elements have been:

A. Economic

1. *Change from a subsistence to a money economy.* This change, consciously encouraged by colonial governments and European enterprise in order to increase the export of primary products, introduced the cash nexus and economic individualism, altered the patterns of land tenure and capital accumulation, and, in general, widened the area of both individual prosperity and insecurity.

2. *Growth of a wage-labor force.* This development has resulted in the proletarianization of substantial numbers of Africans, which has weakened communal or lineage responsibility and rendered those concerned vulnerable to economic exploitation and grievances.

3. *Rise of a new middle class.* Laissez-faire economics and African enterprise, coupled with opportunities for university and professional education, have been factors contributing to the growth of a middle class. This class is most advanced in Senegal [Ghana], and Southern Nigeria, where it has developed despite successive displacement or frustration by the intrusion of Levantines and the monopolistic practices of European firms.

B. Sociological

1. *Urbanization.* The concentration of relatively large numbers

of Africans in urban centers to meet the labor demands of European enterprise has loosened kinship ties, accelerated social communication between "detribalized" ethnic groups, and, in general, contributed to "national" integration.

2. *Social mobility*. The European-imposed *pax* coupled with the development of communications and transport has provided the framework for travel, the growth of an internal exchange economy, and socio-political reintegration.

3. *Western education*. This has provided certain of the inhabitants of a given territory with a common lingua franca; with the knowledge and tools to acquire status and prestige and to fulfill aspirations within the new social structure; and with some of the ideas and values by which alien rule and colonialism could be attacked. It has been through western education that the African has encountered the scientific method and the idea of progress with their activistic implications, namely, an awareness of alternatives and the conviction that man can creatively master and shape his own destiny.

C. Religious and Psychological

1. *Christian evangelization*. The conscious Europeanization pursued by Christian missionary societies has been a frontal assault upon traditional religious systems and moral sanctions. Moreover, the Christian doctrine of equality and human brotherhood challenged the ethical assumptions of imperialism.

2. *Neglect or frustration of Western-educated elements*. Susceptibility to psychological grievance is most acute among the more acculturated Africans. Social and economic discrimination and the stigma of inferiority and backwardness have precipitated a passionate quest for equality and modernity, and latterly self-government. Rankling memories of crude, arrogant, or insulting treatment by a European have frequently been the major wellspring of racial bitterness and uncompromising nationalism.

D. Political

1. *Eclipse of traditional authorities*. Notwithstanding the British policy of indirect rule, the European superstructure and forces of modernity have tended to weaken the traditional powers of indigenous authorities and thereby to render less meaningful precolonial socio-political units as objects of loyalty and attachment. There has been what Professor Daryll Forde calls a "status reversal"; that is, as a result of the acquisition by youth of Western education and a command over Western techniques in all fields, there has been ". . . an increasing transfer of command over

wealth and authority to younger and socially more independent men at the expense of traditional heads . . ."

2. *Forging of new "national" symbols.* The "territorialization" of Africa by the European powers has been a step in the creation of new nations, not only through the erection of boundaries within which the intensity of social communication and economic interchange has become greater than across territorial borders, but also as a consequence of the imposition of a common administrative super-structure, a common legal system, and in some instances common political institutions which have become symbols of territorial individuality.

These are a few of the principal factors in the European presence which have been contributors to the rise of nationalism.

There are a number of explanations for these areal variations. One relates to the degree of acculturation in an area. This is a reflection of the duration and intensity of contact with European influences. The contrast between the advanced nationalism of the British West Coast and of Senegal and the nascent nationalism of British and French Central Africa is partly explicable on this basis.

A second explanation lies in the absence or presence of alien settlers. On this score the settler-free British West Coast is unique when contrasted to the rest of Africa. The possibility of a total fulfillment of nationalist objectives (i.e., *African* self-government) has been a powerful psychological factor which partly explains the confident and buoyant expectancy of West Coast nationalists. On the other hand, as previously noted, the tendencies toward accommodation or terrorism in the white-settler areas is a reflection of the absence of such moderating expectancy.

Certain African groups exposed to the same forces of acculturation and the same provocation have demonstrated radically different reactions. The Kikuyu versus the Masai peoples of Kenya, the Ibo versus the Hausa peoples of Nigeria, and the Creole and Mende of Sierra Leone are cases in point. It is suggested that the dynamism, militancy, and nationalist élan of the Ibo peoples of Nigeria are rooted partly in certain indigenous Ibo culture traits (general absence of chiefs, smallness in scale and the democratic character of indigenous political organization, emphasis upon achieved status, and individualism). Much of the same might be said for the Kikuyu peoples of Kenya.

Differing colonial policies constitute another cause of these areal differences. Nationalism is predominantly a phenomenon of British Africa, and to a lesser extent of French Africa. Apart from the influence of the foregoing historical, sociological, and cultural variables, this fact, in the case of British Africa, is explained by certain unique features of British colonial policy.

It was inevitable that Britain, one of the most liberal colonial powers in Africa, should have reaped the strongest nationalist reaction. A few of the principal features of British policy which have stimulated nationalism deserve mention:

1. *Self-government as the goal of policy.* Unlike the French and Portuguese who embrace their African territories as indivisible units of the motherland, or the Belgians who until recently have been disinclined to specify the ultimate goals of policy, the British have remained indiscriminately loyal to the Durham formula. In West Africa, this has enthroned the African nationalists; in Central and East Africa, the white settlers.

2. *Emphasis upon territorial individuality.* More than any other colonial power, the British have provided the institutional and conceptual framework for the emergence of nations. Decentralization of power, budgetary autonomy, the institution of territorial legislative councils and other "national" symbols—all have facilitated the conceptualization of a "nation."

3. *Policy on missionaries and education.* The comparative freedom granted missionaries and the laissez-faire attitude toward education, and particularly post-primary education, has distinguished and continues to distinguish British policy sharply from that of non-British Africa.

4. *Neglect, frustration, and antagonism of educated elite.* Not only have more British Africans been exposed to higher education, but the British government until recently remained relatively indifferent to the claims and aspirations of this class, which forms the core of the nationalist movements.

5. *Freedom of nationalist activity.* The *comparative* freedom of activity (speech, association, press, and travel abroad) which British Africans have enjoyed—within clearly defined limits and varying according to the presence of white settlers—has been of decisive importance. It is doubtful whether such militant nationalists as Wallace-Johnson of Sierra Leone, [President] Nkrumah of [Ghana], the Dauti Yamba of the Central African Federation, could have found the same continuous freedom of movement and activity in Belgian, Portuguese, and French Africa as has been their lot in British Africa.

All of this suggests that African nationalism is not merely a peasant revolt. In fact, as already noted, nationalism where it is most advanced has been sparked and led by the so-called detribalized, Western-educated, middle-class intellectuals and professional Afri-

cans; by those who in terms of improved status and material standards of living have benefitted most from colonialism; in short, by
those who have come closest to the Western World but have been
denied entry on full terms of equality. From this comparatively
affluent—but psychologically aggrieved—group have come the or-
ganizers of tribal associations, labor unions, cooperative groups,
farmers' organizations, and—more recently—nationalist movements. They are the Africans whom British policy has done most to
create and least to satiate.

Normally, a colonial nationalist movement directs its efforts towards the attainment of two main objectives: (1) the achievement
of self-government, and (2) the creation of a cultural or political
sense of nationality and unity within the boundaries of the area of
the nation to be. Nationalists are obliged to adopt the second objective because imperial powers either did not or could not establish
political boundaries which embraced only one self-conscious cultural unit; and certainly those powers made no conscious effort to
build nations. The nationalist dilemma is that in most cases pursuit
of the primary goal (self-government) lessens the likelihood of
achieving the secondary goal (cultural and political unity). Put another way, the drive behind African nationalism in many instances
is not the consciousness of belonging to a distinct politico-cultural
unit which is seeking to protect or assert itself, but rather it is the
movement of racially-conscious modernists seeking to create new
political and cultural nationalities out of the heterogeneous peoples
living within the artificial boundaries imposed by the European
master. Their task is not only to conduct a successful political revolution and capture power, but also the painful job of national political integration.

The major factor conditioning the development of a particular
nationalist movement, therefore, is the degree of internal politico-
cultural unity, tolerance, or compatibility amongst the peoples of
the area moving into its national era. Disunities can exist in a given
territory for a variety of reasons:

1. Traditional pre-colonial hostilities and cultural incompatibili-
ties such as exist between the Kikuyu and Masai peoples of Kenya,
or the Ibo and the Tiv peoples of Nigeria. In some instances these
have been exacerbated as a result of imperial policies; in others as a
consequence of the mere fact of lumping them together and endeavoring to impose territorial uniformity.

2. Tensions between groups resulting from unevenness in development, acculturation, and the acquisition of modernity. These can
be the product of original cultural differences (i.e., the variations

between groups in their receptivity and adaptability to modernity —e.g., the Ibo and Hausa); historical circumstances (i.e., differences in the duration and intensity of the European impact—e.g., the Creoles of Freetown vs. the Mende peoples of the Protectorate of Sierra Leone); or of constitutional reforms pointing towards African self-government. One could argue that Ibo-Yoruba hostility in Nigeria is the product of all three factors. Just as the advance towards independence precipitated a cleavage between Muslims and Hindus in India, so has the development of nationalism and the move towards self-government in Africa brought to light a multitude of disunities. Fear of domination by the more advanced and acculturated groups—European or African—is one obvious explanation.

3. Tensions between the Westernized elite—the nationalists— and the traditionalists and the masses. This nationalist disability has tended to be exaggerated in the past, usually by imperial spokesmen endeavoring to repudiate the nationalists or to isolate them from the traditionalists. The intensity of the cleavage varies widely according to circumstances. In several areas such as the Protectorate of Sierra Leone, the Northern [Region] of [Ghana], Western and Northern Nigeria, amongst the Kikuyu in Kenya, and in Northern Rhodesia and Nyasaland the educated nationalists and some leading traditionalists have cooperated in varying degrees.

4. Differences within the ranks of the Westernized elite. These disagreements—and one is struck by their persistence, strength, and virulence—may arise from several causes, including normal competition for power and prestige or honest differences over aims, timing, or methods to be employed in the nationalist drive. Such differences as separate Messrs. Fily-Dabo Sissoko and Mamadou Konaté in the French Sudan; Lamine Gueye and Léopold Senghor in Senegal; Félix Houphouet-Bougny and Kouame Binzéme in the Ivory Coast; [President] Kwame Nkrumah and Dr. J. B. Danquah in [Ghana]; the Sardauna of Sokoto, Obafemi Awolowo, and Dr. Nnamdi Azikiwe in Nigeria; Eliud Mathu and Jomo Kenyatta in Kenya; and Harry Nkumbula and Godwin Lewanika in Central Africa, have very materially affected the course and strength of nationalism in the territories concerned.

These nationalist disabilities are the product of a complex mixture of hard historical and cultural facts, of changes introduced and differentials created by the Western intrusion, as well as of the provocations of the nationalist drive itself. The success of any nationalist movement will in a large measure depend upon the extent to which these internal tensions are softened or dissipated. The latter will depend, in turn, upon the degree of repressive opposition, or unwitting or intentional cooperation, of colonial governments; upon the development of pan-territorial political associations, the membership of which is rooted in all ethnic groups and in which there is free vertical mobility into the "upper crust" which that membership constitutes; upon the emergence of pan-territorial economic-interest groups (e.g., middle-class associations or labor organizations) ; and upon many other sociological processes . . .

It would be naive to argue that a large measure of politico-cultural integration is required—as distinguished from being desirable —in order for a nationalist movement to succeed in wrestling self-government from an imperial power. Most successful colonial nationalist movements have been organized and led by small minorities which have been able either to gain the support of the masses or to capitalize upon their inertia and apathy. It would be unrealistic, however, to contemplate the success of a movement which did not have at least a minimum of unity or tolerance within the "upper crust," even though it be of the sort displayed by the unstable truces negotiated from time to time between the Sardauna of Sokoto, Mr. Obafemi Awolowo, and Dr. Nnamdi Azikiwe, the regional leaders in Nigeria.

A few of the many factors which might be observed and evaluated in order to determine the probable success, as well as the territorial implications, of an African nationalist movement or nation-building endeavor are as follows: (1) the degree of internal social mobility, economic interchange and interdependence, intermarriage and commensality, and the intensity and level of social communication among the ethnic groups comprising a given territory; (2) the location of population clusters and "core areas," as well as of "sub-national" regions of more intense economic interchange or of cultural focus; (3) the powers and functions of "sub-national" political institutions (i.e., regional, tribal, etc.), and the degree of *meaningful* participation in them by the Western-educated elements; (4) the rate at which "national" institutions and activities are capable of attracting and absorbing new social strata from all ethnic groups into the "national" life (e.g., the ethnic composition of the central administrative and technical services) ; (5) the centrality and nationalness of educational institutions, particularly the professional schools and universities; (6) the degree of pan-territorial circulation of nationalist newspapers and literature and the extent to which these play up "national" events and personalities; (7) the differentials in the material development, per capita income and wealth, the acquisition of modern skills and knowledge, and the concentration and capacity for accumulation of capital amongst the different sub-national areas and ethnic groups; (8) the ethnic makeup of the Western-educated categories and particularly of the active membership of nationalist or proto-nationalist groups; (9) the development and extent of usage of a trans-tribal pan-territorial language, be it English, French, Portuguese, Swahili or Hausa; (10) the compatibility of the "detribalized" basic personality types produced by the indigenous cultures; (11) the extent to which the territory concerned embraces total cultural groups, or, put another way, the degree to which artificial colonial boundaries have [split] ethnic groups whose division may be the source of later irredentism; and (12) the rapport between the Western-educated nationalist elements and the traditionalists, including the existence of nativistic tensions or economic grievances which the nationalists could manipulate or exploit in their mobilization of mass support.

Results obtained from inquiries along these lines would go far to explain the present orientation of a nationalist movement, as well as possible future trends. And yet an emphatic note of caution should be sounded: objective forces of integration and disintegration are powerful determinants in the nation-building processes, but so also are subjective factors. By all laws of geography and economics Northern Ireland should belong to Eire, and East Pakistan to the Republic of India; but they do not. By the same laws, the Gambia should belong to Senegal, Guinea to Sierra Leone and Liberia, Mozambique to the Central African Federation, and so forth; and yet present trends suggest that such will not be the case. The principal forces currently operating to shape Africa's emergent nations are either tribalism or a nationalism following artificial imperial boundaries; and, with few exceptions, neither of these is directed towards the creation of political units which the geographer or economist would classify as ideal. In this respect, of course, Africa is not unique.

The foregoing raises the crucial question of whether it is possible for the peoples of Africa—in their own interest—to avoid the balkanization implicit in the full application of the national principle to their continent. So long as the rest of the world is organized according to that principle, and so long as the national idea universally embodies aspirations which cannot be satisfied by other forms of human organization, the answer would seem to be in the negative. The quest for racial equality and acceptance is as important an ingredient in the African revolt as is the desire to determine one's own destiny. Rightly or wrongly, self-government within the confines of the sovereign nation-state has become the supreme symbol of the equality of peoples. The only possible alternative would be broader Eur-African political groupings or self-governing plural societies in which emergent African leaders could play what they would feel to be an equal role. In the light of the persistence of national self-determination as a symbol, and particularly in view of the growing strength and contagion of African nationalism, the future of such multi-racial experiments will depend in a large measure upon the rapidity with which European governments and leaders provide for such a role.

7  THE THREADS OF GHANA'S CONSTITUTION

Peter R. Gould

When two cultures come into contact with one another both are likely to borrow and adapt certain elements in the culture of the other. We of the West, for example, have taken and absorbed into our culture much that Africa has to offer, especially in the field of music and plastic art, and Africans in turn have borrowed much from the West. The willingness on the part of Africans to accept Western ideals, institutions and values has swung violently in the past two decades. Twenty years ago there was a general feeling that any Western thing was better than any African thing; and Africans, in the effort to copy the European and American, blindly rejected African culture as inferior. Then the pendulum swung the other way and, led by the strident poetry of French-speaking Africa that clarioned the ideal of *negritude,* things indigenous to Africa were exalted and alien elements spurned. Today both types of extremists are listened to less than they were, and there is a growing desire and willingness to absorb and adapt those things offered by the West and East that can lead to a better life in the modern world, while preserving, at the same time, the best of Africa's heritage.

Often the Western and African way are inextricably mixed; take, for example, the story of the trade union leader at one of Africa's principal ports, an important member of a thoroughly modern and Western institution. After a period of unsatisfactory service, during which the rank and file members became more and more restless and dissatisfied, the trade union leader was finally dismissed. Now in the West dismissal means a declaration of no confidence, a vote and an expulsion order. The trade union leader turns over his duties to his successor and leaves. But this was not the way leaders were dismissed in this particular African town. The only experience the union members had of dismissing a leader was the destoolment of a chief; somewhat similar to the dethronement of a king. Destoolment means disgrace, and a chief undergoing the ordeal has his badges of office torn from him, his clothing rent and his head and body cuffed by those removing him from his office. And this was precisely the way the trade union leader left: his jacket torn, his tie askew, cuffed, jeered and spat upon as he made his way to the door of the meeting hall.

Or take, as another example, the manner of debates and the way they are resolved. In a Western democracy issues are debated by the Government and Opposition parties, amendments are offered to be accepted or rejected, and finally a vote is taken in which members of the parties register their approval or disapproval of the issue at hand. But this is an alien way for much of Africa, which, it should be remembered, had thoroughly democratic discussions of tribal and village issues while much of Europe was still being governed by baronial fiat and decree. Traditionally, those taking part in African debates change their minds on the merits of the issue as their persuasions are altered by the arguments of the opposing sides. Gradually, one side convinces and wins more and more of those participating until no more remains to be said: at this point the minority registers its disapproval by walking out. No votes, no party whips, no calls to maintain the honor and integrity of the party, just debate on the merits of each and every individual issue, and a silent, disapproving walkout. Does it, or should it, come as a surprise, then, to hear of an African Opposition Party walking out of the national council chambers before a vote is taken? Here again, for all the forms and trappings of Western parliamentary debate, is the traditional African way asserting itself as a more meaningful way for Africa. Even the honored trappings are being molded to suit the "African Personality"; the mace becomes the kyiame stick of the linguist, traditional drums and horns announce the opening of Parliaments, the two sides of the house become a

U-shaped forum, and, as the Leader of the House in Accra said recently, "the term 'Opposition' has confused many minds and caused so much misunderstanding . . . that the terms 'Government Side' and 'Opposition Side' should be abolished."

Constitutional ideas and ideals from the East and West are also being selected with care to be molded and shaped to the needs of Africa. Below are some of the principles enumerated by Article 14 in Ghana's Constitution; principles to which any incoming President must make a solemn declaration of adherence. Read them slowly and thoughtfully, and savor the way in which the ringing tones of Rousseau and John Locke ("That the powers of Government spring from the will of the people . . .") mingle with the Marxian ideal of social justice ("That every citizen should receive his fair share of the produce . . .") which twines in turn with values that Africa feels should be fostered and preserved ("That the union of Africa should be striven for . . . That Chieftaincy in Ghana should be guaranteed").

> *That the powers of Government spring from the will of the people and should be exercised in accordance therewith;*
>
> *That freedom and justice should be honored and maintained;*
>
> *That the union of Africa should be striven for by every lawful means and, when attained, should be faithfully preserved;*
>
> *That the Independence of Ghana should not be surrendered or diminished on any grounds other than the furtherance of African unity;*
>
> *That no person should suffer discrimination on grounds of sex, race, tribe, religion or political belief;*
>
> *That Chieftaincy in Ghana should be guaranteed and preserved;*
>
> *That every citizen of Ghana should receive his fair share of the produce yielded by the development of the country;*
>
> *That subject to such restrictions as may be necessary for preserving public order, morality or health, no person should be deprived of freedom of religion or speech, of the right to move and assemble without hindrance or of the right of access to courts of law; and*
>
> *That no person should be deprived of his property save in accordance with law, and that no law should be made by which a person is deprived of his property without adequate compensation other than a law imposing taxation or prescribing penalties for offences or giving restitution for civil wrongs or protecting health or property.*

8 ❉ WILL DEMOCRACY WORK IN AFRICA?*

Julius Nyerere

I have very often heard doubts expressed about the possibility of maintaining democratic freedom in Africa, but I have been struck by one thing which most of the doubters and critics have in common. They have not bothered to define the essentials of the democracy they are speaking of; they have usually confined their idea of it to certain democratic institutions, or forms, which have been developed in particular countries as the result of local circumstances and national characteristics peculiar to those countries.

For instance, the British critic who speaks of "democracy" has a picture in his own mind of what democracy should be. This picture includes the Parliament buildings, a party in power within those Parliament buildings, and another party within the same imposing buildings, which is not yet actually in power but with hopes of getting into power if, and when, their turn comes to win a general election, and in the meantime enjoying the title of Her Majesty's Official Opposition. In other words, to the Briton, democracy is an institution consisting of a debating house in which one group is "for" the motion, and another is "against" the motion, and each group is quite distinct from the other. Similarly, the American critic has his own picture of democracy. Each is confusing the machinery, or structure, with the essence. To such critics an organized and officially recognized Opposition has become almost the essence of democracy.

I may be over-simplifying the basis of the criticisms and doubts, but that is certainly the way in which most people argue when they question Africa's ability to maintain a democratic form of government. They assume that, if a country is governed by one party, the government cannot be a democratic one. In doing so, I suggest, they ignore three important factors.

The first is this: that a country's struggle for freedom from foreign domination is a patriotic struggle. It leaves no room for

*From Julius Nyerere, "Will Democracy Work in Africa?" Reprinted with permission from *Africa Special Report* (Washington, D.C.), Vol. 5, No. 2, February 1960.

differences. The issue, at that stage, is a simple one, and one which unites all elements in the country. As a result you find—not only in Africa but in other parts of the world which face a similar challenge—the growth, not of a "political party," but of a nationalist movement.

It is this nationalist movement which fights for, and achieves, independence. It, therefore, inevitably forms the first government of the independent state. It would surely be ridiculous to expect that a country should voluntarily divide itself for the sake of conforming to a particular expression of "democracy" which happens to be seen in terms of a government party and an opposition party; and to expect the country to do this in mid-stream and during a struggle which calls for the complete unity of all its people.

Democracy has been described as a "government of the people, by the people, for the people." Surely, if a government is freely elected by the people, there can be nothing undemocratic about it just because nearly all the people, rather than only some of them, happen to have voted it into power. Indeed, it appears natural that young nations which emerge as the result of a nationalist movement having united their people, will be governed at first by a nationalist government as distinct from a party government. No one should therefore jump to the conclusion that this means such a country is not democratic or does not intend to be democratic.

Today, when there is this conflict between East and West, Africa is fortunate in that there is still to be found on this continent a form of organization of society which fundamentally solves the conflict between the individual and society. It should be possible, therefore, for Africa to use both its own basic structure and the self-criticism of Western Europe in order to evolve from them a form of society which can satisfy both sides.

We are not so naive that we do not realize the problems which new countries must face, and the anxious times through which such countries must pass. Nor are we unaware of the efforts, and even sacrifices, which people in new countries may be called upon to make in the national interest and in the process of consolidating their newly-won freedom through economic reconstruction. But, even when all this is granted, there should be no conflict between our commitment to freedom for the individual and our need for national effort. In fact these can work together harmoniously as long as the emphasis is on the national interest as implying the interests of the individuals who comprise the nation.

Another factor which is generally forgotten by these critics is that the presence of an organized opposition as a visible symbol of democracy is not, in fact, universal. It is, rather, the Anglo-Saxon's symbolic demonstration of his own democracy and implies the existence of a class struggle. In my opinion, the two basic essentials to democracy are freedom of the individual and insurance that the government of a country is freely chosen by the people.

The third factor which is conveniently forgotten by the critics of African democracy is the history of Africa. In traditional African society, the African never was—nor thought himself to be—a cog in a machine. He was a free individual in his own society and his conception of government was personal, not institutional. When "government" was mentioned, the African thought of the Chief. Unlike the Briton, he did not picture a grand building in which a debate was taking place. The colonizers of Africa did little to change this. In Colonial Africa, you mention "government" and the average person immediately thinks of the district commissioner, the provincial commissioner, or the governor.

When, later, the "mad" African—like myself—reads Abraham Lincoln and John Stuart Mill, and demands that government should become "institutional," what happens? The district commissioner, the provincial commissioner, and the governor—the very ones who have come to symbolize "government" in their persons—resist this demand. We have to keep on insisting and agitating until, at the eleventh hour, our demands are granted, elections take place, and "government" becomes—almost overnight—an "institution." But this happens only a very short time before the country achieves independence.

Under these circumstances, it would be surprising if the pattern of democratic government in Africa were to take on, immediately, the shape familiar to the United Kingdom or to the United States of America. But it would be unfair to assume, therefore, that this unfamiliar shape which democracy might take in Africa meant that such government was any less dedicated to the preservation of the rights of the individual.

In the world today there is a conflict between the advocates of the freedom of the individual and those who champion the primacy of the state. When one examines the differences between the ideologies of the Eastern and Western powers, one can reduce them generally to this very conflict. The West seems to have exaggerated its idea of freedom beyond the point where freedom becomes license; to have accepted a society in which—provided a man does not too obviously steal or murder—he can defend any form of self-indulgence by calling it the freedom of the individual. The Communist world, largely I think as a reaction against this exaggeration, has swung like a pendulum to the other extreme: the individual in a Communist society is secondary to something called the state. Here, then, I think, is the problem: where does society, or the state, draw the boundary of its rights and obligations? And where does the individual? It is a problem which has not yet been solved by either side in a way which can be accepted by the other.

In primitive African society, this question of the limits of responsibility, as between the individual and the society in which he lives, was not very clearly defined. The traditional African community was a small one, and the African could not think of himself apart from his community. He was an individual; he had his wife or wives—and children, so he belonged to a family, but the family merged into a larger "blood" family which, itself, merged again into the tribe. Thus he saw himself, all the time, as a member of a community. But, he saw no struggle between his own interests and those of his community—for his community was, to him, an extension of his family. He might have seen a conflict between himself and another individual member of the same community, but, with the community itself, never. One must not think that the African is therefore a "natural Communist." He is not. To him, the wage is his wage; the property is his property; but, his brother's need is his brother's need—and he cannot ignore that need. He has not yet learned to ask: "am I my brother's keeper?" The African is not "communistic" in his thinking; he is, if I may coin the expression, "communitary." He is not a member of a "commune"—some artificial unit of human beings—he is of a genuine community, or brotherhood.

9   **BALLOTS IN THE BUSH***

D. Kirby

In 1954 a commission under the chairmanship of Mr. Bryan Keith-Lucas, Senior Lecturer in Local Government at Oxford University, was appointed by the Governor of Sierra Leone to recommend measures of electoral reform in the territory. Although this

* From D. Kirby, "Ballots in the Bush: A Case Study in Local Elections in the Bo District of Sierra Leone," *The Journal of African Administration*, Vol. IX, No. 4, October 1957. Reprinted by permission of the Controller of Her Britannic Majesty's Stationery Office.

step was taken largely as a result of criticism of the existing system of indirect elections to the Legislative Council in the provinces, the terms of reference included the franchise of all local government bodies as well as the Legislative Council itself and in this context the tribal authorities were held not to be local government bodies.

The Protectorate of Sierra Leone is divided into twelve districts, each in the charge of a district commissioner as the local representative of the central government and having since 1950 a district council as the major local government unit. Each district contains between seven and fifteen chiefdoms which are the indigenous political units, and each chiefdom is ruled by a paramount chief and tribal authorities. The chiefdom is divided into a number of sections—usually between four and twelve—each is the charge of a section chief and every village in the section has its village headman.

All the chiefs and headmen are assisted by various "big men," the chief assistant being the speaker, who acts for the chief or headman in the latter's absence.

By the District Councils Ordinance of 1950 district councils consisted of the paramount chief and one representative from each chiefdom in the district, and in chiefdoms with three thousand taxpayers or more, one additional representative for each one thousand taxpayers after the first two thousand. There were also three additional members nominated by the councils themselves, and the district commissioner was a member *ex-officio*, and until 1955 *ex-officio* chairman. The chiefdom "second representatives" (as they were invariably known even when there were three or four of them) were elected by the tribal authority in each chiefdom.

The tribal authorities consist largely of village headmen and their speakers "elected" generally from hereditary ruling families by the inhabitants of the village concerned, and section chiefs and their speakers "elected" by the other members of the tribal authority in the section. These elections are subject to the approval of, and are usually conducted by, the paramount chief and his speaker or speakers, who are themselves elected strictly from members of chiefdom ruling houses by the tribal authority, which after election they head. All these people are elected for life but may be deposed for misconduct—in the case of a paramount chief only after very great difficulty. Additional members are similarly "elected" by the taxpayers to bring the total representation for each section to one tribal authority member for every twenty (formerly forty) taxpayers. These members are now usually elected for a limited term of three or five years.

No special procedure for elections to the tribal authority or from the tribal authority to the district council was laid down. In almost all cases they proceeded by public acclamation when—as was usual—the nomination was unopposed, and by open vote, the counting of hands, when it was contested. Almost without exception the method of canvassing was to make customary presents to the paramount chief and other influential members of the tribal authority. Although many educated and able councillors were produced by this traditional native method the second representatives were in general nominees of the paramount chief and customarily voted with him in the council meetings. The ordinary taxpayer had in effect little say in these elections and resented this, whilst most of the chiefs considered that it was right and proper that elections should remain "chief's business"—a sentiment not uninfluenced by their vested interest in the existing situation.

The 1956 legislation provided that paramount chiefs should remain *ex-officio* members of the district council but that the additional chiefdom representatives, one for each thousand taxpayers in the chiefdom, should be elected by secret ballot on a franchise including all persons liable to pay local tax (i.e. all adult male residents) together with women who are literate or who own real property.

One of the most important features for ensuring the effectiveness of this wide franchise is that registration of voters in so far as taxpayers are concerned is automatic. The commission considered this vital because experience in Freetown and elsewhere in West Africa had shown that where those qualified to vote were obliged to register in order to do so, only a small proportion took the trouble. For simplicity the law provides that each chiefdom should be divided into single member constituencies.

The chiefdoms containing less than two thousand taxpayers were designated as a single ward. With the aid of the chiefdom clerks, the tax assessment lists, and a large-scale map, there was no difficulty in dividing the remainder into wards each containing approximately one thousand taxpayers. Great care was taken to see that the division of traditional ethnic groups was avoided wherever possible.

The intention to hold an election for the district council on the new franchise later in the year and a brief outline of the probable procedure was first explained to the tribal authorities by the district commissioner or his assistant early in 1956. The main object of this tour, which took place before the election legislation was published, was to supervise the collection of local tax. No opportunity was lost for further explanation at all subsequent public gatherings.

It was not possible for any administrative officer to tour the district for the express purpose of explaining election procedure after the publication of the legislation, but an elections assistant—a retired forest ranger re-employed to help with the elections—did make such a tour. He found difficulty in many places in gathering people together because of the absence of co-operation of some of the chiefs. A Public Relations Department team also visited all the more accessible chiefdoms giving a cinema show which included a film of secret ballot elections in [Ghana]. About a dozen pamphlets on "How to Vote" were also sent to each chiefdom for distribution. In general, meetings were possible only at the chiefdom headquarters, and in the remoter chiefdoms even these had only one meeting.

The provisional voters' lists were taken from the local tax assessment lists which theoretically included every adult male resident in the chiefdom for six months of 1955. The names of the taxpayers in each village and of each village in the ward were arranged in alphabetical order.

This considerable task was performed initially by the chiefdom clerks in each chiefdom and checked by the elections assistant. It was hoped that the provisional lists would be completed within a month of the issue on the 1st of May of the instructions for their preparation. Unfortunately, owing to the newness of the conception of alphabetically arranged lists to chiefdom clerks and to their preoccupation with routine occupations such as revenue collection and court work the lists for only half the forty-four wards were completed even by the fifteenth of June. The remainder were brought into the district office on that day and completed hurriedly by any clerk or literate messenger who could be spared for the purpose.

The tax lists themselves were by no means accurate. Because of the frequent movements of taxpayers from chiefdom to chiefdom in search of diamonds many persons on the assessment lists did not pay the tax and many newcomers who did pay were not on the original lists. Efforts were made to correct the lists after tax collection but especially in the alluvial diamond areas and the large towns these efforts were not entirely successful. Although the liability to pay tax rather than its actual payment was the qualifying factor, these complications were to add to the confusion.

As a result of these difficulties the provisional voters' lists were most inaccurate. They were nevertheless completed and distributed to wards in time for publication on the thirtieth of June.

The law provides that objections and claims of omission should be submitted to the returning officer within ten days of the publication of the provisional lists. Although scores of persons qualified to vote had been omitted no claims or objections were in fact received by the tenth of July. (None was made until polling day.) There was therefore no need for the revising court to sit and the revising officer had only to sign the provisional lists to convert them into the registers of voters. As over two thousand signatures were needed, this was no mean task.

For a number of reasons including speed, simplicity, and security, it was decided to hold the elections in all forty-four wards on the same day although the difficulties of doing this with the limited staff available were appreciated. A suggestion was made that polling should be spread over three days to ensure that news of the election reached all parts of the district and to allow for the travelling of voters in the bad weather, almost certain at the height of the rainy season. It was finally decided that because of the added difficulties of securing boxes and papers overnight in remote polling stations, polling should be confined to one day. As a result of this the limited staff made it necessary to restrict the number of polling stations to only one in each ward in spite of the fact that some wards were as much as twenty-five miles between furthest boundaries with few or no motor roads.

All the assistant returning officers reached the chiefdom headquarters at which the nominations for all wards in the chiefdom were to be received by eight a.m. on the thirty-first of July, the due time and date. In all cases a large crowd including the full tribal authority had assembled at the [courthouse of the chiefdom] by ten a.m., many of them apparently under the impression that elections were to proceed then by the old method.

In twenty-three of the forty-four wards their representative had already been chosen in the traditional manner—doubtless with all the usual intimidation and corruption—and only one candidate was nominated. In another ward the opponent of a lawyer withdrew his candidature fifteen minutes before the closing time for nomination after a discussion "in chambers" with the lawyer and other big men of the chiefdom. In another the assistant returning officer was compelled to refuse the nomination of an unpopular candidate because none of the half-dozen or so literates in the town would agree to witness the thumb print of his illiterate proposer and seconder, and in yet another, a nomination paper was refused because it had clearly been forged on behalf of an absent candidate by one of his relatives. In one chiefdom the assistant returning officer, after receiving one nomination for each of the five wards and being told by the chiefs there would be no more, left after three hours. He had to return five days later and wait the statutory eight hours, but no further nominations were made.

This left only nineteen contested seats out of forty-four. Two other candidates expressed the wish to withdraw between nomination and polling day but were dissuaded from doing so. A third withdrew his candidature by letter the day before polling day so that in the event only eighteen contests took place.

The short-comings of the register of voters became apparent on nomination day when the names of several of the nominated candidates could not be found on them although they produced current tax receipts. That their omission was probably not deliberate was indicated by the fact that one of those whose names were omitted was a chiefdom clerk who had prepared the voters' list himself. Fortunately all those concerned were also qualified by birth so that no nomination had to be refused for this reason.

Candidates, in order of nomination, chose the symbols to be attached to their ballot boxes for the enlightenment of the illiterate majority. The most popular symbol was the traditional farmer's machete; the least popular was the *balanji,* a musical instrument little used in the area.

Polling stations varied from the luxury of permanent buildings which provided shelter for the officials and waiting voters with a well-lit office for a polling booth, to the primitive verandah and dim interior room of a leaking mud and thatched house, or even temporary structures of palm leaves erected for the occasion. The most serious fault of the last two categories was that they were far too small. All the polling staff, whose numbers at each polling station it had fortunately been possible to double as a result of the many unopposed nominations, were at their polling stations with all opening formalities completed by eight a.m. on polling day, the thirteenth of August. Interest was surprisingly brisk in all except the three urban wards of Bo Town, the district headquarters. In most places there were soon over one hundred voters waiting. In the well organised wards these were quickly formed into orderly queues, and in others a noisy but good-natured mêlée persisted most of the morning. It was evident from the holiday mood of the crowds that they found the strange new procedure for elections most entertaining and a welcome break in monotonous routine.

The gross inaccuracies of the voters' registers quickly became glaringly obvious. Many were not in proper alphabetical order; more did not show the number of the tax receipt issued to each voter—a very necessary method of identification. Dozens of tax-payers who produced valid tax receipts could not be found on the lists at all. Some of them were prominent citizens who had paid tax for many years in the ward; they grew most indignant when informed that their names had been omitted. Some presiding officers issued tendered ballot papers in order to mollify them (tendered ballot papers are by law not counted and should strictly be issued only to persons in whose name someone has already voted). The native custom whereby each man has several alternative names, some of which he may have forgotten, and the unfamiliarity of many of the officials with this engaging habit also added to the confusion.

Various successful devices were tried by enterprising assistant returning officers to speed the sluggish stream of voters through the polls. In many wards voters from each village had come to the polling station in a body. The queues were therefore organized in order of villages and the entire voters' list for each village was read out, voters coming to the presiding officer to collect their ballot papers in answer to their names. In others the registers were split into two parts and two queues were formed. If a voter's name could not be found quickly by the presiding officer or the assistant returning officer he was referred to one or other of the polling assistants. The latter, if and when he traced the name, gave the voter a slip of paper marked with his number on the register and returned him to the presiding officer who then quickly checked against his copy of the register and issued the ballot paper.

There were no violent incidents although last minute canvassing was often heated. The one police constable and two chiefdom messengers allocated to each polling station proved adequate to maintain law and order. The remaining chiefdom messengers held at readiness at the chiefdom headquarters and a police unit at district headquarters in case of trouble were fortunately not needed.

The ballot boxes and documents were duly sealed at the close of the polling at five p.m. by the presiding officers and delivered to the assistant returning officer for counting at the chiefdom headquarters the same evening, or where this was not practicable early the following day. The counting of the votes caused surprisingly little difficulty. The only matter found in the ballot boxes other than ballot papers was a few tax receipts: these were returned to the owners. The reconciliation of used, spoiled and unused ballot papers was effected accurately and quickly.

The results were in all the circumstances surprisingly good. Of a total of 7,374 ballot papers issued to voters only 61 were spoiled, having been placed on top or near the ballot boxes instead of inside them. Only 17 were not traced. In one of the most remote wards, Gbo Chiefdom, a total of 747 voters cast their votes for the three candidates—a poll of more than 63 per cent of the electorate. Several other rural wards also achieved polls of over 50 per cent. At the other end of the scale, in the three urban wards in Bo Town, the percentages of the electorate who voted were only 16, 20 and 27 per cent respectively. The most convincing of the many possible reasons adduced for this curious disparity between town and country were first that the district council did little work in the town to arouse interest comparable with that aroused by the construction of motor roads in the country, and secondly that secret ballot elections were no longer a novelty in Bo, the Town Council having been elected by that method the previous year. The average poll in the eighteen contests was 37 per cent, a figure which is believed to compare favourably with the results usually achieved in local authority elections in West Africa, especially where the registration of voters is not automatic.

The main conclusions to be drawn from this early experiment in democracy would seem to be as follows:—

(i) In these early stages the main temptation to corruption lies in approaching intending candidates rather than the voters themselves. The penalties for discouraging nominations by intimidation or bribery must be widely publicised and rigorously enforced.

(ii) The time for preparation was insufficient. At least six months should be allowed between the enactment of the legislation and the actual poll. As a result of this haste publicity was also inadequate. The ideal would be a lecture on why, and a demonstration on how to vote, in every large village. Prospective candidates should themselves receive advice on publicity matters for the first few elections.

(iii) The season should be carefully chosen. In this election, bad weather and farming operations (e.g. bird-scaring on upland rice farms) kept away many voters and caused acute inconvenience to others. In most of Sierra Leone the best month would be January after the harvest and before brushing farm, or April towards the end of the farm-burning season.

(iv) There is much to be said for a suggestion that the voters' lists should record names in order of tax receipt numbers rather than alphabetical order. Under the present system, however, this would change every year: there is therefore even more to be said for arranging the names on the tax assessment lists in alphabetical order (they are at present recorded in extended family groups) and issuing the individual tax receipts as far as possible in the same order. This would greatly facilitate the preparation of voters' lists and the tracing of names.

(v) Polling stations must be big enough to accommodate all staff and a number of waiting voters without overcrowding. The polling booths should be adequately lighted. There were in this election no incidents of the kind reported to have occurred in another West African territory when an old and one suspects short-sighted lady could not find the exit from the booth and finally climbed through the grass roof in panic. The stygian gloom of some polling booths visited during this election lent credence however to such dire possibilities. To preserve the secrecy of the vote all shutters had been closed even where windows were well above eye-level.

10  WHAT SHOULD OUR POLICY
    TOWARDS AFRICA BE?—A*

*United States Senate Committee on
Foreign Relations*

The United States has never had a positive, dynamic policy for Africa. Until very recently, we have looked to the continuing control by friendly European powers as a guarantee of stability and dependable cooperation and have been reluctant to acknowledge the principle of self-government as fully applicable to its peoples. Yet in 1960 we shall be dealing with 9 or 10 fully inde-

* Excerpts from *United States Foreign Policy: Africa: A Study Prepared at the Request of the Committee on Foreign Relations United States Senate by the Program of African Studies Northwestern University* (Washington, D.C.: Government Printing Office, 1959).

pendent states in Subsaharan Africa alone, and a decade later with perhaps more than twice that number.

The fact that since World War II Subsaharan Africa has been effectively stable has reinforced a tendency to show little concern for the discontents of African peoples. The events regarded as critical in their impact on international relations may, indeed, have exerted a negative influence on our thinking about Africa. That is, they diverted attention elsewhere and created a climate of opinion dominated by official and popular attitudes almost entirely irrelevant to the realities of the African scene.

Official statements repeat our historic position with respect to the aspirations of African peoples for self-government. However, these ideologically significant declarations are so qualified, as they hasten to add that self-government is only for those who can demonstrate that they are ready for it, that they lose much of their effect. Thus, Mr. Acheson, in 1949:

> The United States supports the nationalist aspirations of those peoples who are progressively advancing toward the charter's goal of self-government or independence. It is the policy of our Government . . . to support the attainment of freedom by all peoples who, by their acts, show themselves worthy of it and ready for it.

Mr. McGhee, in 1950:

> . . . It has been our traditional policy . . . to assist . . . in the . . . advancement of dependent peoples along the road to eventual self-government or independence. We realize, however, that the evolution of dependent peoples toward political maturity must of necessity be an orderly process of events, if it is to succeed.

Mr. Dulles, in 1958:

> The United States supports political independence for all peoples who desire it and are able to undertake its responsibilities.

Mr. Satterthwaite, in 1959:

> We support African political aspirations when they are moderate, nonviolent, and constructive and take into account their obligations to and interdependence with the world community. We also support the principle of continued African ties with Western Europe. We see no reason why there should be a conflict between these two concepts.

A position of this kind nettles the Africans because of the qualifying caveats, while the European governing powers react to the presence of our traditional affirmation.

We write many prescriptions for self-government. African leaders must be able to withstand "extremist" pressures, and forsake "short-term" domestic political rewards; they must show moderation; they must be able to "rise above mere chauvinism" in border disputes; they must show preference for democracy as a political form; they must expand the area of their competence as legislators; they must be friendly to the metropolitan powers, recognizing the colonial contributions and showing a willingness to continue or expand existing ties with a metropole; they should demonstrate a preference for free enterprise, at least to the extent of choosing a "mixed" economy; they should be receptive to Western economic cooperation.

As for the African peoples, a continuing theme states our preference for steady evolutionary political progress as opposed to sudden, radical change; we feel that there should be a sufficient number of trained African civil servants; that there be an increasing literacy rate and school enrollment; that there be adequate medical facilities; that minority rights to persons and property be respected; and that there be no discrimination on the part of Africans against non-Africans living in their country.

Admittedly, it is not easy to adjust the machinery of policy-making to the rate of change in contemporary Africa. There is little question that where no conflict exists between the emergent African state and the governing European power, and when adequate notice of change is given, the United States can adapt preexisting policy to meet the new situation. Our recognition of the Sudan and of Ghana was immediate, and we have recently raised the consulate in Yaoundé, French Cameroons, which we established only 2 years ago, to the level of a consulate general in anticipation of the change in status of that country from trust territory to an independent state. But the establishment of Guinea found us without even a consular agent in its capital. Moreover, we required over a month to recognize a government that had come into being in accordance with procedures laid down by our French ally; and we showed extreme caution in granting aid requested of us by this new country.

Acceleration in the rate of change in Africa is clearly shown in the materials . . . of this report. It makes little difference, especially in that part of the continent lying south of the Sahara, which territories are considered. It is apparent in the drift to newly built urban centers, in the incorporation of Africans into mining, large-scale agriculture schemes, and industry. It is reflected in the continuous increase in world trade as shown in imports and exports, in the growth of schools and school populations, and the number of African university graduates and postgraduate students in institutions of higher learning in Africa itself and in the rest of the world. It is evident in many nationalist movements that have appeared; in the way in which Africans have learned to employ parliamentary procedures to achieve constitutional reform, where they have been allowed to do so; in the greater pressure of Africans for administrative responsibilities.

These unities in the changes taking place in Subsaharan Africa cut across earlier tribal and linguistic groupings. They readily move over present political boundaries, as delimited by treaties among the colonial powers, because of the arbitrary nature of these frontiers, which reflect few of the ethnic, geographic, or economic realities of the continent. And they do this despite the fact that for a half-century or more, the peoples of the several governing powers have become accustomed to different kinds of administrative procedures; have been taught different European languages; have grown up under different educational systems; and have been exposed to different forms of European values, institutions, and customary modes of behavior.

Here, however, a caution must be entered. Change is valued in our society. Because we find the changes that have been taking place in Africa so compelling, we allow them to obscure the force of antecedent tradition that underlies the continuities in the African scene. Though the changes in African ways of life are apparent even to the casual observer, lying beneath the innovations are the pre-existing cultures of the continent, which turn out to be no exotic and romantic survivals of an earlier day, doomed to extinction, but functioning realities of the present.

If we will but look, we will see the power of tradition manifested everywhere. In the political field, we can see it in the pull of tribal affiliations as against national allegiances; in the difficulties being faced by the newly independent African countries that arise out of a need to determine the position of traditional rulers in a modern state; in the problem of adapting the mechanisms and even more the ideologies of parliamentary democracy by peoples who for centuries have utilized different means of reaching political decisions.

Similar phenomena confront us in the economic sphere: in attempts to transfer agricultural work-patterns to the rhythms of industrial labor; in efforts to accommodate a tradition of sharing wealth, income and responsibilities for social welfare among members of a kin-group to the requirements of an economic system based on individual initiative; in the new forms which African labor unions are taking. We can see this same mechanism functioning in the religious field, as in the case of the many independent African Christian churches which incorporate elements of European and African theology and ritual, and in addition have become centers of political activity. There is also a growing synthesis of European and traditional influences in the arts.

It is thus of the greatest importance for an understanding of contemporary Africa, and hence for the future of African-American relations, that we think in terms not of change, but of adjustment. In doing this, we must fully recognize the values Africans find in African ways of life. We must also recognize that adjustment is not unidirectional. Just as Africans are adjusting their ways to meet new needs, innovations from Europe and America are being given new shape and meaning as they are integrated into African life.

What is at stake here is essentially the direction which the future affiliation of the new African states will take, in terms of the friendships that can accelerate or stand in the way of attaining world peace. The most hardheaded approach to our foreign policy dictates that we phrase our statements and base our action on a recognition of the maturity of African peoples in terms of their own cultures, and of the validity of their own ways for them. The Prime Minister of Ghana, in his opening address at the All-African People's Conference of 1958, put the case quite unequivocally:

> Some of us, I think, need reminding that Africa is a continent on its own. It is not an extension of Europe or of any other continent. We want, therefore, to develop our own community and an African personality. Others may feel that they have evolved the very best way of life, but we are not bound, like slavish imitators, to accept it as our mold. If we find the methods used by others are suitable to our social environments, we shall adopt or adapt them; if we find them unsuitable, we shall reject them.

CONCLUSIONS AND RECOMMENDATIONS

CONCLUSIONS

1. The dynamic character of the drive of African peoples toward self-government makes it apparent that in the near future we will be dealing in Africa with many governments controlled by Africans.

RECOMMENDATIONS

1. U.S. policy, in furthering its own best interests and in accord with the action of some of our NATO associates, should be guided by expectation of the primacy of Africans in all Subsaharan Africa.

CONCLUSIONS

2. U.S. policy during the past decade has been based on the assumption that Africa, as a continent under the control of our NATO associates, can be given minor consideration.

3. The broadest interests of the United States lie in furthering amicable relations with the peoples and governments of Africa and in promoting mutual understanding as an instrument of world peace.

4. It is important that communism and African nationalism not be confused. The choices that African States will make as regards the world struggle will be influenced by the use of perceptive insights into African needs cast in African terms, and by understanding African aspirations in the light of patterns based on pre-existing traditional values and modes of behavior.

5. Africans have shown concern about the problem of "balkanization" of the continent, and of strong states preying on weak ones. They are in-

RECOMMENDATIONS

2. The United States must treat Africa as a major policy area, to be approached on a level of equality with other policy areas, particularly Europe, where African-American interests are involved. U.S. policy in Africa must be *flexible,* in view of the variations in the African Continent and the rapidity of the changes occurring there; *imaginative* in view of our traditional sympathy with the aspirations of peoples to direct their own affairs; and *positive* in shaping aid programs with a view to African needs rather than cold war instrumentalities.

3. U.S. policy in Africa must facilitate the implementation of mutual interests with African countries. It should favor their development free from outside interference, with governments that will live at peace with their neighbors and serve the best interests of their peoples, as these are defined in terms of their own values, functioning so as to reduce racial tensions where these are a factor.

4. The United States should recognize that for African states a policy of nonalinement is in the best interests of the West and of Africa. On the assumption that most of Subsaharan Africa will soon be released from colonial controls, the United States must take the position that our strategic requirements there will be subsidiary to political considerations, and military aid secondary to technical assistance.

5. The United States should view with sympathy efforts to create wider associations of African States which will promote political and economic

CONCLUSIONS

sistent that future independent African States be free to assert their own personalities while benefiting from wider affiliations within the continent.

6. The experience of the United Kingdom in West Africa and of France in the French related territories, like that of the United States in the Philippines, has demonstrated that elimination of uncertainty as to the future of non-self-governing peoples by the establishment of specific timetables or specific measures for the legal attainment of independence is particularly effective in lessening tensions and assuring future good relations.

7. Examined in historical perspective, the present differences in opportunity and reward between African, Asian, and European groups in the multiracial societies of Africa are found to be the end result of the circumstances of early contact. Resistance to change in the existing system of stratification is based on long-established attitudes which are reinforced by tensions of the kind found wherever entrenched social, economic, and political positions are challenged.

8. The problems in international relations presented to the United States by the multiracial countries of eastern and southern Africa arise from the handicaps that racial inequalities in these countries and the tensions resulting from them impose in furthering the cause of the democracies in world opinion.

RECOMMENDATIONS

stability, and facilitate the extension of aid in the economic and technical fields.

6. The United States should extend to all African dependent territories the policy applied to Tanganyika, favoring the issuance of specific statements by the responsible authorities about when and how self-government is to be attained, since the more peaceful the transition to self-rule, the greater the likelihood that present orientations toward the West will be maintained by newly independent states.

7. The United States should exert its influence to assure peaceful resolution of conflict in the multiracial states of Africa. It should urge recognition of the interests of all concerned and the implementation of their rights, without regard to ethnic affiliation.

8. The United States must demonstrate that in Africa it applies its domestic policies aimed at achieving interracial good will and equality. Examples of this would be the extension to all government operations there of existing legislation forbidding dealings by government agencies with firms that practice racial discrimination; having U.S. missions apply nondiscriminatory rules in personnel policies as regards local staff;

CONCLUSIONS

RECOMMENDATIONS

and requiring U.S. firms operating in Africa to show that they have used all legal means to comply with this principle in order to receive tax concessions.

9. The fact that we have never had, and never have aspired to have African dependencies, plus the attitudes generated over the years by the work of missionaries, scientists, and others, have made our contacts with Africa essentially of the person-to-person variety. Private organizations, however, can no longer provide the amounts needed to carry on the educational and research activities that are requested of us. Hence, substantial governmental contributions are essential if the historic continuity of our earlier contacts with Africa, and the resulting benefits from them, are to continue.

9. The United States should greatly increase appropriations for African exchanges and educational programs of all kinds. Support should be given to projects that link American scholars and their counterparts in Africa, thereby making available to African countries our best educational resources. The number of fellowships for Africans to study in American institutions of higher learning and technology should be materially increased. Existing programs to train specialists sent to Africa as technical experts or members of the Foreign Service, in the human aspects of their work, should be extended.

10. The rapid shift of power and responsibility to independent African States, with the resultant withdrawal of overseas administrators, has created a shortage of trained and experienced management and advisory manpower that is likely to persist for some time. Africans fully recognize the needs created by this situation, and look to the United States, the United Nations, the former metropoles, and other countries and agencies for aid in providing essential personnel.

10. The United States, in order to play its role in providing technical aid for newly independent and emerging African countries, should facilitate steps to establish career services for technical assistance personnel on the international level in cooperation with other countries, through the United Nations and through its own governmental operations.

11. The proportion of U.S. loans, grants, and technical assistance to African territories has in past years comprised but a minute part of its total world commitments. Metropolitan countries have provided important assistance to their overseas de-

11. The United States should immediately reappraise its aid programs for Subsaharan Africa in order to determine their adequacy in the light of the needs of the area and of American interests. To compound the effectiveness of future contributions,

CONCLUSIONS

pendent territories, but new provisions must be worked out as these territories become independent.

12. As in most nonindustrialized areas, a basic problem of Subsaharan Africa is the low level of average income with resulting deficiencies in health, education and standard of living. Though the countries of Africa have shown a determination to rectify these deficiencies, they are handicapped by the fact that their essential capital resources, like those of trained personnel, are inadequate.

13. Despite its subsoil resources, and the industrialization that is possible in view of the hydro-electric potential in Subsaharan Africa, farming will continue to constitute a major sector of African economies. The needs of farmers, however, are not customarily taken into account when loans and grants are projected, because of the difficulties in organizing and administering programs of aid on this level.

14. There are still great gaps in American knowledge about the ways in which African economic problems can be overcome. In order that technical assistance and loans and grants may best be used to develop stable and prospering states in Africa, a

RECOMMENDATIONS

efforts should be made to develop regional arrangements, roughly analogous to the Colombo plan, that will provide a framework for cooperation among the countries of Subsaharan Africa, the European Economic Community, the British Commonwealth, the United States, and other nations willing to participate in measures to promote economic growth in the area.

12. U.S. grants, loans and technical assistance, whether given directly or through international agencies, should be channeled toward aiding countries of Subsaharan Africa in building up an infrastructure of facilities in such fields as transportation, communications, health and education, where local resources of capital and personnel are inadequate to permit these countries to implement these basic aspects of their developmental plans.

13. U.S. fund-granting agencies and international bodies on which the United States is represented should extend the range of their operations to provide for research into problems of soil management and the development of effective methods for growing, processing and marketing crops. These matters should be included in the agenda of discussions and negotiations for loans or grants to the gove-nments of African countries.

14. U.S. Government agencies, including the International Cooperation Administration, should be authorized and encouraged to initiate studies of how technical assistance and loan or grant funds can best stimulate long-term economic growth

CONCLUSIONS

great deal more needs to be learned about the character of these societies.

15. There is little evidence that moves looking toward expropriation or unduly heavy taxation of foreign holdings by newly independent African States are to be anticipated. Thus far, U.S. private investment has been relatively restricted in Africa, both as to number of firms involved, total amount invested, and geographical spread. Enough data are in hand, however, to indicate that greater opportunities for profitable operations exist than has been realized.

RECOMMENDATIONS

and stability. In fulfillment of this objective, U.S. Government agencies should make maximum use of the growing body of knowledge about African societies gathered by non-governmental institutions.

15. To encourage American capital investment in that continent, the Department of Commerce should extend the series of economic studies of African countries treating of their commercial and industrial potentials. The United States should also extend the use of methods developed for guaranteeing private investments in newly independent African States, such as the International Cooperation Administration's investment guarantee program, which at the same time will promote the interests of these countries.

WHAT SHOULD OUR POLICY TOWARDS AFRICA BE?—B*

Mr. HERSKOVITS. Senator Fulbright and gentlemen, events in Africa in the 6 months that have elapsed since our study was submitted to the Committee on Foreign Relations underscore the need for implementing the recommendations made there.

The rapidity of change, particularly in political developments looking toward the attainment of self-government, demonstrates how important it is that U.S. policies be "guided by expectation of the primacy of Africans in all sub-Saharan Africa" (recommendation 1), and how essential it is that these operations be flexible,

* Excerpts from *United States Foreign Policy: Hearings before the Committee on Foreign Relations United States Senate: United States Foreign Policy—Africa* (Washington, D.C.: Government Printing Office, 1960).

imaginative, and positive (recommendation 2). If, as is commonly said, 1960 is a year of destiny for Africa, we must be ready to cope with the shifts in its power structures with wisdom, understanding and generosity.

The position we take on questions involving the multiracial states is regarded as the test of our intent against which our acts and our statements are to be projected. The favorable world reaction to the forthright statement of Prime Minister Macmillan giving the British position on South African racial policy underscores the point.[1] We would be well advised to make our own position clear emphatically, and in any event to range ourselves at his side whenever and wherever opportunity offers.

Certainly, at the very least, we can refrain from identifying ourselves with multiracial countries whose practices are such that close association with them must handicap us in the current world struggle. When a responsible U.S. diplomat, speaking over the radio in the Union of South Africa last October, called for the United States and the Union to be "partners" in Africa, this cannot but give support to those who are ready to attack the motivations of U.S. operations in Africa.

Our friends, moreover, cannot but be the more confused when they read of this radio address and contrast it with the statement made by the U.S. representative in the Special Political Committee of the United Nations on December 9 last, in the debate over the treatment of the Asians in the Union, in which he rejected practices involving "maladjusted ethnic relationships of which those in South Africa are an unfortunate example."

With the ever-growing strength of African nationalism, the importance of consistency in statement and act becomes greater since, as predicted, this strength is more and more making itself felt in the multiracial African states. The realism with which Belgium has faced the imperatives of African aspirations in the Congo has already had its repercussions to the east, and must already have been felt in the Portuguese territories of Mozambique and Angola.

Developments of major importance for U.S. policies concerning modes of granting economic and technical aid must be noted. Recommendation 11 of our study had to do with the desirability of implementing this through multilateral arrangements, particularly through groupings organized in accordance with the pattern of the Colombo Plan.

In recent months the European Economic Community has become more active in promoting African loans and grants, while

[1] See Harold Macmillan, "The Wind of Change," in this volume.

Secretary Dillon has brought together the nations of Europe for the purpose of formulating a joint approach in helping the under-developed countries raise their standards of living by improving educational resources and technological competence. On March 7 a new aid program for Africa was announced by the Secretary General of the United Nations.

In private conversation, African leaders have expressed consider-able reserve when the first two of these developments have been discussed, because of their political implications. At the second All-African Peoples Conference, held during January, in Tunis, EEC proposals were subject to criticism on the grounds that the aid to be given by this group represents what is termed "the new imperialism."

The group assembled by Secretary Dillon, it is noted, includes all the colonial powers. Association with it, the argument continues, lays the United States open to accusations of being a party to a new form of domination over newly independent countries. It is essential that those objections be fully analyzed and assessed when shaping policy, in order that we avoid an ambiguous role in the current ideological struggle, given the force of anticolonialism in influencing affiliations.

The various United Nations plans, particularly the United Nations Special Fund for underdeveloped countries, being under the widest international control, avoids many of these dangers. The more recent proposal is especially important because it indicates specific methods for establishing an international corps of techni-cians to aid in development schemes, as is suggested in recommen-dation 10.

United Nations auspices in all cases minimize suspicions that have arisen out of the ad hoc, bilateral arrangements which in the past the United States has tended to favor, but which, significantly, the United Nations Economic Commission for Africa at its Tan-giers meeting rejected in principle, while favoring multilateral ar-rangements.

Whether aid is given through the United Nations, however, or through multilateral organizations of industrial countries, or by means of bilateral arrangements, the United States should insist on the inclusion, from the initial organization stage, of recipient as well as donor countries.

The new nations of the world are sensitive to anything that sug-gests a return to their earlier status of dependency. They must be in a position to participate in planning, directing and implementing assistance at all stages. "Enough of charity" was how it was phrased at the Tangiers meeting.

It is difficult to change a habit of thinking, but the habit of thinking colonially must be given over if the new countries are to be convinced that aid programs are not motivated by concerns of continuing control over their destinies. It is, in these terms, better to speak of economic cooperation rather than economic aid, to the end that psychologically, as well as on the levels of economics, politics and technology, we may achieve understanding and friendship with the Africa of tomorrow as well as of today.

Senator GREEN. I have no doubt my colleagues have some questions they would like to ask. Senator Hickenlooper, have you any?

Senator HICKENLOOPER. Yes. Your discussion this morning, Mr. Herskovits, is a very comprehensive one and I think it is a very excellent summary of your report. The African problem is recognized by everybody as a very difficult one. I have the impression at times that these various African nations want our help but they do not want to call it help. They claim great independence of thought and spirit and yet they are constantly wanting assistance. What is their attitude and how does that square with independence of action, and so on?

Mr. HERSKOVITS. May I call your attention to what I said at the end of my statement about using the phrase "economic cooperation" instead of "economic aid"? All over the world today, new nations are as sensitive as we were in the early days of our own independence about anything that seems to imply dominance by an outside power. I feel that one of the reasons they come to us is because they trust us.

Senator HICKENLOOPER. Well, they say they do not.

Mr. HERSKOVITS. Some of that is for home consumption. I am sure we all understand how that works.

Senator HICKENLOOPER. Well, I think they had better change their tune a little bit and say something for our consumption if they are wanting our assistance.

Mr. HERSKOVITS. It seems that we are going to have to exercise a certain measure of understanding of the way in which human psychology works. Here are people who have been thinking, not in terms of world problems, but almost exclusively in terms of getting out from under colonial rule and what they have been deprived of because of the colonial status under which they have lived. Now they want some of the things that they see other nations have.

I do not know to what you particularly refer, and, of course, no one has to come to me asking for aid, but when I have discussed such matters with African leaders I have found that what they are saying is, "We want to be considered as much as any other country when these problems are set up."

Senator HICKENLOOPER. There are a number of highly capable and, in my opinion, highly intelligent leaders in each of these countries. I have met a number of them, and they seem very dedicated people, at least at the outset. When I say "at the outset," I mean one never knows what power will do to a leader as time goes on. Many leaders who start out with great dedication and high ideals become rather oppressive later on. But the ones I have met, I am convinced have great dedication and a very high competence. They have a great mass of people in those countries who are really quite primitive.

Their governments are composed of a small cadre of leaders. The great mass of people, whether it is because of colonialism or whatever, have just not experienced the responsibilities of self-government. What is going to happen in the next few years with this type of government? Will there be a trend toward more dictatorship in those countries? Is there a capability within the peoples of the countries at the moment—based on experience, let us say, because I think capability is there whether experience is there or not—to exert the basic rights of individuals or will they follow their leaders right into a dictatorship or some type of autocratic government?

Mr. HERSKOVITS. If I may slip into my role as an anthropologist for a moment, I would like to indicate that even the earliest travelers were impressed with the degree to which African societies had developed effective and, in many cases, quite complex systems of government.

As we got to know African cultures better, we began to see that there is a kind of democracy there, where the sort of procedure we use in arriving at a decision, where you raise your hand and the majority rule, is not present. In African practice you talk out a problem until you get unanimity.

Senator HICKENLOOPER. Let me say, we have that going on in the Senate right now.

Mr. HERSKOVITS. So I have heard.

Senator HICKENLOOPER. Do not misunderstand me, I am not a believer in attempting to impress our system on some other group.

I am not so sure our system would be best for certain other peoples who have different backgrounds, traditions, and history. However, I think there are certain basic rights that ought to run through different social systems.

I have had the impression that in a number of African countries, they have had, as you mentioned a moment ago, a very high, complex, and traditional system of government, of justice, of human relations, and of property that had worked very well for a long time. The difficulty was that some of their forms did not quite coincide with the colonial powers' idea of what justice was. I have the impression that the colonial powers went in and tried to superimpose a certain concept of justice on an age-old system that had worked very well, and all they did was confuse these people. Now they are in a state of confusion as to what is right and what is wrong. I think that has been especially noticeable in the Kikuyu tribe in Kenya which had really a very complex and highly organized system of government but which has now been utterly confused to a point that they do not know what they are doing. They do not know what is right and wrong. They are going to have to have some reorientation, some readjustment of their concepts. Either they must go back to their older forms or try to learn about the new ones.

Mr. HERSKOVITS. Senator, you have put your finger on what, so far as I am concerned, is the basic problem in Africa, the degree to which there is retention of the old in the face of requirements of the new; I am not worried about the readjustment that must take place. I do not think the Africans have become as confused as it seems on the surface, so that they will not be able to work out an amalgam between the various elements that have gone into their experience. All people do this; as far as we know, it has been happening as long as there have been human societies, and I see no reason to suppose the Africans, after a time where there will be undoubted periods of adjustment, will not work this out.

Senator HICKENLOOPER. Without doubt they will eventually work out a system under their own responsibility which probably will fit their particular needs better than any other system will fit it. But I am concerned about the immediate future, and the possibilities of totalitarian influence coming into Africa, the invasion of Communist ideas, the blandishments and the glittering promises of communism, in order to get a foothold there and to saddle their doctrines on these people as opposed to what we think should be an orientation toward a free system of individuality and responsibility.

I think in this transitional period there is a great danger of this because people in confusion sometimes follow the leader who talks the loudest and makes the greatest promises. Although things may, perhaps, work out all right in future generations, it is the present that is our problem.

Mr. HERSKOVITS. As I said, I am not too disturbed on that score. If there is any one thing that African leaders with whom I have discussed this problem have said, it is, "We do not want to exchange one form of domination for another."

Senator HICKENLOOPER. Well, have they not done that?

Mr. HERSKOVITS. No. Where?

Senator HICKENLOOPER. Well, as a matter of fact, there are a number of these African leaders now who are virtual dictators.

Mr. HERSKOVITS. Do you mean dictators in the sense of being Communist dictators? I do not quite understand.

Senator HICKENLOOPER. I mean dictators in the sense that some of these leaders, who have recently come into power, have used various devices and means to suppress opposition.

Mr. HERSKOVITS. There is this possibility. But I have not seen it yet. For example, there is still an official opposition in Ghana.

Senator HICKENLOOPER. It has to be a little careful.

Mr. HERSKOVITS. When I listened to Dr. Danquah on Mr. Huntley's television program from Ghana, he did not seem very careful to me. And he is still talking.

Senator HICKENLOOPER. I do not know. I am just asking.

Mr. HERSKOVITS. Frankly, I think it is a bit dangerous to think of African matters in terms of European patterns expressed in European words. You may very likely have something that looks to us like totalitarianism, and yet will have great popular support; and I mean real and not imposed popular support. Thus there is no question about the fact that Convention People's Party, the ruling party in Ghana, has very great popular support.

Now they are doing some things that people accustomed to systems like our own, who have been brought up to believe in the values of such systems, do not like.

Senator HICKENLOOPER. That gets down to the question of how far we should go in supporting and encouraging the development of systems which are inimical to what we believe to be a basic system of governmental and political conduct.

Mr. HERSKOVITS. My fundamental position is that this is not anything we can do much about, unless it be in terms of giving or refusing loans. The principle of noninterference is particularly important here where we are dealing with young nations. They are going to have to work out their own destinies, and all we can do, it seems to me, is to watch the progress with understanding and sympathy. As long as they stay inside their own borders, we must help them to develop the kind of economic and educational structure that seems to me is the best insurance against the kind of happening that you are afraid of.

Senator LAUSCHE. Now, then, you recommend that we approach the giving of aid by standing in the distance. Do you anticipate that the Soviets will follow that course?

Mr. HERSKOVITS. I do not think they are going to be allowed by the African nations to do anything else.

Senator LAUSCHE. You think they will follow it?

Mr. HERSKOVITS. I think they will have to.

Senator LAUSCHE. You think the African people will prevent them from doing anything else?

Mr. HERSKOVITS. They do not want to trade one domination for another. I have not talked to a single African leader, and I may say that I have had opportunities to talk to some of them quite confidentially, who has expressed enthusiasm for the Soviet system. Some of them say, "Well, I may be a Marxist, but that is a different thing than political communism."

Senator LAUSCHE. That will be their attitude? What do you think the attitude of the Soviets will be?

Mr. HERSKOVITS. I think they are going to try to get everything they can.

Senator LAUSCHE. You believe that it will be to our advantage to follow the course which you recommend for our country, even though the Soviet follows an imperial course?

Mr. HERSKOVITS. That is right.

Senator LAUSCHE. What is your appraisal of the good faith and the genuineness of purpose of most of the colonial powers in granting independence and autonomy? Have they shown that they recognize the coming of the day when there will be independent nations in Africa?

Mr. HERSKOVITS. I find it difficult to think of any human group as having either horns or halos. I feel that in all human situations, both elements of self-interest and of idealism enter.

I think that the colonial powers have shown wisdom in bowing to the inevitable. I do not think they are doing this for altruistic reasons. Having done it, I think they are going to try to help these countries develop their potentials in a reasonably disinterested way.

Senator LAUSCHE. Just one more question: You have outlined the course you think we ought to follow. Do you see any dangers that might arise if the course which you recommended is followed?

Mr. HERSKOVITS. Frankly, I think the greatest danger we face is if in Africa we do the thing that we have done so often in various other parts of the world, and that is to try to outdo the Iron Curtain countries in something they are doing, rather than take a stand on the basis of our own ideology and our own history.

Senator LAUSCHE. Where have we tried to outdo the other countries?

Mr. HERSKOVITS. An example is the case of Guinea, where we did nothing until after Czechoslovakia moved.

Senator LAUSCHE. Yes. But you must recognize that we moved far in advance of the Soviets in trying to help people.

Mr. HERSKOVITS. Of course.

Senator LAUSCHE. Our program of aid began a decade before the Soviet program began.

Mr. HERSKOVITS. That is right.

Senator LAUSCHE. Then you would have to say that from the standpoint of altruism, we are far in advance of the efforts of the Soviets?

Mr. HERSKOVITS. I think that is true, in fact. But I do not think we are given credit for it.

Senator LAUSCHE. Why do you say that we react to what the Soviet [Union] and her satellites are doing in that area? Hasn't the Soviet [Union] been reacting to what we have been doing, for example, by going into Egypt?

Mr. HERSKOVITS. If we go back to the point that Senator Hickenlooper raised with regard to the United Nations, I realize that it is exceedingly difficult for the United States to take the same stand on colonial questions that Russia does. I also take it for granted that the stand we do take is a more honest one than the one that the Soviet [Union] takes, which I think is rather cynical.

Nonetheless, the imputed difference in the stand of the Soviets and ourselves on colonial issues is one of the things that has made a deep impression on Africans. I do not know the answer to that.

Senator CARLSON. I want to read one sentence of your report:

> In giving aid to African countries, we must balance making funds available for military purposes against helping them with their development requirements.

Did you find in your visits with the leaders of these countries any demand for military assistance?

Mr. HERSKOVITS. Almost none. But I think that anyone trying to do the kind of study that I was doing, who did not envisage this possibility or the possibility of an arms race in Africa being induced from outside, would be derelict in his duty.

Senator CARLSON. What has been the situation with the countries who have developed these nations—Belgium, France, and England—have they devoted much time to training the natives from a military standpoint?

Mr. HERSKOVITS. Very little. Actually, what forces exist in these countries are more in the nature of a police force than anything else. Military forces such as the Senegalese battalions of the French Army, were and have been used principally outside Africa.

Senator CARLSON. The reason I was interested is because we have these military assistance programs. Can you see in the future any possibility that there might be requests for military assistance and, in that case, would we not be looked upon with suspicion as a nation that is trying to build up Africa as a great military bulwark in support of our own program?

Mr. HERSKOVITS. If such requests were made and if we responded to them we would be under such suspicion, which I suspect might even be justified. I would regret very much seeing this.

Senator CARLSON. In other words, you do not see anything at the present time that would lead us to give our aid toward building great military support in that area?

Mr. HERSKOVITS. No. And I think it would be very dangerous for us if we did. After all, in the last few years we have discovered that arrangements for bases, particularly in countries that are colonial territories that become free, can be precarious if not dangerous.

Senator CARLSON. One of the unfortunate situations we face among free nations in the world is that we are accused of being militaristic, although it has not been proven and I do not think it is a fact.

That is all, Mr. Chairman.

11   A NEW AMERICAN POLICY TOWARDS AFRICA*

The Africa League

PAST U.S. POLICY TOWARDS AFRICA

How has the United States reacted to the new events in Africa? On the whole, we have not seemed to understand them. Too often we have responded only to immediate crises which could not be ignored. In these responses, our policy has been determined in the first instance not by African considerations at all, but by non-African ones. These stem from our official interpretation of the cold war, which has dictated the terms of our alliance in NATO with the colonial nations of Western Europe.

It is true that, in the last few years, the State Department has begun to give increased attention to African problems. We now have an Assistant Secretary of State for Africa. New consulates have been opened. Career men no longer consider assignment to an African post as an indication of the disfavor of their superiors.

Nor have we totally forgotten our historic sympathies with anticolonial revolutions. But we tend to remember them on those occasions which do not require choosing between an established European ally and a new African nation. It is not coincidence that Britain fairly readily transferred power in Ghana and Nigeria, and that our government maintained steady cordiality toward the independence claims of these two nations. But where the interests of our European allies and of African nationalists conflicted, there

* From The Africa League, *A New American Policy Towards Africa* (New York: February 1960), pp. 16–29. Reprinted by permission.

U.S. policy has vacillated and illustrated our ignorance of the facts at issue. Decisions have been made which we believe were neglectful of true U.S. national interest.

There are many illustrations from the recent past. We irritated Moroccan nationalist leaders by negotiating only with France for military bases on Moroccan soil. They did not forget this when it came to renegotiating with us for those bases after Moroccan independence. We have sided against the Algerian nationalist leaders on big issues and small: we voted against them at the U.N.; we backed contracts between U.S. oil firms and the French government for the Sahara concessions even when we had been warned by the Algerians that they would not honor the agreement; we made it difficult for Algerian nationalist representatives to enter the United States; we did not control the final destination of arms we contributed to European defense, and so France used them in the Algerian war. It was with American planes that the French bombed the Tunisian town of Sakiet-sidi-Youssef beyond the border of the Algerian war. Yet, as has been obvious for several years, Algeria will soon be independent. The government of an independent Algeria will remember these facts, and it will color their attitude towards us.

We were so dependent on French official sources for news of their part of tropical Africa that we were totally unprepared for recent rapid developments. We had no policy ready when Guinea unexpectedly voted herself to independence in De Gaulle's referendum. While the new nation was eager, enthusiastic for it, we delayed recognition too long. When it finally and inevitably came, it appeared unwilling, and to that extent gave unnecessary offense. In February, 1959, we organized the defeat of the resolution sponsored by the independent African states and calling for U.N.-supervised elections in French Cameroon prior to independence in January, 1960. Unrest is following independence. We should not be surprised; indeed we ought to be prepared to assume some of the responsibility for it. For the elections which produced the present Cameroon government were widely thought to have been rigged by the French administration. A government produced under such circumstances is not in a strong position. Internationally supervised elections would have provided an opportunity for reconciling deep internal differences in French Cameroon, and so would have helped give legitimacy to the government which must cope with the forces of disintegration that appear after independence.

What was the value to the U.S. of taking sides against Africans and in favor of our European allies on questions of African policy?

The arguments used to support those decisions were deduced from priorities accorded to the maintenance of the NATO alliance. Far too little consideration was given to those by-products of this priority, which in fact worked against our interests in the cold war: that only a token contribution to NATO was made by a colonial power like France, whose forces were engaged in Algeria; that overseas colonial rivalries slowed down the pace of European economic and political integration; that the Communist nations could appear as the only champions of the anti-colonial movements.

Priority to the European regional alliance was a hangover from a past phase of the cold war, when our strategy assumed a military clash with the Soviet Union within a time-span which reflected our expectations of Soviet actions under Stalinist rule. Now the terms of the cold war itself are changing. It is becoming less a rivalry which might be resolved at any moment by the use of arms, and therefore the existing industrial complex of Western Europe is of less crucial significance. It is becoming more one in which the developed powers—particularly Russia and the United States—must justify their systems and their values to the leaders of the underdeveloped nations who are shopping around for the best ways to integrate their nations, rapidly transform their economies, develop their resources and therefore achieve equality at the international level. Russia has already indicated her recognition of this by expanding her scholarship assistance, signing trade pacts and offering technical assistance as well as capital to the new African nations.

United States policy has not adequately responded to these new realities. We still have a reserve of credit among Africans which we should not dissipate carelessly. We once fought a revolution for freedom from colonial rule. We have longer and deeper contacts with most African nations than any non-colonial power. Many African leaders still turn with optimism to what they hope will be a sympathetic American government, ready to understand and to help.

POLICY SUGGESTIONS

Though our policy has been inadequate in terms of the problems presented by African political development, it is still possible to develop an American policy for Africa which accords both with the needs of the area and with our national interests.

The United States is faced with fundamental decisions concerning its relations with the underdeveloped areas of the world. Our policy for Africa must be examined in terms of the problems of Africa, and not as a mere by-product of our relations with the Soviet Union or Western Europe. Such an attitude harmonizes not only with our interests in the international situation but with our positive and traditional values of freedom and democracy in government.

We stand for these values. This does not mean that it is either right or useful to tell other peoples what kind of government they should have. Democracy, if it is to exist in the sense in which we know and value it, must be rooted in modern social conditions which do not yet exist in Africa. The best two ways for us to serve the cause of democracy are to act as does a nation that believes in it, and to help Africans lay the basis for the kind of social and economic system in which democracy might eventually take root. Meanwhile it is both useless and offensive to Africans for us to blame them for not having a multi-party system, for example, when such a system can only exist where development has led to the differentiation of a nation's society into a national rather than sectional interest groups, and an understanding and acceptance of institutions in which these differences can be resolved. Our policies can make a difference in some areas when we choose between supporting Europeans or Africans, traditional or modern elites, forces of national and international integration or of anarchy. We can be a decisive factor in helping economic development or, by not doing so, in encouraging stagnation. If our policies do not cope with these issues, then we are not dealing with those questions which are most important for the future of Africa.

Establish the Priority of African Interests. Numerically Africans are in the majority on the African continent. Democracy means majority rule. This poses few problems for us when we consider West Africa, but many more when we come to the European-dominated areas of South, Central and North Africa. There Africans seek government based on racial equality as rooted in a universal franchise. From these expressed African goals it does not follow that African nationalists are racists. On the contrary, their demands are the basic demands of democracy, and must be met if democracy is to find hospitality in Africa. We must constantly demonstrate our belief that where the interests of Africans and privileged white settlers conflict, the interests of Africans have priority. Racial discrimination in any form—the guest list of our Embassy dinners in South Africa, the admissions policy of a U.S.-owned theater in Southern Rhodesia, the hiring policy in U.S.-financed governmental or non-governmental projects—is to Africans evidence that we do not practice what we preach.

Whose definition of African interests should we follow? Where we are in a position to choose, we should give support to the modern African elite because they want to take the steps which bring about necessary social and economic changes. The modern elite—the men who have partly rejected the traditional values, who think of national and international rather than sectional and ethnic interests—are only a small group in most African states. Their position is not yet secure, for they are but a minority even in the new independent states of which they form the governments. Their hold on the affections of the rural population is often slender. A reduction in their numbers because of war (Algeria) or of divisions among them (between northern and southern Sudanese) weakens the nation. In societies like those of Africa, unrest spreads quickly. Tunisian and Moroccan stability is increasingly threatened by the Algerian war; people living in Chad, Niger, [Mali] and Mauretania grow restless because of it. If the influence of the modern elite breaks, then there is danger of chronic disorder, of communal and ethnic violence in which no authority can for long maintain peace. In such disorder men become dangerous both to themselves and to their neighbors. They are far indeed from a situation in which the values of freedom and democracy can exist.

However, in United States policy the interests of Africans must take priority over the maintenance of order or the *status quo*. Order unacceptable to the majority of the people—colonial rule—can be maintained only with increasing resort to force and, as Kenya during Mau Mau, breeds in its turn disorder of the most destructive kind. The corrosive nature of Mau Mau was less in its use of violence than in the fact that it came to express rejection of modern egalitarian values. It came about as a result of the authoritative political system which then existed in Kenya. Europeans denied the African elite the right to organize to express town and rural discontent. Rural discontent mounted even as educated Africans saw no way to put their modern values into practice, and so began to doubt them. The implications for South and Central Africa are obvious.

Herein lies a dilemma. The modern African elite does not constitute the legal government in many parts of Africa, and the lawful governments in many instances use their power against that elite. Furthermore, the dogma of national sovereignty in diplomacy requires that we do not intervene in the internal affairs of another nation.

We believe this dilemma is more apparent than real, however. The notion of national sovereignty, while perhaps fundamentally applicable to nineteenth-century diplomacy, is not sufficient by itself to guide the United States through the twentieth-century network of relations among nations. A country as powerful as ours intervenes whenever it acts or does not act. Each time we distribute aid, make a loan, send out technicans or exchange delegations, we intervene in internal affairs, particularly in countries which are in the midst not only of political but also of social and economic revolutions. We too often retire behind simple assertions about sovereignty. It is far better that we be aware of the extent to which we are in fact intervening, and therefore conscious of our responsibility for the results of our actions internationally.

Welcome Independence Based on Racial Equality. Africans still living under colonial governments will soon be independent, with or without our agreement. We should welcome that independence, and make it clear to Africans and Europeans alike. In this way, we can help reduce the violence and make the inevitable transfers of power as constructive as possible. We should favor independence, however, on one condition: that it is based on universal suffrage in which race makes no difference in the counting of votes. Freedom and equality are among the values which we claim to support at home and abroad. It would be a negation of those values to favor independence, for example, in the Central African Federation under its present European-dominated government. Already our claim to these values is suspect in Africa because of our checkered history of race relations.

We should indicate our acceptance of independence in Africa in small as well as large ways—in the choice of diplomatic personnel for Africa, for example. We need first-rate representatives in Africa to bridge the cultural gap, far wider than with Europe. We need good reporting from awake, informed Americans. We would then not have to rely so heavily on European sources of information. Our acceptance of independence is a prerequistite for all adequate cultural relations. And these must greatly, rapidly, improve, particularly in those African nations where Europeans of the extreme Left or Right have both painted distorted pictures of the United States.

Finally, we must express our acceptance of the new Africa with a tact indicating respect for African sensitivity to outside interference or even so much as a patronizing manner. The ideas of *négritude* reflect this sensitivity, even while glorifying things African—

much as the "self-reliance" preached by Ralph Waldo Emerson or the intoxicated enumeration of all things American sung by Walt Whitman illustrated nineteenth-century American sensitivity to foreign patronage, advice or instruction.

Support African Moves Towards Unity. The drive towards unity is a major force in politics within and among the new African nations, although there are strong differences among African leaders as to the form it should take. Unity is related to the ability of the modern elite to stay in power, and linked to finding satisfactory solutions for the problems of integration, economic development and foreign relations. It is in the United States' interest that the modern elite manage to remain in power, and so solve these problems. Therefore, it is in our interest to support these moves towards unity, since a divided elite means even more divided nations in Africa.

What kind of moves towards international unity in Africa should we back? Those made by popularly supported African governments. We should understand, also, that the trend towards unity finds expressions not only in governmental meetings, but in meetings of other groups: political parties, in the All-Africa People's Conference, or trade-unions, for instance. Activity in these areas reflects the same sentiment of self-reliance, the same intense desire to find their own path that underlay the drive for independence.

In West Africa the new African governments have made numerous moves towards unity: the Ghana-Guinea- [Mali] Union, the Sahel-Benin Union. There exist conflicts, or potential conflicts, among the African governments making these moves. Some lead towards real unity; some only achieve larger disunities. We must keep out of these conflicts, for only Africans can resolve them. Similarly, only they can find the right form to contain their drive towards unity: federation, confederation, alliance. It is the business of the United States to back unity in West Africa, but not to dictate whose unity or what kind.

We must not back moves towards political unity involving any European-dominated governments, however. Africans fear, not without reason, that in a federation with even one such constituent unit the pace of progress towards racial equality is determined by the state with the most discriminatory system: Kenya in East Africa, Southern Rhodesia in the Central African Federation. In these places Africans reject federation, and formulate their political demands within territorial frontiers, such as Nyasaland. From the experience of South Africa, they believe that if white settlers dominate at the time of independence then Africans may have an even harder time achieving equality than under a colonial system. In such areas, therefore, United States policy should support internal political equality before either independence or unity within federations.

These exceptions apart, we should keep in mind that unity within and among nations is important because it lays the basis for rapid and efficient economic development. A united elite is more likely to take decisions which reduce the sharp differences between the rates of development of different areas within nations—differences which add to national instability. Unity among nations helps promote a scale of regional planning required by areas like West Africa. Political and economic divisions reinforce each other. The present differences between the franc and sterling zones in Africa help maintain political divisions. It would indeed be a waste of resources if in post-independence West Africa there were a repetition of the type of inefficient development which characterized the region under colonial rule. Parallel railroad systems, for instance, were built simply because the British and French administrations did not cooperate. Such plans as the Volta River project of Ghana, Konkouré in Guinea, or Inga in the Belgian Congo raise, now or in the future, problems of priorities both for African and foreign investors. The fewer the frontiers, the simpler the task of planners, the easier to raise the standard of living.

Many African nations will want to continue cultural and other ties with European nations. Provided these ties are the result of the willing agreement of both sides, no one can or will object. Such ties, and Africa's growing contact with other parts of the world, will reflect Africa's desire to maintain fruitful international contacts while creating an identity all its own. In this way it will serve its own interests best and be more likely to create a truly democratic, truly independent society.

Help Train Personnel. These nations must first train their people. Since World War II thousands of Africans have studied abroad, and some dozen new universities have opened their doors. In most countries, however, the supply of engineers, teachers, technicians, administrators, doctors, and other professional staff is still very short.

Most serious, perhaps, is the shortage of people with intermediate skills: nurses, midwives, agricultural assistants, secretaries, mechanics, lower-rank supervisors, veterinarians, clerical accountants. Many of the people who acquired these intermediate skills have, amid tough competition, reached the top of the educational ladder within their countries; many accumulated more prestige through nationalist activities. Frequently, they are drafted upward into positions of greater responsibility than those for which they were educated. There they no longer make use of their special skills, and must rely on subordinates with little or no special training. Men with intermediate skills are indispensable in a modern society; without them administrative, technical and social services flounder and the energy of highly-trained people must be frittered away on jobs which ought to be left to assistants. Training in these intermediate skills must be closely related to local conditions, and far too many people must be turned out quickly and at a young age for it to be economic or advisable to send them all abroad. A country can for a while afford to train its engineers abroad, but not its secretaries.

An increase in the number both of top-level professional people and of those with intermediate skills depends almost entirely on the secondary school facilities. This is the educational bottleneck in most of Africa. There are too few secondary schools, and so only a small percentage of those who learn to read and write in the primary schools can continue their studies.

Neither the schools nor management have produced anything like the necessary numbers of Africans qualified to supervise at a lower level of production in African industry. As a result, low-level supervisors are brought from Europe at high wages, which raises the cost of production. In large measure the productivity of African labor depends on the quality of the supervisors and on their relationship with the workers. If conditions favorable to development are to exist in Africa, then facilities to Africanize rapidly this supervisory personnel must be created both by governments and by private industries.

The United States government should develop rapidly an expanded program of educational assistance to the new African nations. This program must be designed to meet the shortage of trained African personnel both on an emergency and a long-term basis. Of course, the details of such a program must be worked out with each country concerned, but the broad lines should be the following:

> A. A vast expansion of the scholarship program for postgraduate training of Africans in the United States, and, in areas where local university facilities are inadequate, for undergraduate training as well.

B. Allocation of funds and technical aid to help the new African universities grow as rapidly as possible.

C. A series of programs designed to help the African government expand their secondary school facilities: by making funds available on a grant-in-aid basis for the construction and supply of the new schools; by sponsoring capable United States high-school teachers who are willing to serve in African high schools and help fill the gaps in staff until the local universities do so.

D. Allocation of funds and services useful to African governments sponsoring emergency vocational training programs, both for young people and for adults.

E. Emergency measures to increase the supply of supervisors for industry, for example, an industrial internship program for African foremen or potential foremen and office managers in both private and public enterprises in the United States.

F. Aiding the trade-union movements to develop adequate programs of training for their leaders, and of workers' education.

The expansion of education in all its forms must, of course, be carefully planned. There is always a danger of allowing education to outrun job possibilities. Though this is not yet a difficulty in most African countries, the experience of some Asian countries counsels care and balance.

Expand Aid and Technical Assistance. We must make the same generous gesture to the new nations of Africa that General Marshall made to postwar Europe. We must vastly increase the public funds we allocate for use in Africa, and enlarge our technical assistance services. We must help meet African needs directly and through the United Nations. Although there are, of course, local variations in these needs, broadly they fall into three categories: intensive construction of transport facilities; modernization and diversification of agricultural production; industrialization.

U.S. aid should be available to African governments for essential ports, railroads and roads. Ports and railroads are needed to make the economy more adaptable, roads to knit people together. They extend the hinterlands of cities, stimulate the production of food for sale in the rural areas and cut the price of food in the cities. Thus they increase the real income of the city wage-earner and add to the money income of the villager. Roads stimulate the movement of people and ideas and so dilute ethnic particularist sentiment. The existing network of rail communications runs from port to interior. Roads are an indispensable adjunct to them if the internal market is to grow.

Our aid should also be available for use in agricultural development. Expanding farm production is the fastest way to increase the
income of the average African, and that increase provides a firm
base for industrialization. If resources now devoted to subsistence
production were absorbed into the money economy then the mass
of the village population could begin to buy manufactured products.
The internal market on which the survival of industry in Africa
depends can exist only where roads go to the village and money to
the villager.

More, better and more varied crops depend on other things than
transportation, however. They depend on improved agricultural extension services, and on good agricultural research. The United
States has considerable experience in this field. The International
Cooperation Administration should be encouraged to expand its
agricultural work in Africa.

African governments place high priority on industrialization,
and for it they need a great deal of cheap power. At present most
of the energy used in Africa is derived from imported, and therefore expensive, fuel oil and coal. African leaders know that African rivers constitute a huge power reservoir; an estimated 40% of
the world's water power potential is in Africa. Some of that potential is already realized, because of dams constructed at Owen's
Falls in Uganda, Le Marinel in the Congo, Kariba in the Rhodesias and Edéa in Cameroon. There are on paper plans for the construction of more dams at Konkouré in Guinea, on the Volta River
in Ghana, and for the vast Inga project in the Congo.

All these plans are for areas where water power and its prospective use are found together, since mineral deposits needing processing are located near projected dams. Capital is needed if the
African potential for hydro-electric power and for metal-process-
ing industries is to be realized. In most of these hydro-electric projects, construction depends on the availability of long-term low-
interest loans. Of necessity most of the capital must come from
outside of Africa. Sufficient private foreign capital cannot be expected, in spite of the favorable conditions which African governments offer. Therefore, the United States government is receiving
appeals for public investment in these hydro-electric schemes. We
should entertain these requests favorably.

For a variety of reasons, except in the Union of South Africa,
Liberia and Northern Rhodesia, the volume of U.S. private investment in Africa is negligible. Many new African governments, such
as Tunisia, Ghana and Nigeria, are taking measures to attract
foreign private capital. The United States government should help

African governments in this by extending guarantees to private investors against the risks of war, expropriation and currency restrictions. Encouraging private investment in Africa, however, is no substitute for public loans and aid. For Africa needs to invest in works which cannot be expected to pay for themselves. Roads, ports, and dams do not pay for themselves directly. They are justified by their contribution to over-all economic growth. They are a basic responsibility of government, in Africa as elsewhere, and we can be of great assistance.

In the matter of personnel (both diplomatic and technical) and aid, we would be wise to keep in mind the comparative return of quality and quantity. Often one ill-advised, badly-chosen person can make errors of tact and judgment which defeat the serious effort of many others. The answer is not always quantity; it may be quality. The new African nations have come into being on an enormous surge of courage and energy. At this time of their crisis they are not living by economics alone. They are living by will-power, slogans and a dream of the future. Every revolutionary country, our own included, lives for a short time more on aspirations, ideas and courage than on rigid economic realities. We should have learned, by 1960, that gifts and resentment often go together. How the gift is given makes the difference. We have learned lessons, some of them bitter, in Europe and Asia. Let us attempt to send to Africa men and women who are not simply skilled, but who are flexible, sensitive, able to act on and speak about the real values—and problems—of a democratic free nation.

If our nation will have the foresight—such close-range foresight by now—to take hold of the advantages naturally ours: the echoes in Africa of the words of our own fight for independence, the vitality of an egalitarian country, our true and often misunderstood generosity, the vast humanitarian effects made possible by a technical society—we will be in a frame of mind to weigh individual decisions. So often the outcome of policy decisions depends on when they are made. Things change very fast in Africa, and there ought to be in our policy a steady course through caution to a willingness to make use of opportunities quickly. We must recognize that only by keeping constant our fund of information about Africa will we be able to make the quick decisions which must be made, and which must be made on the basis of what is to come, rather than what has been.

Part Two

ECONOMIC CHANGE

Closely interwoven with the rapidly changing political scene, and hardly separable from it in reality, is the economic revolution, another face of the "rising tide of expectations" sweeping the African continent. In the United States, the richest nation on earth, with our economic institutions increasingly geared towards overseas aid, we are going to see our relationship to the new Africa affected more and more by the economic and technical needs of the new nations emerging there. It is perhaps with this realization that Sir Oliver Franks, a former British ambassador to the United States and chairman of one of Britain's largest banks, proposed that we of the Western world should re-examine our common objectives. For nearly a decade and a half our energies have been absorbed by the Cold War, and our thinking has been oriented almost entirely along an East-West axis. Now, closely bound up with the tensions of the Cold War, but clearly distinguished by their importance from them, are the problems associated with our relationship to the underdeveloped areas to the South. In brief, we are not only going to have to shift but to double our thinking, and give equal attention to the new North-South axis, the overwhelming importance of which is only now becoming apparent. It is easy to reason in a hard-boiled manner why we must change our thinking, easy to note that our strategic posture demands it; but perhaps we should not be afraid to admit that the shift will also come about because for us there is only one answer to the question "Am I my brother's keeper?"

Much of the economic aid for Africa will be used to develop the basic requirements of all chronically underdeveloped areas: adequate roads, railways, and communications to speed the flow of goods and people; medical and public health services to ensure a healthy population; schools and community development teams to teach people to read and write; machines to increase productivity; and power to turn the machines. Yet all these developments may come to nothing without the rapid growth of the most important economic sector of all—agriculture. Basic to the growth of all African economies, underpinning all the hopes for industrial development, is an increasingly productive agricultural sector of the economy. Industrial plans demand workers, and these must come from the land and be fed from the land; Africa's burgeoning cities demand more and more food for their exploding populations; thus the productivity of the agricultural sector becomes the key to all development. Professor Neumark, of the Food Research Institute of Stanford University, raises some of the basic questions that must be answered if African agriculture is going to buttress securely the present development plans. What we have seen over the past decade is the increasing inability of traditional methods of cultivation to cope with the problem. Output per man has not been able to keep pace with the rapidly growing needs of many areas because the traditional shifting agriculture, no matter how suitable once, is geared to the needs of another era. Today the furrows must follow the contour, grass burning must be stopped to give the land a cover, new varieties of seeds must be introduced, and new ways must replace the old if Africa is to build upon a firm foundation.

All too often a glib answer is given to the problem of increasing agricultural production—mechanize. But, as the results of some bold but foolish mechanization schemes have shown us, the answer is not that easy. As P. Staner, a former Belgian administrator in the Congo has noted, ". . . the mere purchase of a machine does not remove all difficulties . . . it may aggravate and multiply them." Machines may replace men, but if other tasks are not immediately available serious social problems arise; machines may replace fatigued muscles, but must themselves be maintained and repaired by skilled hands; machines can clear and plough vast areas, but the cost may have to be measured by the red-brown sluggish waters of the local streams bearing the precious topsoil to the sea. The answer is not, cannot be, simple. In the Union of South Africa, man's attempts to push agriculture into marginal areas has had devastating consequences, so that today the people talk of the problem of "desert encroachment." But careful investigations by scientists, among them D. F. Kokot, an agricultural expert on a research team that probed into the problem, have shown that the problem is not a natural one, it is rather a problem brought about by man himself with his annual fires, his ploughing of the thin soil and his introduction of too many cattle for the land to bear.

The problems of soil erosion, annual firing, and overgrazing are the constant worry of African agricultural officers and specialists and, as in many parts of Asia, these basic problems are compounded and aggravated by systems of land tenure and inheritance geared to the requirements of an earlier age. For example, in Kenya a piece of land held by a Kikuyu is divided among all his sons upon his death. The result of the inheritance system can be seen stamped upon the land as a mosaic of tiny fragmented holdings, few of which are capable of being worked economically. As an administrative officer in Kenya, G. J. W. Pedraza, notes, the decreasing ability of the land to provide crop yields capable of supporting a rapidly growing population has forced the government of Kenya and the Kikuyu people to consider programs of land consolidation, and today the very landscape is changing as the old fragments are gathered into new farms laid out and managed with extreme care so that the land will bear for future generations.

If steadily increasing agricultural production is the basis for industrial development plans, solving the agricultural problem does not automatically clear away the problems of industrialization. One of the world's leading economists, Arthur Lewis, a former economic adviser to the Ghanaian Government and now Principal of the University of the West Indies, made an industrial study of the Ghanaian economy that has become a classic of realistic appraisal. A strong proponent of increasing agricultural production to provide the capital, labor and, ultimately, the main market for industry, Professor Lewis points out one fact so often overlooked by many eager to develop their economies: it is *not* capital or technology that is the basic need—people can be taught technical skills, and capital is usually available for sound investments—it is rather *managerial experience* that is in such short supply. All the business schools in the world cannot teach a person this; he has to learn by doing, and this is why most governments of underdeveloped areas rightly insist upon bringing local people into managerial training positions.

A program of industrialization also needs men, and often Africa is viewed as a vast, untapped pool of cheap labor. The cost of labor, however, cannot simply be measured in terms of low hourly wages; it is in the productivity of the labor supply that the true cost must be found. Here Africa scores abysmally low. In many areas chronic malnutrition and a host of debilitating diseases cut a man's output to a fraction of what it might be, and when, as in many of the new cities, a man overwhelmed by the solitude of his new rootless life no longer has the old ends to work for, that fraction is reduced still further. I remember myself in West Africa visiting a sawmill, which had been shipped lock, stock and saws from the United States. In this country it was operated at peak output by twenty-six men. In Africa it required ninety-six, partly, it is true, because every worker had his relatives put on the payroll, but mainly because years of inadequate diet and weakening parasitic disease prevented the men from maintaining high rates of output hour after hour.

If we recognize that development capital is often available from private, national and international sources for sound industrial investment, we must also note that money for the less exciting, day-to-day costs of government and social services is not. Usually, money for these purposes must be found by the countries themselves, thus raising one of the most difficult economic questions of all—taxation. For, as the African Studies Branch of the Journal of African Administration notes, development "gives rise to recurrent charges . . . and it is largely from taxation that these recurrent charges must be met." Thus, if development plans are to succeed, the administrative base must be secure; that is, government payrolls must be met, roads and harbours must be maintained and money for the thousand and one small budget items must be found. But taxation in Africa is not easy; even today most of the tax revenues are indirect and the individual, unless he is a farmer growing an export crop, goes free. The trader, particularly, escapes paying his fair share of the tax burden, for where no books are kept who is to say what the tax shall be? In Africa, as elsewhere, everybody has a poor year when the tax collector knocks. Yet many of the traders of Africa are extraordinarily astute, and some are immensely wealthy. It is no secret that some of the women cloth traders of West Africa have an annual turnover of $250,000, and if we grant that these are the exceptions then we also have to admit that the average is still very respectable. Often a large trader starts out with very little, but if he is skillful he can turn over what little he has many times very quickly. One of the most famous ways is "gold-coasting," a system of short-term commodity borrowing from a commercial company, and it is fitting that a description of this should come from the United Africa Company, which so often and unwittingly must have provided the gold-coasting start of many an African trader.

All too often the rapid pace of economic development simply conjures up thoughts of huge, impersonal development plans that send new roads and railways ripping through the bush and new power dams soaring, and whose impact and success are measured in equally impersonal national income figures. We forget what a road may represent at the local level, what a new dam means in terms of resettling people, and how a small portion of a national development plan may pull one thread of a cultural web to change and distort the rest. Such change has come to the Kipsigis people of Kenya in a mere twenty years, and is described in a "before and after" case study by an agricultural officer, C. W. Barwell, whose work over fifteen years in the area provided one of the bases for the profound changes that have taken place. So great have been the changes, so rapid the acceptance of new ways, that it is doubtful that an African Rip Van Winkle would know the land today. Clothing, utensils, land tenure and cultivation, transportation, diet and local government—all have changed beyond recognition under the impact of a changing economy. And all over Africa, for all the impressive projects in concrete and steel, for all the vast economic changes that are taking place, it is ultimately at this local level that the greatest changes of all will occur, for if the elite are the source then these people are the sustenance of the "rising tide."

13 ☸ THE NEW INTERNATIONAL BALANCE*

Oliver Franks

I have been asked to discuss the broad subject of economic relations between Europe and the United States, with particular attention to some specific questions. To tackle this assignment one must first be clear about the general approach. Let me explain what I mean. It makes all the difference whether we are thinking of the economic relations between Europe and the United States as a going concern, and are interested in improvements or modifications to it, or whether we suppose that these relationships have entered a basically new phase so that most questions have to be worked out afresh.

The first suggestion I wish to make is that our common objectives of policy have changed, that it is not particularly easy to be sure what our present objectives should be, and that the first job is

*Excerpts from Sir Oliver Franks, "The New International Balance: Challenge to the Western World," *Saturday Review,* January 16, 1960. Reprinted by permission of the *Saturday Review.*

to identify them. It is only if we have success in this task that there is a chance of answering the specific questions put to me.

It seems to me that the economic objectives to which we have been accustomed in Europe and the United States since the Second World War paralleled the attempt to answer the dominant political and strategic problem, that of East-West tension polarized in Washington and Moscow. The two aims we tried to realize were, first, the recovery of Western Europe and, secondly, the strengthening of world liquidity so that the international exchanges of trade would not break down through lack of the means of payment.

Throw your mind back to the second half of 1947, when concentrated work first began on the Marshall Plan. Who can forget how doubtful any real recovery of Western Europe seemed, how easily the collapse of Western Europe might have tilted the world balance decisively in favor of the East and Communism? When I was at the Paris Conference in the late summer of 1947 it was only a matter of weeks before France and Italy ran out of dollars with which to pay for bread grains—and this in a world in which there were no surplus bread grains outside North America. Only twelve years ago Europe was on the threshold of catastrophe, while lack of gold or inadequate reserves of acceptable currencies in many countries made any lasting revival of international trade a dim and distant prospect. At this point you will allow me, as a citizen of Britain, to observe that while these two great aims—the recovery of Europe and the building up of reserves and liquidity in most of the Western world—were common objectives of the peoples on both sides of the Atlantic and while cooperation between them was genuine and strong, nothing at all could have been achieved without the broad, imaginative, constructive initiatives of American policy. The Marshall Plan itself, the whole story of aid and assistance, the steady liberalization of the international trading policies of the United States during the period, are historical evidence of this truth.

But why do I dig back twelve years into the past? To remind you how greatly things have changed. In the late 1940s and through most of the 1950s we were quite clear about these international economic objectives in the Western world and worked steadily towards them; there was no problem of identification. But now Europe has recovered. Think, too, how much the problems of world liquidity have been eased. No doubt it would be foolish to talk of ultimate or enduring solutions or hope that no further difficulties will arise. But consider how international trade has revived, how the manufacturing industries of Western Europe have been rebuilt, how the reserves of their central banks have been increased, and how the gold stocks of the free world are better distributed. When we add to all this the increase in the resources of the International Monetary Fund and the increased strength of sterling, one of the two great international trading currencies, surely the contrast between now and the late 1940s is absolute. We have moved into a different sort of world.

This is why it is important to ask what are now our common objectives of economic policy on the two sides of the Atlantic. I suggest that today we have two, and they are related to a change in the broad political and strategic posture of our Western world. Earlier the problems of East-West tension were dominant; now we have a North-South problem of equal importance. It is connected with the former but has its own independent and equal being.

I mean the problems of the relationship of the industrialized nations of the North to the underdeveloped and developing countries that lie to the south of them, whether in Central or South America, in Africa or the Middle East, in South Asia or in the great island archipelagoes of the Pacific. If twelve years ago the balance of the world turned on the recovery of Western Europe, now it turns on a right relationship of the industrial North of the globe to the developing South.

I believe that there are questions which need discussion in a forum which brings together the industrialized nations of the North if they are to be successful in finding means and measures commensurate with their aims. In saying this I am in no way undervaluing the work of existing institutions. I should be particularly sorry if it were thought that I underestimated, or failed to appreciate the great work which has been done and will continue to be done by the International Bank, the Monetary Fund, and the GATT.

What are these questions? Let me give a few examples. There is the question of how much the industrialized North can channel into the developing countries. There are questions of whether the necessary growth and economic stability in the industrialized countries can be sufficiently foreseen and provided for to make a given scale of constructive help possible. There are questions of the appropriate shares to be borne by the different nations of the industrialized Atlantic world. There may be questions of priority and order. There are certainly issues of coordination and programming. At present coordination between us is quite inadequate. There is no general program. There is instead a pronounced lack of continuity.

Just as twelve years ago the balance of the world depended upon the fate of Western Europe, so in these coming years it will surely turn on the destiny of the newly developing countries.

We all know that many of them intend to develop at all costs. It is no use wondering whether it is wise. We developed ourselves earlier and they are now going to develop themselves in turn. They face a vicious circle. Low living standards and free, broadly democratic societies cannot produce sufficient savings for the rapid economic development they will not forego. They need more capital to increase output; low output prevents sufficient saving for capital.

This circle can be broken in one of two ways. It can be broken by tyranny which, by enforcing hardships on the people and holding down their standard of living, forces the savings for rapid development. Or it can be broken by capital from outside which gives a free society the chance both to develop and to remain free. This vicious circle for country after country will be broken one way or the other in coming years.

We have already had evidence in the Middle East of how real and how urgent these problems are. I do not understate when I say that the world balance will shift decisively against us if we fail to devise adequate means to realize the twin objectives I have identified.

Growth with stability is a necessity for the survival and success of the Western world. So is a right answer to our relationship to the developing peoples and a proper allocation of our resources to this cause. If we can look at our worries in terms of these broad aims and work out the answers together, then we have a guiding thread to prevent us from going wrong. This goes for the future of the European Economic Community; it goes equally for the European Free Trade Area, and for the destiny of the larger group which I hope will result from these two. It applies just as strongly to the choice of methods to deal with the American deficit on the balance of payments. This is why I have stressed the importance of identifying our common objectives and, since they are now new, at least in emphasis and priority, the need for an informal means by which our governments can argue things out afresh and harmonize our approach to the new jobs we have to do in the world.

14   SOME ECONOMIC DEVELOPMENT PROBLEMS OF AFRICAN AGRICULTURE*

S. D. Neumark

African agriculture is often described as consisting of two different sectors—the subsistence or self-sufficient sector, and the export or cash-crop sector. However convenient such a division may be for some purposes, it is misleading if subsistence farming in Africa is considered to be identical with self-sufficiency in the literal sense. The latter implies an economy in which farmers produce all the means of their subsistence by and for themselves. Being by definition independent of the outside world, they are not supposed to produce a surplus for the market. Whether this type of non-exchange economy is of any importance in Africa is doubtful.

At the other extreme, there are single-crop producers who are dependent on export markets for the disposal of their crops, and for their daily needs, food and clothing, which must often be brought from abroad in exchange for an export crop. Diversification and increased production of crops for home consumption has been advocated from time to time as amelioration of the hazards of monoculture and dependence on fluctuating world prices. Yet many producers find it more economical to concentrate on one export crop and to buy their requirements from the outside. On the other hand, the so-called subsistence sector, so eminently suited for diversification, often contributes very little in the way of exchange. This can be explained neither by inability of the subsistence sector to produce a surplus, nor by a lack of familiarity with the processes of exchange.

The purpose of this brief study is to direct attention to the basic economic conditions essential for the development of this subsistence sector. The problem is stated in its most general form and

* From S. D. Neumark, "Some Economic Development Problems of African Agriculture," *Journal of Farm Economics,* Vol. XLI, No. 1. February 1959, pp. 43–50. Reprinted by permission.

no attempt is made here to discuss the detailed problems of specific areas. Ample published evidence indicates that the economic and technical problems to which attention is here drawn are fundamental and common to most parts of sub-Saharan Africa.

In recent years the demand for the products of African agriculture, both for export and for internal consumption, has been increasing rapidly. The rise in internal demand is due to growth of population, and also to the increase in income which arises from expansion of the export industry and from proportionally large growth of the nonagricultural population engaged in trade, mining, industry, transport, service industries, and government employment. Additional investment in production for export, as well as for local industries, in public utilities, and in administration, will increase still further the local demand for agricultural produce.

Whether African agriculture can keep pace with such an increasing demand depends upon factors both economic and technical. On the technical side, the capacity of the land to maintain human and animal life is being reduced by soil deterioration and soil erosion. Agricultural development is inhibited by the traditional system of "shifting cultivation," while a backward agricultural technique, largely responsible for low productivity per man, makes excessive demands on African labor resources. But of even greater significance is the fact that the largest sector of agriculture in Africa, the so-called subsistence sector, and the people engaged in it, contribute very little to the rest of the economy. Admittedly, the labor force employed in the rest of the economy comes mainly from this subsistence sector, but even so, this sector ties up an excessive amount of labor.

African indigenous agriculture has thus reached a stage in its development which calls for radical changes not only in the prevailing system of production but also in the existing transport and marketing facilities. Before the nature of these changes can be discussed, it is necessary to analyze the present economic basis and condition of the subsistence sector which has as yet played only a very minor role in Africa's modern economic development.

The main technical issues involved are largely encompassed by the problem of shifting cultivation, the possibilities of mixed farming, and questions of land tenure. As is well known, shifting cultivation, an almost universal practice in the forest zones of Africa, is a system under which a piece of land is cleared, cultivated for several years, and then allowed to revert to bush until it has regained its fertility. A new area must then be cleared of bush for crop cultivation. Depending on the demand for land, the resting period for land varies from one year upwards, but usually is between four and eight years. It is clear that indefinite continuance of such a system is only possible as long as there is an abundance of land. But with increased population density, both human and animal, and an expanding demand for agricultural products, the resting period of both arable and pastoral lands has been considerably reduced. Exhaustion of the soil is largely due to loss of organic matter by decomposition when annual crops are cultivated, especially in the tropics where the high temperatures accelerate the process. At each cultivation the humus content of the soil is progressively depleted with the result that the soil gradually loses its organic matter and its crumb-structure and hence the capacity to absorb rainfall. It is true that artificial fertilizers are capable of restoring essential mineral elements, but they cannot replace the humus content as does organic manure. Unless its organic matter is maintained, the soil thus becomes prey to erosion, and climatic conditions in many parts of Africa are especially favorable to the development of erosion. While preventive medicine, improved sanitation and veterinary science tend to cause rapid increases in both human and animal population, soil deterioration accompanied by soil erosion tends to reduce the capacity of the land to maintain human or animal life.

Mixed farming, where conditions permit, is probably the best means of maintaining and improving soil fertility and thus making permanent cultivation possible. What are the conditions and consequences of mixed farming in Africa? One of the essentials of mixed farming is the keeping of cattle. By replacing hand or hoe cultivation with a plough drawn by animals, the farmer can increase his cultivated area and have a supply of manure which will not only maintain his soil in good condition but will also enable him to obtain better yields from his land. At the same time, mixed farming in Africa could achieve a great economy in the use of land. Increase in the farm unit, combined with an increased yield per unit area, should result in a very considerable increase in the volume of production of farm crops. Furthermore, keeping cattle would mean an increased supply of animal protein in the diet of the people. In areas where it is impracticable to keep cattle, green manuring, composting, etc., depending on climatic conditions, may prove effective in incorporating organic matter into the soil. Draft power in such areas might be supplied by tractors.

Close study of the basic conceptions which regulate the customary tenure of land in the various regions of Africa will be necessary before new farming systems are introduced. The indigenous systems of collective or communal land holding were evolved under conditions in which the supply of land exceeded the demand. Modern conditions of pressure of population on the land, and the growth of the exchange economy, are all tending to favor consolidation of holdings. However, such changes as are taking place in the existing system of land rights are slow and inadequate to advance agriculture on a broad front along modern lines.

ECONOMIC ISSUES

In general, an improved system of agriculture and up-to-date methods of production would result in increased agricultural output. It would lead to an increased supply of food, especially protein-rich food, which would improve the diet of the people. Furthermore, by raising the productivity per man much labor at present tied up in agriculture would be released for other employment. This is crucial to economic advancement.

However, the problem is not entirely technical. It is not enough to put a new system or improved methods of farming at the disposal of the agricultural producer. The new system and the improved methods would also have to prove economically advantageous.

Essentially, the whole problem of agricultural development of Africa, as elsewhere, revolves around market opportunities, either locally or abroad, for farm produce. As elsewhere, the provision of transport and marketing facilities has been the *sine qua non* in agricultural development. The whole development of production for export has depended upon the provision of bulk transport, equally for plantation production and for the peasant production which predominates in Africa. River transport has made accessible the forest zones along the Niger, the Gambia, the Congo, and other rivers. New areas have been opened up by railways reinforcing the effectiveness of river transport, as on the Congo, and also making the savannas available for commercial crops. On the other hand, there are potentially productive but isolated hinterlands from which surplus agricultural produce cannot reach the consuming centers owing to inadequate transport facilities. Farmers in such remote areas have, in fact, no good reason for producing a surplus which cannot be easily marketed. Under such circumstances, the only means of improvement open to these people is to export labor to territories where economic development is more advanced.

It would therefore seem that the sector of African agriculture now largely outside a wider exchange economy could be greatly advanced by linking up the underdeveloped hinterland with the urban and industrial centers of consumption in a closer system of interregional trade. The point has now been reached where produce of the hinterland is needed for internal consumption, for support of the nonagricultural population in industry, mining, trade, public utilities, etc., and as a basis for further expansion of local industries.

The essential points emerging from this brief discussion may now be formulated in a more general way. Economic development of Africa on a scale sufficient to raise permanently the standard of living of the whole population depends, among other things, upon the development of the so-called subsistence sector of agriculture, in which, at present, the great majority of the people are occupied. Such development must necessarily take the form of a closer complementary economic relationship between the insufficiently developed agricultural sector and the economically advanced sector. This is an essential condition not only for the development of the subsistence sector, but for the economy as a whole and, in particular, for the establishment and expansion of local industry.

The so-called subsistence sector of agriculture is already under great stress, expressing itself in the form of increasing pressure on land resources and increasing desire and need for money income. This situation calls not only for changes in prevailing systems of production, but also for an improvement in transport and marketing facilities. For it can hardly be overemphasized that lack of transport and related marketing facilities present, in general, the most considerable obstacle to the exploitation of the latent opportunities for the development of interregional trade in Africa.

INCENTIVES

Underlying the foregoing discussion is the tacit assumption that the provision of transport and markets would evoke the appropriate response of the African peasant. What proof is there, one may ask, that if better transport and wider markets were provided, more production would be forthcoming? In Western societies economic motivation is fairly general and constitutes the main driving force for what is called economic progress. How general is economic motivation in economically underdeveloped countries, and to what extent can it be relied upon to serve the purpose of economic development? Indeed, one commonly finds among economists the notion that the supply curve of the subsistence producer is backward rising, i.e., the more money you offer the less marketable output you get. One used to hear from mine operators in Mexico that higher wages merely accentuated absenteeism. Similarly in Africa, one often hears from employers of African labor, whether in agriculture, in industry or domestic service, that higher pay does not offer a dependable inducement to greater effort or more regular work. In many underdeveloped countries, there is lack of initiative and unwillingness of the peasant to improve his methods of production.

All this does not necessarily conflict with the available evidence that there are people in underdeveloped countries who do respond to economic incentives in the expected way. However, the question is not whether some people in underdeveloped countries do or do not respond to money incentives; the question is rather how significant this response is in underdeveloped countries and under what circumstances it operates. Before the nature of this problem can be discussed, it is necessary to examine first what seems to be and what is really a lack of response to economic incentives.

The problem of economic incentives in its bearing on underdeveloped countries may be divided into three broad categories:

(1) *Response to ordinary economic incentives demonstrably normal*

To this category belong not only all cases where supply rises or falls in response to prices, but also cases in which lack of response is more apparent than real. For instance, a supply curve for a certain commodity on a certain market day may appear perverse, but it may appear so only because the producer has found more lucrative alternatives.

(2) *Lack of response due to circumstances over which the individual has no control*

To this category belong institutional and tribal deterrents such as indigenous systems of communal land holding as well as lack of transport and marketing facilities. Clearly, where lack of initiative or response arises from circumstances over which the individual has no control the remedy is along the lines of economic and social improvement.

(3) *Lack of response arising from an economic system in which demand for money is a target demand*

The concept of *target demand* needs some explanation. Briefly, it relates to the nature of the demand for money in a subsistence or an embryonic exchange economy. In a developed exchange economy money stands for all the things money can buy. The demand for it is nonspecific in the sense that money does not have to be embodied in real things, or earmarked for any specific purpose, in order to exercise its influence as a spur to greater efforts. As against this, the demand for money in a subsistence or embryonic exchange economy is derived from a demand for *specific* things for which there is a felt need. Once a limited objective has been attained, any further exertion to earn money would be meaningless. Such a demand for money may be called a *target demand.* In a fully developed modern exchange economy, target demand for money,—as, for example, when a person makes a special effort to earn additional money for a specific purpose—is ordinarily of relatively little economic or social significance. But in an embryonic exchange economy, operating as it does on the fringe of a developed exchange economy, the amount of labor or goods that members of such an economy are prepared to offer for sale in the market is determined by the target demand for exchange media rather than by price, cost, and profit. There is nothing perverse or irrational about such behavior.

Lack of response to economic incentives does not arise from the innate characteristics of the people, but before economic incentives can come into play in an embryonic exchange economy there will have to be a general and pervading change in social and economic values.

Such changes are, in fact, taking place. As more and more people in underdeveloped countries are drawn into the orbit of a continuous exchange with the outside world, their needs are undergoing radical changes. The number of people in Africa, and elsewhere, who respond in a positive way to the usual economic incentives is, so far as one can weigh the evidence, steadily increasing. To a large extent this growth has been the result of opportunities provided by better transport and wider markets.

Large-scale exploitation of minerals has, among other things, led to the emergence and rapid growth of urban centers of population and industrial development, notably in southern and central Africa. There has been an exceptionally rapid development in French tropical Africa in recent years, mainly as a result of the large investments made in public and private enterprise. Although the French achievement has been very impressive it is not an isolated case. In other parts of tropical Africa too, the expansion of crop production for export has given rise to a similar, though less rapid, process of urban development.

All these developments point to significant changes in the social and economic life of African countries. One important aspect is the effect of African urbanization on agricultural production for local consumption. The presence of a nonagricultural population with a relatively high purchasing power now presents a ready outlet for the so-called subsistence crops for local use. In other words, not only export crops but also food crops for the local market have become profitable and have thus attained the status of cash crops. Moreover, as the local market presents the African peasant with new opportunities for earning a cash income, it also frees him from too much dependence on a single export crop. Such a development constitutes a new stage in African evolution which is bound to affect the whole structure of the primitive subsistence economy.

As may be expected, the degree and diversity of exchange production is related to the distance and transportation facilities to market with exchange production for local consumption assuming very large proportions in the immediate vicinities of large urban centers. On the other hand, in areas remote from the railroad terminal with poor road and marketing facilities, little is grown for overseas export, and the amount of surplus disposed of locally is small. Under such conditions, the balance of money income has to be earned by the temporary export of labor. Indeed, the phenomenon of migrant labor in Africa is closely related to the comparative lack of transport and marketing facilities, since workers can travel great distances on foot even where little else may reach the market. Thus the export of labor, in a to-and-fro migration pattern, from remote and least developed areas to market points, has become for many such areas the most significant form of exchange with the outside world.

To sum up, one of the great needs in Africa is a link between the so-called subsistence sector and the rest of the economy. The missing link is seen in transport and marketing facilities. This is not to say that the governments in Africa do not realize the importance of transport. On the contrary, all economic development plans throughout Africa south of the Sahara have devoted a substantial part of the planned expenditure to transport and communications. Yet the mere development of communications does not in itself represent a coordinated policy for the development of the subsistence sector of agriculture. Some official policies, in fact, have often consisted of no more than road building and other transport improvements, leaving the rest to take care of itself. In contrast, there are those who advocate direct investment in small-scale agriculture as a cure-all, without reference to transport, markets, or marketing facilities. To do no more than build roads is unimaginative; but to do no more than invest capital in small-scale farms is blind. In fact, capital spent on technical improvement of production may be largely wasted unless transportation and marketing facilities are made available simultaneously.

15 🐝 PROBLEMS OF AGRICULTURAL
        MECHANIZATION*

P. Staner

The development of mechanization in a new country is an indubitable manifestation of progress, for it implies a perfecting of working methods and a progressive increase in incomes. Well conceived and wisely applied, mechanization frees the workers from the more irksome and unhealthy tasks, and introduces an element of skill and personal initiative into the humblest duties. If, on the other hand, such mechanization only aims at raising productivity and profits, it leads to [production line techniques] and the transformation of men into more or less perfected robots.

The agriculture of the Congo is participating in the general [economic] evolution and is reaching a stage where manual labour no longer enables it to satisfy the constantly growing needs of the domestic market or the development of the foreign trade. The producers are desirous of improving their standard of living and of achieving a degree of comfort which the hoe and machete are unable to give them. Mechanization, the very principle of which was a subject for discussion several years ago, has become a topical problem.

What is the situation with regard to mechanization in the Congo?

The Congo is too vast and heterogeneous, the economic and social conditions too variable, for it to be possible to lay down general rules in this domain. The trials already accomplished, and those which are in progress, are principally concerned with resolving particular problems of a local nature. Analysis of them will

*From P. Staner, "Agricultural Mechanization in the Belgian Congo," *Sols Africains,* Vol. III, No. 4, October–December 1955. Reprinted by permission.

make it possible to lay down, not a general doctrine, but a few basic principles enabling us better to situate the problems awaiting resolution.

The mechanization of methods of production must justify itself not only from the technical, but also the economic and human standpoints. The mere purchase of a machine, even a good machine, does not automatically remove all difficulties; on the contrary, it may aggravate and multiply them, for it introduces basic modifications, almost always unexpected and often unpredictable, into the agricultural system, the organization of the enterprise and the financial balance of the latter.

Mechanization should not, therefore, be carried out just for mechanization's sake, but applied only when the replacement of muscles by motors offers irrefutable advantages. At present, mechanization may be justified in cases where it is less costly and more productive than manual labour; where it makes possible agricultural operations that the native is physiologically or psychologically unable to execute himself; where it liberates manpower for other tasks; or, in certain exceptional cases, where political or economic factors having no connexion with agriculture, make it necessary to develop rapidly the production or the standard of living of the population.

The field of action for agricultural mechanization is wide, but is closely dependent upon local conditions.

In *forest* regions, the processing of products at present accounts for more than half of the work devoted to *food* drops. Practical solutions to the problems of shelling or husking maize, rice, Job's tears, ground-nuts; of drying, storing and protecting products, have already been applied and have considerably lightened the work of the farmers.

The mechanization of cultural practices properly so called, will be more difficult to achieve, as the clearing of tree stumps and the levelling of termitaries are arduous and costly operations. Trials of tree-felling with chainsaws have given interesting results, and the process could be extended to most native settlement colonies and, especially, to lumbering enterprises.

The utilization of mechanical methods in the cultivation of *perennial crops* is limited to the maintenance of the spaces between the rows with rotary cutters, weed cutters or simply heavy harrows. Systematic trials conducted by large private firms have led to encouraging conclusions, although they have confirmed the necessity of controlling the tree-felling operations and of adopting judicious methods of clearing.

In *Savanna* regions, mechanization may be applied to a wider range of tasks. In addition to the remarkable results obtained by the *Compagnie Sucrière Congolaise,* attention may be drawn to the work carried out in the province of Kivu by the *Mission Anti-Erosive* (erosion control, land improvements, tillage, irrigated riziculture) and by the *Groupe d'Economie Rurale du Bas-Congo* (land improvement and intensive dry cropping), and the progressively extended utilization of mechanical tillage in certain native settlement colonies of the province of Kasai.

Less study has been given to the maintenance and improvement of *pastures* by mechanical methods, but this will become a matter of necessity in the near future, in regions where the reserves of land are limited.

Finally, the importance should be mentioned of mechanical instruments in lumbering and wood-working, and the increasingly frequent utilization of motor pulverizers and sprayers for *disease control* in perennial or annual plantations.

As can be seen, agricultural mechanization may assume different forms and affect all phases and fields of agricultural activity. In applying it, however, account must *always* be taken of the cost as well as of the possible reactions of the soil and the human milieu; in general, it may be considered that its success will depend upon the degree of intensity of cultivation which it makes possible, and upon the increased prosperity which may result therefrom for the peasants.

Buying a tractor is not enough to modernize an enterprise: the equipment must be correctly used, maintained, repaired and overhauled.

Mechanization requires, if failure is to be avoided, a highly developed infrastructure: competent and competing commercial agencies and technical services; modern, well-managed garages; the organization in each enterprise of well-equipped workshops and a good spare-parts service; establishment of a simple but efficient inspection and accounting system; training of drivers, mechanics, etc. Failure to appreciate these fundamental requirements has caused many disappointments, and has come near to compromising the very principle of mechanization in Africa.

Mechanization will make it possible to establish plantations in lightly populated regions, and agricultural colonization will receive a new impetus. Furthermore, the inevitable increase in the numbers of skilled workmen, drivers, mechanics, solderers, artisans, etc., will lead to a general rise in the economic standing of the workers and in their technical capacities and vocational standards.

Mechanization will also exert a determining influence on the rural masses. Integrated into a policy of intensification of cultural methods, it will help to liberate the peasants from the inferiority complex that weighs upon their vocation, to render their lives more attractive and interesting, and to change them from humble toilers engaged in a thankless occupation, into progressively better qualified and remunerated specialists.

These blessings are not unmixed, however: the introduction of mechanization could shake the very bases of the traditional society and lead to an accelerated evolution of the customs and the psychology of the rural inhabitants. The field of action of the tractor cannot be arbitrarily limited: its use will be extended, sooner or later, to all phases of agricultural activity. Furthermore, simple mechanical tillage involves the clearance of the ground, planned fallows, fertilizer—in other words, the elimination of shifting cultivation, the establishment of a complex organization of the enterprise, and the placing in common of certain means of production. This progressive industrialization is hardly compatible with the matriarchal system or with certain elements of native land tenure; a technocratic hierarchy would be substituted for the hereditary hierarchy of the clan. Hence, to avoid dangerous upsets, agricultural modernization must be accompanied by a patient and wise programme of education, in order to accustom the native of the Congo to organizing his work, co-ordinating his efforts and exercising the responsibilities which will gradually be allotted to him.

In this connexion, the future importance of the organization of native colonization schemes in the Congo and Ruanda-Urundi is already clearly shown. This new organization of the African rural structure makes it possible to eradicate shifting cultivation, which is so harmful to good soil conservation, and to facilitate the social evolution of the inhabitants. But these colonization schemes are not the final stage of the evolution of the rural populations: they only represent one stage, an important one, withal, of their progress. The rational regrouping of the peasants in allotments will provide a field ready to hand for our effort of intensification and of reasoned application of mechanical methods. It will enable us successfully to make the necessary adaptations without obliging the Congo natives to bear the brunt of the inevitable trial-and-error connected with any new experiment and without imposing a tension on the native community which would jeopardize its integrity and its future.

16 DESERT ENCROACHMENT IN SOUTH AFRICA*

D. F. Kokot

For forty years or more there have been repeated murmurings about the deterioration of natural conditions in South Africa. There were tales of heavy stock losses due to drought, of failing springs and of boreholes in which the water receded ever deeper and deeper. Pastures were not as good as in the days gone by, unpalatable alien plants were invading areas where sweet grass has reigned supreme. Summer dust storms from the arid west darkened the skies. So farmers, scientists, and legislators and even the dwellers in the cities, became alarmed and established committees to study the problem and devise means of meeting the ghostly menace to their well-being.

In earlier times we talked about the drought problem; in recent years a more picturesque expression has captured the popular imagination, so now we talk about desert encroachment. But what does it all mean? Are we merely fighting a phantom enemy conjured up to hide our own sins, or are we face to face with the threat of the desert, steadily stealing upon our once fertile pastures and inexorably pushing us ever eastwards to the regions of higher rainfall?

In the Senate of the Union of South Africa the problem of drought was discussed in 1914 and so serious did it appear that a Select Committee was appointed to study the matter. In the resolution appointing the Committee reference was made to the "steadily increasing severity of the annual droughts" and the "alarming increase" of soil erosion. The investigation was not a very thorough one but the conclusion was arrived at that there was no evidence to indicate that the rainfall had diminished. It should be explained that amongst farmers it was very commonly believed that the rainfall of South Africa had seriously diminished. The Committee

* From D. F. Kokot, "Desert Encroachment in South Africa," *Sols Africains*, Vol. III, No. 3, July 1955. Reprinted by permission.

came to the conclusion that the desiccation which had taken place in many parts of the country was largely due to faulty methods of farming.

Only six years later, in 1920, the position had become even more alarming and an important "Drought Investigation Commission" was appointed to make a very thorough study of the problem of increasing desiccation. This time a very painstaking investigation was carried out and the causes of desiccation carefully analysed. Again the conclusion was reached that a diminution in rainfall was not a cause of deterioration but a number of harmful farming practices were enumerated as contributing factors.

In the thirty years since the appointment of the Drought Investigation Commission many changes have come about in South Africa. The population has nearly doubled, and wars and other factors have driven the people to depend more upon the produce of their own land. The pressure on the land has therefore increased tremendously.

To understand the reasons why this pressure has resulted in such marked deterioration one must appreciate the peculiar climatic and topographical conditions which exist. In the first place there are very few localities, and these very limited in size, where the rainfall is adequate in quantity as well as satisfactory in seasonal distribution. One-third of the Union receives less than 20 inches (508 mm) of rainfall per annum and only 3 percent receives more than 40 inches. But not only is the rainfall inadequate in quantity; its bad seasonal distribution is such that it is seldom possible to grow crops throughout the year although temperatures will allow this nearly everywhere. More than two-thirds of the Union receives 70 percent or more of its rainfall during six months of the year only. South Africa is mainly a summer rainfall area, but a small section, the south-western tip of the continent, enjoys a winter rainfall similar to that of the Mediterranean lands. This unequal seasonal distribution of the rainfall, combined with its erratic occurrence from year to year, has provided the stage for some of the most spectacular deterioration which has taken place anywhere in the world in so short a time. A powerful factor aiding the deterioration is the elevated character of the central plateau with its steep river gradients to the sea.

In 1947 an ecologist (Dr. C.E.M. TIDMARSH of the Union Department of Agriculture) working in the Karoo (an arid to semi-arid region) found great difficulty in re-establishing the vegetation which he believed formerly grew there, even when such causes as overstocking had been removed. This led him to the conclusion that some factor had appeared which had brought about a permanent change in natural conditions so that these were no longer favourable for the existence of the former vegetation. In a scientific paper he set out his conclusions and put forward the hypothesis that as a result of the destruction by man of the natural vegetation in the arid western part of South Africa, atmospheric and rainfall conditions had thereby actually been disturbed. This destruction of the silver white grass, leaving a dark desert surface had brought about a rise in atmospheric temperatures so that the west winds exercised a desiccating effect on the more humid east. Following upon the reading of the paper it was suggested that the time was now ripe for a review of the evidence bearing on the problems of drought and desiccation. The idea of man influencing the climate was not new. From various parts of the world, and here in South Africa, especially amongst writers of the last century the view was frequently expressed that destruction of vegetation has resulted in decreased rainfall. The complementary view, too, has been commonly expressed that afforestation should be carried out on an extensive scale to promote increased rainfall.

A "Desert Encroachment Committee" consisting of seven scientists, drawn from a very wide field, was accordingly appointed in 1948 and its report has just been released. (The writer of this article was a member of the Committee.) The Committee devoted its attention mainly to those marginal areas where the vegetation has shown a very marked decline. By taking evidence at numerous places it tried to establish the nature and extent of the changes which had taken place and were still in active progress. In addition to the evidence collected on the spot from farmers the Committee received memoranda from a number of scientists and studied the opinions of many others.

One of the most valuable items of evidence was a map prepared by one of the members of the Committee showing the present day plant distribution over the Union. Combined with this he presented two other maps, one showing the assumed plant distribution before the arrival of the Bantu from the north, and the Europeans from the south. The other map showed what he anticipated the plant distribution would be like after a hundred years, if the present trends continued. The Committee accepted the general validity of these maps although the attempt to reconstruct the past purely on botanical grounds must naturally be open to serious error and doubt.

The indisputable and alarming fact is that there has been serious deterioration of the vegetation and hydrological conditions. And

everywhere there has been almost terrifying erosion of the soil.
The majority of the Committee were quite convinced that all the
damage that had been done could be explained in terms of the impact of man, with his plough and his domestic animals, upon a land
that was from the very start extremely vulnerable. Two members
of the Committee want to go somewhat further and attribute some
of the damage to a change of climate, partly brought about by
man's initial misuse of the land, but partly linked to a worldwide
rise in temperatures and reduction in rainfall.

Travelling across the Union of South Africa, from east to west
one passes gradually from a region having a rainfall of nearly 40
inches to one of the most desolate areas in the world, where barely
two or three inches of rainfall is recorded. With this vast difference in rainfall there is a corresponding difference in the vegetation, not only in density but in character. The major change in the
vegetation now indisputably going on is a gradual eastward spread
of the desert plants of the west. This means that fewer sheep can
be carried per acre of land. But some farmers do not deplore the
change because they say the plants evolved in an arid climate are
better able to withstand the recurring droughts. Some farming
practices are deliberately aimed at replacing grass by succulent
shrubs able to survive long periods without any moisture.

Whilst vegetation has been deteriorating there has been a parallel deterioration of hydrologic conditions but these have, in the
opinion of the present writer often been somewhat exaggerated.
South Africa was an arid country when the first white men settled
here three hundred years ago, and much that we have done has
tended to accentuate the appearance of aridity. When irrigators in
the lower reaches of a river complain that nowadays very little
water reaches them it is often not so much due to a deterioration of
hydrological conditions as to the fact, that the water is diverted by
higher riparian owners.

Throughout the Union of South Africa soil erosion is trium-
phantly on the march. The rivers that hurry impetuously, from
their sources in the highlands, to the sea are laden with the fruits
of erosion. Red and grey and black the rivers flow carrying at times
as much as 10 per cent of silt. One river in the eastern Karoo (a
region with 10–20 inches of rainfall) has over the last twenty-five
years carried an average of over 4 per cent of silt. Many estuaries
where small sea-going vessels could freely enter are today so
blocked with silt that even a small rowing boat runs aground. An
estimate based on the most recent statistics shows that possibly as

much as 250 million cubic metres of soil are annually swept to the seas.

With all this deterioration going on around us we have turned our eyes to the deserts that lie to the west and we talk of "desert encroachment" and the "threat of the desert." In doing so we have maligned the plants of the desert. Nature has compensated them for the harshness of their habitat by endowing them with the means of surviving the rigours of the desert. They are spreading from the desert to the higher rainfall lands only because we are creating the desert conditions under which they can thrive. The desert plants are not pushing out the grasses. Man, with his plough and his sheep and goats, destroys the grass and the desert plants step in. Examples abound where the destruction has been stayed and forthwith the grass is ready to oust the desert invaders. Not everywhere, however, because it seems that at times the destruction has been so severe that even with the complete suspension of all the forces of destruction the original grass fails to be re-established. It is largely for this reason that Dr. TIDMARSH postulates a change of climate condition.

Ever in the minds of those who look to the skies for the life-giving moisture is the thought that our rainfall is progressively decreasing. Conditions they say are not as they used to be in the "good old days" when gentle rains soaked the land so that the grass grew stirrup high and the cattle were fat and sleek. This problem of the alleged deterioration in our rainfall has been examined by a number of scientists. They all affirm that no such thing can be deduced from the available records of rainfall. The present writer has examined much of the available evidence and has come to the conclusion that no change, either in the quantity or the character of the rainfall, can be deduced therefrom. Not only were the available rainfall figures analysed but also the historical evidence. Yet from this mass of material no clear proof of rainfall deterioration has emerged. If our rainfall is changing the change is taking place so slowly that at this stage no such change can be proved.

Whether the desert is encroaching or not need not involve us in fruitless argument. What is plain for everyone to see is that we are "creating" deserts throughout the length and breadth of the land. On the highveld of the Transvaal hundreds of miles from the Kalahari desert exotic inedible plants are replacing the grass which has been destroyed by fire, by the plough, or by overgrazing; the rainfall is still more than 25 inches. Along the eastern escarpment of the Drakensbergen, where the moisture-laden clouds from the warm Indian Ocean cause copious rain, there is the most frightening soil erosion. Along this same escarpment the perennial mountain streams are in many places drying up. Yet in this very region hydrologic conditions have through control of grazing, the prohibition of grass burning and the planting of forests been almost miraculously improved.

The more one studies the problem the more one realises how extremely sensitive much of the land is. Monoculture, overgrazing and veld burning have set in train processes of deterioration which are always difficult to arrest and in many cases impossible. Slowly, only too slowly, are the people of South Africa realising how much harm has been done, and is still being done, through ignorance or economic pressure or reckless cupidity. But I believe that the tide has turned and throughout the land "conservation" farming is beginning to assume its proper role so that the fruitfulness of this sunny land may be preserved for future generations.

17   LAND CONSOLIDATION IN THE KIKUYU AREAS OF KENYA*

G. J. W. Pedraza

Land consolidation, farm planning and resettlement are being carried out in many of the tribal areas of Kenya. There are, however, considerable differences in the methods employed in the various regions, resulting from the various traditional systems of land tenure, the degree of co-operation of the people and from climatic and other conditions. This article sets out to describe the problem only as it affects the three Kikuyu districts in which there is a general similarity of procedure.

Before the advent of the European, and indeed for many years afterwards, there was no pressure on the land generally conceded

* From G. J. W. Pedraza, "Land Consolidation in the Kikuyu Areas of Kenya," *The Journal of African Administration,* Vol. VIII, No. 2, April 1956. Reprinted by permission of the Controller of Her Britannic Majesty's Stationery Office.

to be the preserve of the Kikuyu. All land was held communally by the ten clans, whose elders had the power of allocation to clan members. Much of the land was under forest, which was, however, steadily destroyed as the people looked for more fertile areas to replace their exhausted patches of cultivation. The problem of an apparent land shortage emerged only with the rapid increase of population, resulting from the cessation of inter-tribal wars and the introduction of medical facilities and famine relief measures.

In the interval between the two world wars, and for some years afterwards, there were three major obstacles to be overcome before any real contribution to the problem could be made. The first, and probably the most difficult, was the suspicion with which the tribe looked upon any move by government affecting land. Land, to the Kikuyu, is a possession transcending in value even that of his wives and children. The process of conditioning the mind of the Kikuyu to the acceptance of better methods of agriculture, in its widest sense was therefore long and tedious. It was aggravated for many years by opposition to progressive measures which emanated from political agitators and by the shortage of trained staff. All these difficulties have now been overcome to a large extent.

The second major obstacle which had to be overcome was the inborn conservatism of the peasant farmer, who was accustomed to the traditional methods of agriculture which had remained unchanged for many years. This difficulty has almost been overcome and the farmer now accepts the fact that he has much to learn, even though he, or to be more accurate his wives, may not relish the additional work entailed.

The third obstacle to progressive farming has been the system of land tenure and inheritance. It is only in the last few years that the leading Kikuyu farmers have accepted the fact that their customary laws on these questions constitute the most formidable barrier to good farming practices. Intensive propaganda and demonstration, together with the removal of subversive influences during the emergency, have resulted in a widespread realisation that the old customs must give way to modern methods. It is now probably true to say that a majority of the tribe wish to proceed as quickly as possible with land consolidation and to follow the advice which they receive on agricultural improvement.

It is perhaps best to look briefly at the customary system of land tenure and inheritance before describing the process of consolidation itself.

As stated above, all clan land is held in trust by the elders of the clan. They have the power to allocate any available land to a member of the clan if he is landless. In practice, however, there is now little land left for allocation. Land may also be inherited once it has been allocated. A third method of acquiring land is by purchase. Until recently, land which had been sold could be redeemed at will by the vendor, on repayment of the purchase price. It was, however, essential to abolish the right of redemption before consolidation could proceed and this has been done by the African district councils of the three districts, acting on the advice of their respective law panels.

The traditional laws of inheritance lead directly to rapid fragmentation and are primarily responsible for the present condition of agriculture in the reserve. A man may have the right to cultivate twelve acres of land, which, in most areas, would, if properly farmed, be an economic unit capable of supporting a wife and family at a good standard of living. He may well, however, have three wives, to each of whom he allots four acres to cultivate on his behalf. Moreover, under customary law the area cultivated by each wife is divided between her sons on the death of the father. The son of the first wife, being an only son, would receive the full four acres cultivated by his mother. The three sons of the second wife would receive one and one-third acres each. None of these areas are economic units but they will nevertheless be sub-divided again on the death of the sons and as a result it is not uncommon for a man to inherit as little as one-quarter of an acre. Furthermore, as a result of other customary laws of inheritance, or through purchase, a man frequently finds that he has a number of fragments of land, often separated from each other by some miles, so that he cannot farm them properly however much he may wish to do so. Finally, insecurity of tenure, resulting from the great volume of litigation over land which was common before the declaration of the emergency, dissuades the farmer from improving his land. Of what use is it, he thinks, to improve my land when I may well lose it tomorrow before the courts?

The effort on the part of government officers to improve the standard of agriculture in the reserve has been going on for many years and has been attended by considerable success in many areas. It eventually became necessary, however, to attack the problems posed by the basic system of land tenure and inheritance before any further spectacular progress could be achieved. This called for agreement by the people to four major changes in custom. They were, respectively:—

(a) the consolidation of widely separated fragments into one holding;
(b) the abolition of boundaries between different clan areas, where the requirements of consolidation make this desirable;
(c) the prohibition of the sub-division of land through inheritance below what is considered to be an economic holding; and
(d) the issue of individual titles, which are necessary to give security from litigation, but which will, in fact, also abolish the authority of the clan elders over land.

These principles have been accepted generally by the leading Kikuyu during the past few years. The majority of the population has also accepted consolidation of the fragments as being desirable, but it is uncertain to what extent the people have appreciated the full implications of land consolidation on their customary systems of tenure and inheritance. It is, however, unlikely that they will sustain any objections which they may have when the great benefits to be derived from the process become apparent.

Consolidation is necessarily a lengthy process. At present no legal sanction exists to authorise either its implementation or its end product. It is based purely on the agreement of the people concerned and is not carried out in any area where there is opposition to its introduction.

Land consolidation teams have been formed in each division of the three Kikuyu districts. Their composition varies between the districts but basically they consist of a team leader; a number of recorders, or measurers, whose main task is to measure up fragmented holdings and to compute the total acreage held by each individual; and a staff of farm planners, who lay out each consolidated holding on sound agricultural lines. All these are Africans who are specially trained for the work. Apart from their specialised knowledge they must be honest, since the opportunities for corruption are innumerable in an exercise of this kind.

Choice of a consolidation area depends on several factors. While the emergency continues, only those areas which are co-operative are likely to be selected. Subject to this condition, it is essential that the people themselves wish to have their land consolidated, since the whole scheme is based on agreement and consent. It is equally essential that the people are prepared to practise good husbandry after consolidation is completed, in order not to waste the time and effort involved. Amongst other considerations are the acreage of the areas selected and the desirability of building up blocks of sufficient size to justify aerial survey at a later date.

Consolidation is carried out area by area, and these areas may vary in size between 1,000 and 3,000 acres. Before measurement can begin, the team must effect exchanges of land, so that the fragments of each man who is to be settled in the area to be consolidated are concentrated in that area. This involves a long process of negotiation but it is hoped that the people will eventually themselves carry out these exchanges in advance of the team, as the desire for consolidation increases. The recorders proceed to ascertain and measure the boundaries and extent of each fragment, and the approximate total acreage held by each man is then computed. No attempt is made to carry out an accurate survey, nor is this possible with the staff and the time available. Clan elders and local people are co-opted to assist in determining each man's boundaries and the team leader is responsible for settlement of the more difficult disputes which arise. Records are kept of the location and measurements of each fragment.

Whilst this work is going on a staff of plane tablers make a topographical map of the area. This shows sufficient local landmarks to enable individual boundaries, and a soil conservation plan, to be inserted later, and includes contours at 12-foot vertical intervals. Although a certain degree of precision is required in the compilation of this map there is no attempt at very great accuracy.

On the completion of these two concurrent stages, representatives of the administration, agricultural, health, education, police and of the other departments which have particular interests in the consolidation area, meet together to plan the future layout of the area. These officers are now in possession of a topographical map of the area, a record of the total acreage held by each man, information concerning the location of each of his fragments and the names of the landless persons.

The agricultural officer first draws in on the map the soil conservation plan for the area. This includes provision for the water consumption requirements of humans and stock, in the shape of dams and boreholes. The next phase consists of marking on the map the area to be occupied by the village. Choice of a suitable site depends on the availability of water, health requirements, accessibility and other factors. The size of the village is governed by the acreage required to house those who own 3 acres or less, together with the acreage required for a church, school, shops, recreation area, community hall, cemetery, medical centre and the police post. Further areas are also reserved on the map for tree nurseries, agricultural demonstration plots, coffee and tea factories and any other facilities which are likely to be required by any of the departments concerned. A road plan, designed to open up the area, is then superimposed. Finally, the total acreage required for all

these public purposes is computed and is found by making a proportionate deduction from the total acreage held by each individual.

Representatives of the administration and agricultural department, together with the consolidation team and clan elders, are
now in a position to put in the new boundaries of consolidated holdings, both on the ground and on the map. At this stage, close supervision is required to ensure that each individual receives land of
agricultural value comparable to that which he has vacated. His
consolidated holding must also contain a proportion of arable,
cash-crop and grazing land, to facilitate planning of an economic
farm. As a general rule, allotments of under 3 acres are grouped
round the village where the owners will have to live, and holdings
of 3 to 6 acres are placed beyond these. Holdings of over 6 acres
are placed still further away from the village. The object of this
grouping is to encourage those with 3 to 6 acres to buy up the
adjacent allotments in order to increase their holdings to an economic size. Those who own less than 3 acres contribute one-quarter
of an acre to their housing plot in the village, whilst the landless
are given a similar plot, for which they will pay rent to the African
district council. The landless and the allotment holders will become
the village artizans and shop-keepers of the future and will also be
available to work as paid labourers on the larger holdings. In this
way it is intended to absorb a large proportion of the surplus population in productive labour. When the allocations have been made
the new boundaries are then agreed with clan elders and owners
and marked in on the topographical map.

During the process of measuring up fragments, the team has
already noted down the cash crops and other improvements for
which compensation will be payable in the event of the owner being
moved elsewhere on consolidation. A scale is laid down for all
items which attract compensation. The rates given are not binding,
but they nevertheless form a useful guide to all concerned. While
they are seldom exceeded, they are frequently reduced, with the
consent of the elders and the landowners concerned. Compensation
is paid between landowners and the transactions are recorded at a
specially convened meeting held after the consolidation has been
carried out.

ENCLOSURE AND FARM PLANNING

Consolidation is followed as soon as possible by enclosure. Boundaries are fenced with the most suitable material at hand and,
where necessary, are also planted up with seedlings, which will

grow into permanent hedges. Immediate enclosure is necessary, both to give the owner an increased pride in his holding and to provide boundary marks which will show up on an air photograph. It is proposed that consolidated holdings should be surveyed by air at a later stage preparatory to the issue of individual titles to land. Meanwhile, consolidation is followed up by a team who make an accurate survey of new boundaries. This forms the basis on which individual farm plans will be made.

Farm planning by the agricultural department also follows the completion of consolidation. In the early stages this planning consists of treating each feature as a whole. The general plan which has been adopted is that slopes of between 0° and 20° should become arable land; those between 20° and 35° should be bench-terraced and planted with cash crops and slopes steeper than 35° should be put down to grass. This will suffice as an interim measure to raise agricultural production without delay. As soon afterwards as the staff position permits, individual and detailed farm plans are made in order to show the farmer the best division of his land between the various food and cash crops and grazing; the cycle of rotation for each portion and the ideal layout for the homestead area with adequate paths of access, paddocks and other improvements.

It is at this stage also that an assessment is made of the need of each individual for a loan to assist him in developing his land. Loans of up to £125 may be paid from African district council or government development funds and these are repayable over 5 years at 4½% interest. The form of loan agreement contains, amongst other conditions, a declaration by the landowner and his heirs that the consolidated holding will not be sub-divided below what is considered to be an economic size.

Soil conservation works are carried out as soon as possible after consolidation, since it is essential to follow up this initial work with measures to raise production and to show visible results to the people. Bush and unwanted trees are cleared and bench-terraces, "cut-off" drains, spillways and narrow-base terraces are constructed, either by the people themselves or by paid gangs. The newly made terraces are then prepared for planting by the application of manure from village cattle sheds and compost which is made on the spot. A proportion of the wages of the paid gangs is paid from development funds and the balance is debited to the loan which the smallholder will receive. This is done in order to extend the life of development funds and of the available loan capital, and also to ensure that the individual makes some contribution towards the work done on his behalf.

There is no doubt that land consolidation and farm planning is of primary importance and urgency in the post-emergency reconstruction policy. It will, in addition, make a major contribution towards the resettlement of the Kikuyu because it results in the increased capacity of the land to carry the population and provides employment, as farm labourers, for a large number of those with little or no land, on the holdings of their more fortunate neighbours. Consideration is, therefore, being given to the staff and finance required to increase the rate of progress, so that consolidation and farm planning of the three Kikuyu districts may be completed within the next five years. Experiments designed to streamline the methods employed are also under way and these indicate good prospects of success. Additional funds required will probably be found by African district councils. Although the cost will be heavy, it would be inequitable and unwise to increase government contributions to this work without making even greater contributions to the agricultural progress of those other tribes which have remained loyal during the emergency. Financial considerations preclude such a policy. In order to lighten the burden, it has been proposed that fees should be charged for preparation of the farm plan and for registration of individual titles. This has yet to be approved and will require enabling legislation.

Land consolidation constitutes an agricultural revolution in the Kikuyu Land Unit and it will have the most profound effect on the lives of the people. The increased prosperity and purchasing power of the individual will lead to a higher standard of living and to a greater demand for goods of all kinds. The effect of this, and of other similar schemes elsewhere, which are aimed at improving the productive capacity of the land will, in turn, have a profound effect on the economy of a country the prosperity of which will inevitably be based on agriculture for many years to come.

18   HOW DOES INDUSTRY START IN AFRICA?*

W. A. Lewis

Industrialisation starts usually in one of three ways: (1) with the processing for export of primary products (agricultural or mineral) which were previously exported in a crude state; or (2) with manufacturing for an expanding home market; or (3) with the manufacture for export of light manufactures, often based on imported raw materials. The main difficulty in the way of capturing the processing of raw materials, and thus of getting the consuming countries to import a finished product instead of its raw materials, lies in the superiority of the consuming countries as centers for manufacturing. This superiority is based both on long experience and also on the scale and variety of their manufacturing industries, which is the secret of efficient production. This superiority was an obstacle even four centuries ago, when England was trying to wrest the processing of her own raw material from the more highly developed Netherlands. Today, the gap between industrialised and undeveloped countries is even wider than it was then, and therefore the obstacles to successful competition are even greater. In this competition the undeveloped country relies usually on two advantages: (a) low labour cost, based on low wages, and (b) an advantage in transport cost, if the material loses weight in the course of processing.

The likelihood of low labour cost offsetting the disadvantages of operating in a non-industrial environment is greatest where labour cost is a substantial element in total cost. Low labour cost is most helpful in industries where the amount of capital used per head is small. Since the processing of heavy raw materials is usually very capital intensive, low labour cost is often not sufficient to offset the environmental disadvantages of local manufacturing. It is more usually an advantage in transport cost which decisively favours the

* Excerpts from W. A. Lewis, *Report on Industrialization and the Gold Coast* (Accra: Government Printing Department, 1953). Reprinted by permission.

130

processing of raw materials on the spot. This advantage arises in the case of those raw materials which lose weight in the process of manufacture. For example, since it takes four tons of bauxite to make one ton of aluminium, transport charges are saved if bauxite is turned into aluminium on the spot, instead of being transported as bauxite to the country where the aluminium will be used. Similarly, it is cheaper to transport sawn timber than the equivalent logs, steel than the equivalent iron ore, sugar than the equivalent sugar cane, and so on. It is not, on the other hand, cheaper to transport cloth than the equivalent cotton, because very little fibre is lost in the process of manufacture. Neither is it cheaper to transport soap to the consuming market, rather than the equivalent oils, or rubber tyres rather than the equivalent latex. The decisive factor locating the processing of raw materials is thus, to summarise, usually not low wage cost, but loss of weight in the process of manufacture. Thus it is not surprising that in [Ghana] the chief cases in which processing before export occurs are the timber industry, where up to 40 or 50 per cent of the weight of the log is waste in sawmilling, the palm oil industry, where the waste, by weight, is even greater, and the removal of precious stones from the useless ores in which they are buried, where the waste is greater still.

To the extent to which industrialisation is financed from domestic savings, it is, in the ultimate analysis, the farmers who provide the wherewithal. In Japan, this was accomplished by levying high taxes and rents upon them; and in the U.S.S.R. it was accomplished by an inflationary process, with the prices of manufactures rising faster than food prices, to the farmers' disadvantage. It is, however, one thing to prise capital out of the farmer when his productivity is increasing year by year, and quite a different matter to prise it out of a stagnant agriculture. When rapid agricultural progress is taking place, it is not very difficult to get a lot more capital out of the farmers, and still leave them with an annually rising standard of living. Much is talked about the speed of Japanese industrialisation; but it is not generally realised that what really made this possible was the spectacular increase in agricultural productivity which was taking place at the same time. Thus the secret of industrialisation is a rapidly progressing agriculture, and, since food production is the major part of agriculture, the number one priority in a programme of economic development is measures which increase food production per head. Without such measures, a country like [Ghana] cannot spare the labour for in-

dustries, cannot find the capital for them and has too small a market
to support their output.

Development, like anything else, has a price. The question is not
whether there are disadvantages, but whether the benefit exceeds
the cost. Even when foreigners make large profits they are still
contributing to development, not only by means of the wages, taxes,
and other expenses that they incur, but also because they train
labour and impart commercial experience to the general population. The most serious indictment that can be levied against foreign
capitalists, in economic terms, is not that foreign shareholders
receive dividends, but that the foreigners are often reluctant to
train up people in the secrets of their craft. For usually the foreigner's most useful contribution to a country is not his capital, but the
new techniques which he brings. If these new techniques are dispersed among the people progress is rapid, and the country soon
becomes independent of foreign patronage. But if they remain the
monopoly of a few foreigners, development must be slow.

The foreigner's most useful craft in these days is not scientific
information, but managerial experience. Science and technology are
taught in schools, and the local people can study them in their own
or foreign universities. The craft of business management, however, can be learnt only in managing businesses. If no one will
employ the local people above the level of clerks, they cannot learn
how to manage industrial businesses for themselves, and their
economic affairs will always be dominated by foreigners. This is the
reason why the foreigners, in those countries where they refuse to be
assimilated, are usually most careful to exclude local people from
managerial positions. It is also the reason why most colonial countries, as soon as they become independent, pass legislation or take
other steps to compel foreign firms to open up managerial positions
to local people. But even non-colonial countries have taken such
measures; thus, when foreigners brought new trades to England in
the sixteenth and seventeenth centuries, the patents of monopoly
which they were granted usually included the condition that the
foreigner must train a number of Englishmen in his craft within a
stipulated period. Whatever the foreigner's faults may be, the fact
remains that [Ghana] needs him more than he needs [Ghana].
Foreign capital does not need [Ghana]. If all the foreign capital
now in [Ghana] were driven out, it would have little difficulty in
being absorbed elsewhere, for the simple reason that [Ghana] is a
very small place relatively to the world as a whole. There are
many places within the sterling area crying for capital—England
herself, not to mention Australia, the Rhodesias, Ceylon and else-

where. [Ghana] cannot gain by creating an atmosphere towards foreign capital which makes foreigners reluctant to invest in [Ghana].

The [Ghana] Government is so short of money that it should be reluctant to take on the ownership and operation of industrial undertakings, except where this is inescapable. It may be inescapable in two cases, in public utilities, and for purposes of pioneering. In the case of public utilities, public ownership is one way of protecting the consumer against exploitation, but it is not the only way. The alternative way is to leave the industry in private hands, but to control its prices or profits, and its conditions of sale. There is no point in entering into controversial discussion here of the appropriate place to draw the line between public ownership and private enterprises. Every government has its own philosophy in accordance with which it draws this line where it thinks fit.

From the point of view of economic development, public ownership as a means of pioneering is much more interesting. In countries where entrepreneurs lack experience or confidence, there is a case for the government to lead the way by establishing industries with its own money, and to show that they can be operated successfully, in the expectation that it can withdraw from industry once the pioneering stage is over. The great exponent of this technique was Japan. There, between 1870 and 1900, the Government started one industry after another, and there is hardly a major industry in Japan today which was not initiated under government ownership. There was, however, no intention of permanent ownership; once the factory had become a going concern, the Government sold out, and turned its attention elsewhere. Also the Japanese Government was quite willing to make loans or subsidies to private entrepreneurs where it thought that this would serve the same pioneering purpose. How far it is necessary for a government to pioneer in this way depends upon the peculiar circumstances of the country. Japan at this time was remote from the centres of the world economy, having newly emerged from complete isolationism. Foreign entrepreneurship was not easily accessible, even if it had been welcome. On the other hand there were old aristocratic classes fairly wealthy which could carry on with industrialisation, once the Government had given its lead. [Ghana] has probably greater access to foreign enterprise, and probably also, because of its egalitarian structure, more need for foreign capital than had Japan. The [Ghana] Government should be willing to pioneer in establishing industries which it thinks will be successful, wherever private enterprise is reluctant to take the lead.

Whatever the reason that may cause the government to establish its own industrial undertaking, it has yet to decide how to cope with management. One way is to advertise for a manager and other staff with experience of the industry. This is seldom the best way. Most of the good managerial staff is already employed by industry, and it is not easy to attract such people away. There is therefore grave danger of entrusting an expensive undertaking to people who are not fully qualified to run it. Moreover, even if the best people are attracted, it is not easy for them to keep up with technical developments in the industry once they have left the firms in which new techniques are being evolved. The alternative is for the Government to employ existing firms, already running their own plants, to manage as well the Government's plant. This may be done simply for a management fee, or preferably there may also be some capital participation by the firm, so that the undertaking becomes a joint enterprise. Such joint enterprises benefit both parties, the Government, whose investment is protected by expert management, and the private firm, whose investment is protected by the fact that the Government is in with it.

To train up African enterprise must naturally be one of the major objectives of economic policy. The role of the foreigner is that of the tutor: a sometimes likeable but usually tiresome fellow, from dependence on whom one wishes to escape at the earliest possible moment. As in politics, so also in economic life, the test of maturity is that the country can proceed on its own without needing any significant foreign help. That is why foreign business men should not be allowed in the country unless they play their part in training Africans to do their job, and this is why, in one sense, the crucial test of an industrialisation policy is not how rapidly it increases employment or output, but how rapidly it builds up African enterprise. This conclusion does not stem from any emotional attitude towards foreigners, who are neither better nor worse than the indigenous people, and neither more nor less lovable; even if we look at the matter on its most pedestrian level, there are simply not enough foreigners available to initiate all the development of which [Ghana] is possible, so progress must be slow unless the African people learn to start and to run things for themselves.

African entrepreneurship is deficient in technical knowledge, in managerial capacity, and in capital. Of these three, the easiest to remedy is the deficiency of technical knowledge. For this can be learnt in technical schools and universities, or by placing Africans in foreign firms, at home or overseas, to learn the necessary techniques. Besides, technique can usually be hired. African business men should not hesitate to employ expatriates who have special knowledge: some already do so, and more should follow their example. For an African to hire a European (or Indian or Japanese or whoever has the skill) should be regarded neither as treachery to the racial cause nor as a source of added prestige; it is often simply the quickest way to establish an African business on a sound foundation.

Lack of managerial capacity is more difficult to remedy. The requirements of business management are five-fold. First, there is the management of physical resources—factory layout, the organising of a smooth flow of work through the factory, materials handling, care of machinery. Secondly, there is the keeping and use of records—of stocks, orders, costs, debits and credits. Thirdly, there is the management of men—selection of staff, discipline, loyalty, esprit de corps, delegation of duties and authority. Fourthly, there is the commercial sense, which cuts out waste, adjusts the use of resources to the flow of output, knows what prices to pay or to charge, and knows how to buy and to sell. And finally, there is the sense of integrity, without which a firm cannot acquire reputation or goodwill, and without which it cannot therefore last. These requirements are listed because their importance is frequently overlooked. It is a common error, in undeveloped countries, to believe that entrepreneurship requires mainly technical knowledge and capital. The truth is the reverse: if people really have managerial capacity they will in most cases be able to find technical knowledge and capital to work with. What makes a business successful is the efficiency of its management, for, given this, all else will follow.

African enterprise cannot be built up simply by lending Africans money. To lend money to entrepreneurs who lack managerial capacity is merely to throw it down the drain. What potential African industrialists lack is not primarily money; it is rather technical knowledge, and experience of factory organisation. If the government lends money it should do this only as a supplement to rendering technical and managerial assistance. In fact, the loan should be made only on condition that the borrower is willing to accept some measure of supervision. In some other countries, where money is lent to small business men, the lending agency stipulates that one of its officers becomes a director of the company to which money is lent, with power to veto certain transactions; in other cases it is content merely to have powers of inspection, and to give advice. In [Ghana] a lending agency should have a staff of persons with managerial experience, who keep in the closest touch with all borrowers, partly to ensure that the loan is used for the purpose for which it is given, and partly to advise generally. This is where the old Gold Coast Industrial Development Corporation went wrong. Since it started in 1948, the Corporation lent money to over 40 small African industrialists. It made 10 loans of £500 or under, 13 loans between £500 and £2,000, and the rest mostly in sums under £10,000. No supervision of any kind was exercised. Much of the money was found not to have been used for the purposes for which it was lent, and a good deal of it was never recovered. A few of the loans helped to establish sound enterprises, but most of the loans proved to be a failure.

The missing link in the chain of industrialisation is often no more than lack of interest and initiative. This is not likely in advanced countries, where there are scores of knowledgeable entrepreneurs ever watching out for new ways of making money. Yet, even in advanced countries many governments, central, state or municipal, go out of their way to create special agencies to stimulate industrialisation, because they consider that likely opportunities may otherwise be overlooked. In an undeveloped country the need is even greater. There is a marked shortage of experienced entrepreneurship, and many profitable opportunities escape attention for lack of knowledge of industry. The government has therefore a duty to do research on the profitability of possible new industries, to try to attract industrialists to start such industries, and to start them itself if it is convinced that they would prove successful, but cannot get others to take the risk.

Should the government subsidise or protect manufacturing industries which could not otherwise pay their way? It is generally agreed that a government ought to give temporary assistance to new industries to help them to find their feet, if it is convinced that they will be capable of standing on their own after an initial short period of running in. Should it also permanently assist industries which would otherwise never be able to pay their way?

The argument that new industries must be able to pay their way represents only a first approach to the subject, which must be modified in the light of other considerations. The most important of these considerations are two variations upon the theme that one must take the future into account as well as the present. In the first place, if we are comparing the relative profitability of agriculture and of manufacturing we must do so not in terms of current prices but in terms of prices expected to rule in the future. Agriculture may be very profitable at present, but if agricultural prices are expected to fall relatively to the prices of manufactures, then we should push manufacturing industry now beyond the immediate point of profitability, as an insurance against future trends. In practice, of course, no one knows how prices will move in future. Hence, the best insurance is to avoid excessive specialisation. And this, in the context of [Ghana] seems to mean that it is worth while to subsidise the development of new industries other than cocoa. Such new industries will include other agricultural crops at present on the margin, as well as some factory industries also on the margin.

The second variation arises out of the fact that it takes manufacturing industry some time to find its feet. A new factory in an under-developed country has to train its labour, almost from scratch, and will have to put up with very low productivity in the first year or two. If it proposes to use local raw materials, it may be some time before the supply of these can be organised in sufficient quantity (e.g. in [Ghana] context, tobacco, limes, pineapples) and in the meantime the factory may have to work below capacity, or to use more expensive imported materials. There may also be difficulty in establishing a foothold in the local market, which is wedded to imported brands, which may be neither better nor cheaper. These difficulties decrease with time. Meanwhile, a subsidy or protection for a limited period is thoroughly justified, so long as there is good reason to think that the factory will soon be able to pay its way.

CONCLUSIONS AND RECOMMENDATIONS

Measures to increase the manufacture of commodities for the home market deserve support, but are not of number one priority. A small programme is justified, but a major programme in this sphere should wait until the country is better prepared to carry it. The main obstacle is the fact that agricultural productivity per man is stagnant. This has three effects. First, the market for manufactures is small, and is not expanding year by year, except to the extent of population growth; consequently it would take large subsidies to make possible the employment of a large number of people in manufacturing. Secondly it is not possible to get ever larger savings out of the farmers, year by year, to finance industrialisation, without at the same time reducing their standard of living; hence industrialisation has to depend on foreign capital, and large amounts of capital for this purpose could be attracted only on unfavourable terms. And thirdly, agriculture, because it is stagnant, does not release labour year by year; there is a shortage of labour in [Ghana] which rapid industrialisation would aggravate.

Number one priority is therefore a concentrated attack on the system of growing food in [Ghana], so as to set in motion an ever increasing productivity. This is the way to provide the market, the capital, and the labour for industrialisation.

Priority number two is to improve the public services. To do this will reduce the cost of manufacturing in [Ghana], and will thus automatically attract new industries, without the government having to offer special favours. Very many years will have elapsed before it becomes economical for the government to transfer any large part of its resources towards industrialisation, and away from the more urgent priorities of agricultural productivity and the public services. Meanwhile, it should support such industrialisation as can be done on terms favourable to the country. That is to say, it should support industries which can be established without large or continuing subsidies, and whose proprietors are willing to train and employ Africans in senior posts. Because industrialisation is a cumulative process (the more industries you have already, the more new industries you attract) it takes time to lay the foundations of industrialisation, and it would be wrong to postpone the establishment of any industry which could flourish after a short teething period.

19  THE PRODUCTIVITY OF AFRICAN LABOUR*

P. de Briey

Over the last 60–70 years tropical Africa has undergone an economic revolution. Its 140 million inhabitants, who for centuries had been producing nothing more than the necessities for subsistence, have now begun living and producing with an eye to the outside world. In other words a market economy has taken the place of the subsistence economy. This change was essential for progress. In the absence of any currency some medium of exchange had to be found for the purposes of education, the treatment and cure of

* Excerpts from P. de Briey, "The Productivity of African Labour," *International Labour Review*, Vol. LXXII, Nos. 2–3, August–September 1950. Reprinted by permission.

endemic and epidemic sickness, the opening of communications and the acquisition of a minimum of industrial equipment or simply for the purchase of goods from Western traders. Africa, however, had no other medium of exchange to offer than its own farm produce or the labour of its people. While the resulting exchange has taken place partly through the sale of produce and partly through the hire of labour, there is a marked tendency in most territories for one or the other of these two forms of commercialism to dominate. Thus, for example, production for market plays by far the more important part in money earning in the indigenous agricultural economies in [Ghana], [former] French West Africa, Nigeria and Uganda, while in Kenya, Northern Rhodesia and Southern Rhodesia wage employment completely overshadows cash cropping.

Thus a market economy made its appearance in Africa. The process was and still is extremely slow. Even now, in tropical Africa as a whole, the major proportion (approximately 70 per cent.) of the resources of cultivated land and of labour (approximately 60 per cent.) of the indigenous agricultural economies is still engaged in subsistence production. Yet the development of a market economy is essential for any improvement in the standard of living of the people. In view of the rising population and the progressive erosion of the soil, to quote only the most obvious factors, there is a need to expand resources and acquire equipment, and this would be difficult in a subsistence economy. At the present stage of development the need for fresh changes is becoming evident. It is clear that transport facilities will have to be improved if there is to be any increase in the export trade. Productivity will also have to be raised to ensure a flow of goods to foreign markets, meet the needs of workers employed in non-indigenous undertakings, and maintain the standard of living of the producers themselves. New sources of production will also have to be discovered, and the reserves of labour must be used more effectively than in the past, possibly by finding work for them in industry instead of on the land.

If the output of unskilled labour in industry were to be taken as a yardstick the picture of the African worker's standards of productivity would undoubtedly be gloomy. It is unanimously recognised that the output of unskilled African workers is extremely low in almost all the undertakings that employ them. An attempt to measure the productivity of labour in a factory in Durban (Union of South Africa) showed that the output of the average unskilled migrant worker was only 29 per cent. of the figure taken as the

optimum. The report of the commission of inquiry set up to investigate the protection of secondary industries in Southern Rhodesia
produced statistical evidence to show that output per head of local
workers was considerably lower than in any other Commonwealth
country. A report published in 1946 expressed a similar opinion of
labour in British East Africa (Kenya, Uganda and Tanganyika).
It stated: "The dominant problem throughout East Africa is the
deplorably low standard of efficiency of the worker"—a view confirmed as far as Kenya is concerned by the report of the Committee
on African Wages published in 1954. The Governor-General of the
[former] Belgian Congo, speaking before the Government Council
in July 1949, was also sharply critical of the low output of workers
in this territory. An inquiry held in Duala [in the Republic of the
Cameroons] found that:

> As compared with a White worker's output, that of a Negro varies
> between one-third and one-seventh or one-eighth, depending on the
> employer and the trade (or within a given trade). The usual proportion
> is about one-quarter. In other words, it takes a Negro four days to do
> what a White does in one. And this opinion was confirmed by all the
> employers that we talked to.

The output of the African wage earner is only one determining
factor in the productivity of the population as a whole. Since his
output is low, his wage is low—enough, perhaps, for his own subsistence but quite inadequate to meet the requirements of a family.
This low level of output among the wage-earning population ought
to be offset by higher productivity among the independent farmers,
the more so since the number of the latter has been much reduced
by the movement into wage earning employment in non-indigenous
undertakings. Those that remain must consequently produce enough
to feed the absent workers, meet the needs of the traditional communities and maintain a flow of goods for exchange on foreign
markets. In fact, however, the productivity of the independent
farmer has fallen off in almost every part of Africa south of the
Sahara. An official inquiry held in 1949 into the economic circumstances of the population in a Ciskei Native Reserve in the Union
of South Africa showed that only a very small fraction (6.8 per
cent.) of the farmers' average income was derived from agriculture. In no village was the fraction more than 10.4 per cent. Much
of the population's income (35 per cent.) was derived from extra-
reserve earnings (probably the wages of villagers who had found
employment in areas some distance away). No indication is given
of the other sources of income. Farm produce consisted of a little

maize and kaffir corn, plus eggs and poultry; the main source of income, however, was the sale of wool.

In the Native Reserves the soil is becoming less and less productive. The official farm census returns show that a total of about 620 million lb. of maize and 148 million lb. of kaffir corn were produced between 1923 and 1927. The corresponding figures for 1935–39, however, were no more than 478 and 122 million lb. respectively. In 1949 the average yields of maize in the area covered by the above inquiry were found to be as low as 30 lb. an acre.

In Southern Rhodesia the soil in the Native Reserves is almost as unproductive as in the corresponding areas of the Union of South Africa. For the years 1936–46 maize yields in the Reserves are reported to have ranged from 1.5 to 2.0 bags an acre, as compared with a yield of 4.5 to 7.0 bags on the European farms. This means that two full acres are needed to support one person (at the desirable rate of 2,850 calories per day).

The problem is aggravated by population increase. Unfertile land and the poverty that goes with it have led many of the younger members of the population to migrate. A report from Southern Rhodesia for 1948 states that a little over half the total male population is absent from the Native areas.

[Other studies in Kenya, the Congo and Senegal] have shown that the exhaustion of the soil and the resulting drop in the incomes of African farmers are tending to become general. What is worse, it is clear that the native farmer is simply unable to increase his productivity, the limit to what he can do being governed by factors beyond his control. African farmers have neither the capital nor the technical knowledge, nor in some cases the cultivable land, to expand their output.

The result of this is that over large areas of tropical Africa output is inadequate, and low living standards and instability are prevalent among both the independent farmers and the African wage earners. The peoples of Africa are poor because they do not produce enough. In order to create wealth they must produce more, so that the surplus production can be used to buy more efficient tools, pay for the cost of education and vocational training, acquire fertilisers for their land, extend the expectation of life through medical care, etc. As it is, they have to eat most of their own output of food or use it to buy clothing and other basic consumer goods.

The position is by no means hopeless. In Africa as elsewhere, the productivity of men depends on a few major factors:

(1) the amount of labour in relation to the available land;
(2) the amount of labour in relation to the available capital;

(3) the methods of production;

(4) the state of the labour force from the standpoint of health, intelligence and character, and its skill and training.

The first three factors must be studied if the productivity of the independent farmers is to be raised. However, in the case of the wage earners, whose opportunities are governed in the main by the society in which they are brought up and the undertakings for which they work, the human factor is the only one that matters. Moreover, in such a thinly populated continent as Africa the importance of man himself is preponderant.

The African is closely bound up with his physical environment, and any assessment made of him must therefore take account of the climate in which he lives, the diseases he suffers from, the food he eats, and the social group from which he comes.

As regards climate, the view has been expressed that with freedom from malnutrition and infection, and when other circumstances are propitious, African society can rise to splendid heights, and that Africans themselves are basically well adapted to their climate. Even if this view is considered overoptimistic, the African climate would not appear to be a major obstacle to the productivity of labour.

In a study of labour productivity in the Belgian Congo, Mr. Arthur Doucy has described the physical condition of workers from the Mayumbe, Tshuapa and Middle Kwilu districts on arrival from their tribal areas. He states:

(1) they all suffer from parasitic worms of the intestines;

(2) some suffer from parasitic worms of the blood;

(3) all have malaria;

(4) all have incipient yaws, for which they have received little or no treatment;

(5) most have or have had gonorrhoea;

(6) many have syphilis;

(7) some of these conditions reduce their haemoglobin level, which in many cases is as low as 65 per cent., i.e. a red blood count of 3 to 3½ million.

This gloomy picture is unfortunately generally true, though the specific infections vary. Dr. Carothers, after mentioning the main diseases to which Africans are subject, adds: "Few Africans are free from all of these, and it would be easy to find examples of persons infected concurrently with malaria, hookworm, bilharziasis, ascariasis and taeniasis, with a haemoglobin level of about 30 per cent., and yet not complaining of ill health. 'Normality' in the

African, even from the standpoint of infection alone, is a rather meaningless abstraction." This description of the pathological conditions found among a high percentage of Africans has a parallel in the reports that have come in from various sources concerning the effects of the chronic malnutrition so common in many parts of Africa. The fact that many African communities are underfed has been placed on record on numerous occasions, notably in 1939 by the British Committee on Nutrition in the Colonial Empire, and in 1949 by the Inter-African Conference on Food and Nutrition held at Dschang in the French Cameroons. Dr. Carothers also writes: "In summary, African diets are lacking in a variety of constituents necessary for physical and mental health. These deficiencies are most widespread and prominent in regard to protein, vitamin A, and certain members of the vitamin B complex. The chief sufferers are the infants and young children, but no age is immune. The classical deficiency diseases are seldom seen, but the bulk of the population lives on the verge of their development, and in periods of stringency they promptly appear.

The effects of chronic malnutrition have not been accurately assessed in Africa, but it appears certain that in vast areas where malnutrition is an everyday occurrence the inhabitants lack vitality and drive.

However far the low standard of productivity in Africa may be attributable to malnutrition and disease, it would be wrong to explain the inefficiency of the African industrial worker wholly in terms of his physical condition. The infections to which Africans are subject take a much stronger hold on them in the rural areas, where medical supervision is virtually non-existent and malnutrition is also more acute. On the other hand it would not be true to say that the African is generally incapable of sustained effort in his native environment. Many observers have testified to the contrary, among them Dr. Ombredane, who writes: "It has often surprised me to see Negroes working from 8 o'clock in the morning until 2 in the afternoon without any break for rest or refreshment, in an effort to finish a hut or a piece of raffia work, a hatchet, a hoe, an ivory figure or a mask that they had started making." Mr. Ryckmans quotes the case of men who think nothing of a 12-hour walk into the jungle to fetch well over a hundredweight of brushwood. Other illustrations can be found in the backbreaking job of clearing farmland and in the many other communal tasks that form a part of African village life. In the case of the farming population, as was mentioned earlier, the explanation of the low level of productivity lies in the inefficient farming methods and the desertion of

the villages by the men. In the case of the wage-earning population, on the other hand, it seems that some other explanation must
be found.

It is natural to look first for a connection between the African
wage earner's indifference towards his job and the new setting in
which he finds himself, involving as it does the payment of a wage
as well as special housing, training, industrial relations and so on.

To a European worker wages are the fundamental incentive to
work. It has often been said of the African worker that wages offer
no inducement and that less effort rather than more is likely to be
the result of higher pay. This bare statement will not stand investigation. In a paper submitted to the Belgian Royal Colonial
Institute, Mr. R. van der Linden has shown how wage increases
in a Léopoldville shipyard between 1939 and 1950 were accompanied by an appreciable rise in productivity. What is true is that
many Africans with crops or cattle to look after in their villages
look for wage-paid employment with the sole idea of earning a
little extra money with which to pay their taxes or to buy some
article. If, having found a job, the wage is increased and they succeed in saving the requisite amount more quickly, they see no further
point in working and either slacken off or try to leave. What is
taken to be a lack of logic, or as a sign of indifference or laziness,
is in fact the outward expression of a perfectly valid piece of
reasoning. Even so, before wages can play the same part in the
life of African workers as in the life of Europeans, money and
economic forces generally will have to acquire the same significance
in the African's social group as in the Western world. At the present time, Africans living in a subsistence economy can still dispense
with wages and not starve. This, however, raises the problem of the
African's relations with his social group—a point to be considered
later.

There is no need to emphasize how much a worker's output can
be affected by his housing. If an unstable worker is to settle, he has
to be given a chance of finding accommodation near his work-place,
and if he is to settle for any length of time some arrangement must
also be made to house his family. Some employers have recognised
the benefits of a stable labour force and have arranged for suitable
accommodation to be built for their employees. This, however, has
not happened in the cities. In most cities the way the African population is huddled together in makeshift dwellings has to be seen to
be believed.

However, while poor housing may discourage a worker from

settling down, it should not be assumed that satisfactory housing will always have the opposite effect.

The value of training is self-evident. C. H. Northcott, writing of Africans in Kenya, states that men "who knew nothing of mechanics and until they reached Nairobi had never seen a railway train, are met in the railway workshops with a display of mechanism so great that it bewilders even a well-educated European." The results achieved with training are in fact spectacular, but no worthwhile training can be given to a worker who stays only six months. Training presupposes a certain amount of stability; before a worker can be trained, moreover, he must be imbued with a desire to work.

It may be asked whether the problem can be solved by satisfactory labour-management relations. While an atmosphere of confidence and understanding can undoubtedly do much to encourage more effective and sincere co-operation on the part of African workers, it cannot guarantee success or higher output. There are certain over-riding factors influencing the conduct of the African worker, and even the best employer is powerless against them.

The analysis of the factors determining a worker's output leads to a fundamental question: Does the African want to work in an undertaking of the Western type? As one author has observed—

> Men of all races work only to achieve some end. If that end is unobtainable, or not valued very highly, they either work light-heartedly or not at all. The African in town is in just this position. His expenditure is limited almost entirely to consumable goods, the kind of bric-a-brac that a traveller picks up on his travels. With none of the tribal sanctions capable of operation, with few kinsmen in town to remind the worker of his obligations, and with no urban public opinion, there is nothing, either in his own social system or in that of the West, to inspire him to greater effort.

The above quotation emphasises the solitude of the normal Negro worker. He has lost his attachment to the land, he no longer takes part in tribal consultations, he no longer shares in the labours, joys and sorrows of his village. The significance of this isolation is difficult to grasp without some knowledge of the African's normal way of life in his natural environment and as a member of his social group. Carothers writes—

> Life in Africa was highly insecure, but the individual did achieve some inner sense of personal security by adherence, and only by adherence, to the traditional rules—rules which received their sanction and most of their force from the "will" of ancestors whose spirits were conceived as powerful and as maintaining their attachment to the land.

There were fears, of course, and misfortunes were almost the order of the day, but even these were seldom without precedent, and for each of these there were prescribed behaviour patterns which satisfied the urge to action, so that the African achieved a measure of stability and, within his group and while at home, was courteous, socially self-confident and, in effect, a social being. But this stability was maintained solely by the continuing support afforded by his culture and by the prompt suppression of initiative.

Limits are placed on the freedom of the individual, for otherwise he would be lost to the community. No culture is absolutely static, for a static culture cannot survive. The African tribal system, like every other, has an infinite capacity for adaptation. But the fact remains that for a man brought up under a system deeply rooted in tradition and so vitally dependent on a code of social behaviour, the change to an entirely different way of living is a great strain. As Carothers observes, change has become a familiar feature of modern Europe and America. For an African, however, the shock is incomparably more violent, and it is natural that when he suddenly finds himself confronted with a way of life in which he is left alone to face a multitude of unknown risks, against which his tribal culture can afford him no protection, his first sensation is one of insecurity. This is a point on which all observers are agreed. Mannoni states that when a Malgache finds his traditional chain of authority in danger, if not actually disrupted, he falls a prey to panic, insecurity and a sudden sense of insufficiency. Balandier also notes that the formation of an urban proletariat has gone hand in hand with a rising sense of insecurity. In a report on Elisabethville prepared on 3 April 1950, Grévisse writes: "The thought uppermost in the minds of the Bantu population of the towns is not a desire for individuality or freedom, as is often mistakenly believed; it is neither more nor less than a desire for some security." But the security an African requires is not of a mystical or instinctive kind; it is physical and economic. What he wants is a guarantee against starvation and an assurance that he can live and grow old in peace with his family.

In Western civilization, men work for money because of the security that it brings or because of the possessions and the prestige that a wealthy man can command. In African society men also sought security and prestige. These were likewise achieved only by hard work, although the concept of money did not enter into the situation. . . . The urban situation, however, demands that the African should work as hard as, or even harder than, he has ever done before but, at the same time, neither his work nor the money that he earns can provide him with the security or the prestige that he would like. The average urban African is un-healthy, badly housed, uneducated, and he lacks any security in town even if he happens to have been born there. . . . The bars to progress are very real to him and he knows that, under present conditions, town life in European employment can offer him little in the way of lucrative employment or future stability. Consciously or unconsciously, therefore, he refuses to cut himself completely adrift from his tribal kinsmen and his tribal background. This tendency is referred to as the "foot in both camps attitude" and is largely condemned on the grounds that a man who attempts to retain a foot-hold in both places cannot be efficient in either. There is considerable truth in this assertion . . . the actual situ-ation is that the urban Africans are poised between two different ways of life or systems of belief. They see clearly enough that the kinship system of tribal days and the monetary system of the West are incom-patible. They see the two systems in conflict and they want to come out on the winning side. At present, however, neither side can offer any longterm advantage. The monetary system of the West offers goods but no security. The kinship system offers few goods but some security. This security, however, is already somewhat suspect because of the break-up of the tribal order. On the other hand, the precarious state of those who are completely detribalised, who have no country home to retire to in their old age, or who have no knowledge of country life, is fully realised. And so the majority of men continue to sit on the fence and attempt to retain such rural security as is available together with as many of the material benefits of town life as they can obtain. . . . Little change can be expected in the low level of efficiency, however, because the motives that are fundamental in prompting a man to work— the desire for security and self-respect—cannot operate.

At first sight it would appear that the way to raise productivity is to do away with the alternative—to assist the worker in severing his tribal ties and to settle him, together with his family, at or near a center of employment. To quote Carothers: "As things are, the chief incentive in the towns is to acquire money quickly with a view to a return to rural living. The ambition to improve one's skills and rise in urban industry cannot develop until the rural boats are burned; but I have no doubt that once these boats are burned and incentives are reorientated these people will work as competently, and ultimately as creatively, as any other men."

This policy of stabilising African workers near a center of em-ployment has been adopted in the [Congo] for some years, and also, though more recently, in Kenya. The policy has been very clearly stated in the Report of the Committee on African Wages:

Of a total of some 350,000 adult male African workers in employ-ment outside the reserves, it is estimated that more than half are of the

migrant or "target" type; that is to say, they are workers who have left
the reserves for a specific purpose—for example, to earn sufficient money
to pay tax, replenish a wardrobe or acquire a wife . . . and return to
the reserves once that purpose has been achieved. Many of them spend
no more than six months outside the reserves in any one year and, for all
practical purposes, they may be regarded as temporary workers. . . . It
is only by retaining his stake in the reserve, and by returning there at
frequent intervals, that the African worker can ensure, both for himself
and his family, the minimum requirements of sustenance, a house in
which to live, and security for old age. It follows that, if we are to in-
duce the African worker to sever his tribal ties, and convert him into
an effective working unit, we must be prepared to offer him, in his new
environment, advantages at least as favourable as those he already enjoys
in the reserve. . . . They are—the payment of a wage sufficient to provide for the essential needs of the worker and his family; regular employment; a house in which the worker and his family can live; and
security for the worker's old age. At a later stage—when we have
reached our objective—consideration will also obviously have to be
given to the problems arising from unemployment among a stabilised
working population.

These changes may be expected to yield positive results. In the
[Congo], undertakings that have been employing stabilised labour
for some years have reported an appreciable improvement in efficiency. Even so, it would not appear that the problem had been
solved. For more than ten years the Union Miniére has made it a
practice to employ stabilised African labour, but one of its advisers,
Mr. Fischer, stated in a report to the General Assembly of the
Belgian Colonial Congress on 6 June 1952 that a spirit of tribal
solidarity still persists even among many of the more enlightened
workers and that in the majority of cases money incentives are
ineffective.

What, then, is lacking? One writer has observed that "before
wages can be fully operative as a factor in behaviour, they will
have to find their proper place in a new pattern of society built up
as a prolongation of the older order." As the same writer has observed elsewhere in connection with the new wage-earning population, it should be possible to resettle them, re-establish their bonds
of solidarity, and rebuild an organic community entitled to protect
their interests and providing them with the guarantees that their
original community is no longer able to afford.

It is interesting to see the progress being made in the British West
African territories, which offer many useful pointers for the future,
inasmuch as development, and especially the development of Afri-

can urban society, has been more rapid there than elsewhere. In these territories, as in the rest of Africa, the rural population have left their homes and families and gone into the towns in search of work. Statistics show that between 1931 and 1950 the population of Lagos increased by 80 per cent as a result of an influx from every tribal group in the country.

> What has happened in consequence of this mingling of people and their shift from rural to urban pursuits is that a new social organization has arisen. This is based on association, principally by occupation and by tribe, and it is taking responsibility for many of the duties tradition-ally performed by extended family and other kinship groups . . . Cole-man reports similarly from Nigeria. There, too, these tribal associations have been organized spontaneously in the new urban centres. . . . "They are the medium," says Coleman, "for re-integrating the indi-vidual employed in an impersonal urban city by permitting him to have the essential feeling of belonging." These Nigerian tribal associations also provide mutual aid and protection, including sustenance during unemployment, solicitude and financial assistance in case of illness, and the responsibility for funerals and the repatriation of the family of the deceased in the event of death. . . . The fact that many kinship groups are no longer economically self-sufficient impairs their solidarity for other social purposes, and the result is that occupational and other associ-ations which cut across tribal and kinship lines have taken over many of the activities previously performed by the extended family, the line-age, and similar traditional organizations.

It would seem at first sight that this immense and diversified effort on the part of Africans to build up an entirely new and integrated social structure for their own protection when the older traditional society is beginning to disintegrate corresponds to former develop-ments in Europe. One immediately calls to mind the rapid growth of the trade unions, the co-operative movement and the mutual benefit societies that came with the Industrial Revolution. There are marked differences, however, between what happened in the West and what is now happening in Africa. In the West the changes sprang from a more or less conscious impulse and developed natu-rally out of the economic and social movements of the past. The political and social structure was disturbed and on occasion under-went far-reaching changes, but there was continuity. In many re-spects the peoples of the West emerged from the ordeal with an even greater sense of national solidarity than before, and the com-munity at large was also strengthened by the access of new sections of the population to the responsibilities of government. Nothing of the kind has happened in Africa. There was no preparation for the brutal changes that the community has undergone since 1850, and the changes came through the intervention of foreign people. The new arrivals were not in any way concerned with preserving the foundations of traditional African society, and the result was unquestionably a weakening of the social structure. In the closing years of the nineteenth century and the beginning of the twentieth, settlement ceased to be confined to small and isolated groups of Europeans (such as explorers, missionaries and merchants), and the formation of an organised and stable European colony using the commercial and industrial techniques of western Europe had a revolutionary effect on the indigenous population, to whom the advent of the European settlers revealed an alternative to farming and to the other traditional forms of tribal life. To the members of a strictly closed society such as then existed on the continent of Africa, the prospect of escape that was offered in this way could only serve to precipitate a crisis. The occupation of African territory by a foreign administration was also accompanied by interference in every aspect of their lives: religion, the organisation of society, feeding habits, farming methods, family relationships, the wisdom of the elders, the education of children—nothing remained intact. The African felt the ground shifting beneath his feet and suddenly perceived that the most stable elements in his experience had been shaken and were untrustworthy. Some of the officials sent out by the colonial Powers to administer and develop the new territories realized the extent to which the African community had been disturbed and tried to preserve as much of the political and social system as they could. Lord Lugard's "dual mandate" had its counterpart in Galliéni's orders for Madagascar and Lyautey's instructions for Morocco. But however well inspired such efforts may be, there are limits to what they can achieve; it is not always possible to preserve a system that is no longer in touch with present-day requirements or with the most progressive sections of the population. In a large part of tropical Africa the social structure is disintegrating, if it has not already done so, and a new and improvised system of society cannot easily acquire the solidity and strength of one that is rooted in tradition. It may be argued that before doing away with the tribal basis of society an honest attempt should be made to give it new vitality and strength. Such an attempt, however, is not always possible. However poor and inadequate the new framework of society may be, it is always better than no framework at all. Consequently, where the traditional system seems to be declining, the possibility of remodelling the whole of indigenous society has to be considered.

All these factors have a direct effect on productivity. Every human being lives, works and dies within the framework of society, and, should it ever be threatened with collapse, his life and work are influenced accordingly. For the African, the problem of security is twofold—collective and individual. The reason why collective security is such an urgent problem is that the primitive society was based on a code of neighbourly assistance that constituted a permanent guarantee for every member of the group. The spontaneous associations that are being formed among the mass of the detribalised working population hold out a promise for the future. In the economic and cultural sphere the community development schemes and other similar ventures, and in the social sphere the mutual benefit societies, seem to have made a great impression, without having any specific political affinities, and should bring out the best leaders among the African population. The community principle behind these projects should make for consultation and so provide a safeguard against arbitrary action. Similarly the efforts made to eliminate racial opposition and discrimination and build up a homogeneous society could undoubtedly do much, with time, to reduce one element of tension that makes for insecurity among the African population.

The African has also a problem of individual security. The straitened circumstances of their families now force the younger generation to make a rapid choice. Their own existence and that of their dependents are in danger; for them this is a new situation, since the livelihood of their fathers and forefathers had always been assured by the communities in which they lived. If the African decides to go to work in a factory he encounters a new form of insecurity; whereas he naturally hopes to find the same neighbourliness and community spirit in his new surroundings that he was accustomed to find in his native village, he is suddenly confronted with antagonism.

> When a tribal Negro agrees to enter the employment of a foreign master, he does so, perhaps without realising it, on the very real assumption that the master will take the place hitherto occupied by his tribal chief, or rather by the tribe in its entirety as represented by the chief, i.e. that he will take him over as he is, and be responsible for every aspect of his life—in fact, be a kind of father and mother to him. If we may be permitted to use precise and rather abstract terms, the Negro looks upon his wages not as payment for work done but as a token of a social contract.

This feeling of insecurity can be partly overcome by the worker's belonging to a union; this gives him a new and vital sense of com-

radeship but stresses still further the antagonism which he finds
so painful.

A number of rural employers in one of the provinces in the
[Congo] have decided, with the assent of the African labour they
employ, to replace the contract of employment by a contract under
which the worker no longer enters into a personal commitment but
simply undertakes to do a job. The agreement is concluded between
the two parties more or less on an equal footing, and the African
worker has no difficulty in finding many precedents for it in tribal
law. This is also true of other contracts, such as the contract of
supply and certain contracts between landlord and tenant. There
are, of course, many types of industrial employment to which contracts of this kind are hardly suited. Even so, the contract of employment itself is flexible enough in many ways. The modern world
has ceased to regard it as the token of a sale in the ordinary meaning of the term and has recognised that the employer is not freed
of all obligations when he has paid for the work. He is obliged
to take account of the worker as a person, and the majority of
Western laws require him to pay a pension to aged workers, compensation to workers injured at their work and even special allowances to workers with large families. Recreation facilities are also
organized. All this is evidence that labour is not a commodity, and
we are therefore forced to recognize that the African's reaction is
essentially the reaction of a human being against an abstract and
rigid legal concept. Yet it should be possible to make the human
factor play an even greater part in the contract of employment by
increasing the number of joint councils of employers and workers
and by making them competent to deal with certain private matters
of immediate concern to the workers and their families.

There are many other ways of encouraging the African worker
to settle down in a normal social system, e.g. by schemes for providing housing at low cost, by affording facilities whereby the
worker can become the owner of a house or land, by stabilizing
workers and their families at or near their places of employment,
by paying wages adequate to support a family, by encouraging
training, and so on. Many of these suggestions are now being followed up in Africa, but there are two aspects of the worker's social
life that have not been given the attention they deserve. The first is
the position of the aged worker. There can be no question of security
for a worker who knows that he has nothing to expect in the way
of provision for his old age in the urban or industrial centre where
he works. His natural inclination will be to keep open some line of
retreat to his traditional environment. He will not work well, will

be content to draw a meagre wage and will choose his own time to leave his employment. A great deal consequently remains to be done to guarantee detribalised workers a pension, and, if possible, a house, and perhaps the chance of increasing their resources from market gardening.

A worker's productivity, after all, is no more than a particular manifestation of human behaviour and should be studied in the context of the whole man. The African has had a very violent shock and has suffered considerably as a result. In a closed society where all precautions had been taken to safeguard the individual against all the hazards of life, a revolution has suddenly exposed him to a variety of hazards for which he is wholly unprepared. He cannot be expected to behave as if nothing had happened. The African of today has no assured future ahead of him and finds it impossible to pin his faith either in the values of the Western world, to which in any event he has hardly any access, or in the values of his former world, whose foundations have been shaken.

20   PROBLEMS OF TAXATION*

African Studies Branch

The rapid political, social and economic advance which is being made in Africa can be sustained only if the people are willing to tax themselves in order to pay for it. Development gives rise to recurrent charges which must be met from annual revenue. Since forms of revenue other than direct or indirect taxation form only a small part of most colonies' revenue it is largely from taxation that these recurrent charges must be met. Taxation has the equally important though perhaps less obviously necessary role of paying for the machinery of democratic government, which will almost certainly be far more expensive than that of Native Authorities.

Advance towards democratic government in Europe and America

* From African Studies Branch, "Methods of Direct Taxation in British Tropical Africa," *Journal of African Administration,* Vol. II, No 4, October 1950. Reprinted by permission of the Controller of Her Britannic Majesty's Stationery Office.

has frequently proceeded from the principle of "no taxation without representation," but that is not quite the way in Africa. There the growth of representative government, both central and local, is not usually matched with a comparable disposition to contribute the taxes necessary to it.

There is no evidence to show that Africans in general object to the principle of taxation or that they are noticeably worse than other people about paying. But broadly speaking the direct connection between the cost of the development, which they are demanding, and taxation seems so far to have escaped their notice.

A sound structure whether of social services or of democratic government cannot depend indefinitely upon outside aid. Nor will the new wealth to be created by the various development schemes help to support the structure unless that wealth is made taxable.

Indirect taxation will continue to provide a large part of revenue, and to this the African community does of course make its contribution. It is, however, impossible at present to compute this contribution but it is certain that it has increased with the rise in the standard of living of many Africans and their increased consumption of taxable goods which were previously used mainly by non-Africans. To take one example, the consumption of imported beer in West Africa has increased manyfold during the last decade.

Nevertheless it is probable that at present rates of duty the yield of indirect taxation has reached its peak. The Governor of Sierra Leone in a speech made in the Legislative Council in December 1949, pointed out that revenue appeared to have reached the top of the rise; new increases in salaries, wages and other costs would have to be met either by increased taxation or by a retrenchment in services or by a combination of both.

The Chairman of the Bank of British West Africa Limited speaking at the Annual General Meeting on 12th July, 1950, also referred to the indications that the "boom" phase is passing. "Improved methods," he said, "and increasing energy are necessary now that greater competition is in evidence from producing areas in other countries . . . Any important fall in revenue due to reduction in world prices will in the absence of further sources of taxation, lead to a curtailment of desirable development schemes."

These comments find echo elsewhere and cast doubts upon the ability of indirect taxation to maintain its high contribution to revenue.

Apart from this, however, there is a doubt whether indirect taxes can ever be adjusted so as to extract proportionately more from the rich and proportionately less from the poor. They have a way of being passed on to the poorest consumer or producer as the case may be.

Moreover indirect taxation is not capable of being used to inculcate a sense of political responsibility and to emphasise the relation between taxes and services. To the average African who does not consume taxed commodities the relation is not evident and to those who do consume such goods the price must seem a form of rationing by the purse and nothing more.

A "snow ball" economy, in which greater tax yields support extended services and these in turn eventually increase taxable wealth, is the object of every territory. If the snow ball is to gather momentum it will be necessary, for political as well as economic reasons, to discover means of applying to Africans a progressive form of direct tax in place of existing regressive systems.

The increase of the economic activity and prosperity of the Africans over the years of British Administration; their increasing production of cash crops; the increasing numbers of Africans working as wage-earners; the growth of a class of comparatively prosperous African traders; the extension of a money economy and above all the rise in prices since the War—all these have gradually rendered the traditional methods of direct native taxation, based usually on a flat rate, ineffective as a means either of drawing from Africans tax proportionate to their actual wealth or of obtaining a significant increase of the yield. Although the flat rate is capable of minor adjustment, the system cannot for example take full advantage of a situation such as that reported from the Lango District of Uganda, where the cash income to growers of cotton leapt from £140,000 in 1948 to £504,000 in 1949 and the average cash income of a taxpayer from all sources rose from £4 14s. 0d. in 1948 to £11 19s. 0d. in 1949.

Moreover largely on account of the economic and social changes of recent years an increasing number of Africans no longer live in tribal units. Yet it was usually for the tribal unit that methods of assessment and collection of the native tax were originally planned.

On the other hand the extension of income tax to the bulk of Africans continues to present almost insoluble difficulties. The technical staff is not available and even if it were the cost of administration might absorb too large a proportion of the yield if large scale evasion is to be prevented. Yet there are signs of concern that the traditional and regressive native taxes may fail to make an equitable contribution to revenue.

It is clear that it is fast becoming insufficient to make a simple distinction for taxation purposes between Africans and non-Afri-

cans since the former grounds of discrimination in favour of the
African community, namely its poverty and economic backwardness
are gradually ceasing, particularly in West Africa, to be valid with
the growth of economic activity and the prosperity of individual
Africans.

Cutting right across the purely fiscal aspect is the administrative
requirement—imposed by the present policy of local government—
of distinguishing between central and local sources of revenue. Nowhere yet has this distinction been fully worked out.

In recent years numerous Committees have been appointed in
various African territories to investigate the problems of raising
the yield of taxation from both African and non-African sources,
of extending its incidence whilst ensuring its fairness and particularly of replacing regressive by progressive forms of taxation.

Similarly problems such as the relation between central taxes and
local rates and the appropriate division of the tax yield between
central government and local authorities have been studied by such
Committees.

Most of these investigations have been confined to individual
territories, but the problems they have wrestled with are of common concern to all Colonial territories. Sir Alan Pim observed that
the experience of the methods employed in neighbouring territories
was of considerable value to his enquiry into the problem in Kenya.

It is in the hope that some similar purpose may be served that
this article seeks to provide, as a basis for comparative study, a
survey of the main existing systems of direct taxation especially of
Africans, in the principal African territories.

The traditions of taxation policy, so far as it was a conscious
policy and not merely the natural response to local economic circumstances, differ between the West African territories on the one
hand and those of East and Central Africa on the other. The demands of recent economic and political developments referred to
above have now brought their needs much into line, but this is
really a recent phenomenon.

Before the 1914 War, West African budgets relied very largely
upon indirect taxation derived from Customs and similar duties.
Direct taxation of the normal kind levied by the Central Government did not then exist in some of these territories. In the East and
Central African territories, then less economically developed than
those of the West, the situation was different. Whilst indirect
taxation, principally in the form of Customs duties, constituted an
important source of revenue, it was direct native taxation in the
form of Hut and Poll taxes which furnished the largest and most

important single source of revenue. Thus in West Africa in the years between 1900 and 1914 Customs revenue contributed generally between a third and a half of the total internal revenue: in East and Central Africa direct native taxation furnished approximately that proportion.

After 1918 the disturbed conditions of trade following on the Great War caused a decline in revenue. Indirect taxation was most immediately affected, but the East and Central African territories which depended more on direct taxation soon found that this too was as seriously, if less immediately affected.

One of the original intentions of the native tax had been to encourage Africans to take some paid work and so make a contribution to the economic development of the territory. It was now found that trade dislocation and economic stagnation diminished the possibilities of such employment. In consequence the sources of native tax began to dry up. In 1921 revenue from Customs in Kenya fell by £100,000 or approximately one third of the previous figure. In 1922–3 in Nyasaland on a total revenue of £257,000 there was a fall in the yield of direct taxation of £30,000 of which figure native tax accounted for £12,000.

A general falling away of revenue both from indirect and direct taxation emphasised the importance of finding a more stable system of direct taxation—one that would be less linked than was then the case to the factors which operated adversely upon indirect taxation. This together with the greatly increased cost of administration after the War obliged Colonial Governments and the Colonial Office to consider a large-scale revision of taxation policies. In the older non-African Colonies attention was given to the extension of direct taxation and particularly the introduction of income tax. Although the African Colonies were less directly affected by the fluctuations of international markets they had even so to contemplate similar measures. Kenya which had proposed the introduction of income tax as a war-time measure made the same proposals again in 1921. However, not only did income tax have to be abolished in the following year but a large reduction had also to be made in the rate of native tax because of economic depression. Northern Rhodesia did introduce income tax in 1921 though this was particularly connected with mining profits and incomes. Nyasaland also introduced income tax tentatively in 1921. The systems in both these territories were wholly revised in 1925–6. Nigeria introduced income tax in the Colony area (Lagos and the district around it) in 1927.

Otherwise income tax was not introduced into any African territory. The old forms whether of direct or indirect taxation were maintained, but serious attention was given to the efficient assessment and collection of the native tax. The middle twenties saw something of a revival of trade and consequently a restoration of revenue and financial stability in both East and West Africa. Then came the slump of the early thirties and old problems returned. In East and Central Africa all territories imposed a Poll-Tax on non-natives and renewed the effort to increase the yield of the direct native tax. Yet as Lord Hailey pointed out in 1938

> "It is correct to say that of recent years administrations have shown themselves impressed by the need for moderation in native taxation; there has been no general tendency to increase the prevailing rates."

It was by efficiency in assessment and collection and by discrimination in the rates of tax rather than by a general increase of them that it was hoped to obtain a greater yield.

In Kenya the Native Hut and Poll Tax had since 1921 been considerably developed into a more modern form of tax payable only in cash and extended from adult males to include women as well. By 1935 its yield constituted the second largest item of internal revenue and about the same time its importance was emphasised by the fall of its yield by as much as £43,000 as a result of drought and locust plague.

In Tanganyika proposals were examined in 1934 for graduating the scale of Native Hut and Poll Tax with assessment of individual incomes by the Native Authorities of each district.

In Nyasaland the yield of the Hut and Poll Tax by 1937 was 45.8 per cent of the total internal revenues of the territory. Its importance led to the appointment of a committee in 1936–7 to enquire into the possibility of improving the efficiency and raising the yield of the tax. This Committee also enquired into the possibility of starting a system of village income-tax, based upon an assessment of the income of each village unit, as was practised in Northern Nigeria at that time and since. This plan for the introduction of a graduated tax on the basis of the income of a community was however found impracticable for reasons which have consistently made assessments of this kind more difficult in East Africa than West, namely, that the Africans live much less in compact units.

In Northern Rhodesia similar difficulties occurred when the yield from Native Poll Tax fell in the early thirties. A review of the whole system of taxation, African and non-African, was undertaken in 1934 which resulted in the committee of enquiry under Sir

A. Pim in 1938, and the Lockhart Committee later the same year.

In West Africa the position before 1939 was somewhat different. There was less dependence upon direct taxation whether African or non-African. Trade continued to provide through the channel of indirect taxation the greater part of the revenue required. In [Ghana] there was in fact no direct tax either on Africans or non-Africans.

In Sierra Leone and the Gambia there was a Poll or Poll and House Tax, known as Yard Tax in the Gambia.

In Nigeria the position was unique. Africans in the Colony area were liable since 1927 to income tax but not elsewhere. It was however at a very low rate as it affected Africans and was collected by the Native Authorities who retained a proportion of it as part of their revenue. For the rest of Nigeria under a separate ordinance there was a well established system of native taxation based on individual incomes from whatever source they were derived. Sometimes it was a community assessment arrived at by calculation from the incomes of representative individuals. The community assessment was allocated to individuals by the Native Authorities either in proportion to their incomes or at a flat rate according to administrative possibility.

These problems of increasing the contribution from direct taxation which were being faced in the 1930's have been greatly accentuated and made more urgent by two new factors; first the outbreak of the second world war, with its effect on trade and on costs of administration, and its stimulus to greater productivity in Africa; secondly the new large scale Colonial Development policy instituted in 1940.

It is to be noted with regard to the first named that the effects of the recent war have been greater in the Colonial, and particularly the African territories, than those of the 1914–18 war. One of its major indirect influences has been the widening of political and social horizons of many African peoples and their consequent demand for an accelerated development of social, educational and other services. These though along the lines of the official development policy require considerable increase in local revenue which can mainly be drawn only from a revised and extended system of direct taxation.

The second factor, the Colonial Development and Welfare Grants, brought this question of direct taxation more directly to a head because such grants naturally presupposed the condition that individual territories themselves would make the maximum reasonable contribution to the cost of the development schemes.

A situation arose in some ways like that of 1919 when after the first war an extension of taxation had to be considered. Accordingly income-tax has now been introduced into every African Colonial territory which had not already got it. Although in many territories it has been made applicable in law to Africans as well as non-Africans, Africans are generally excluded from its operation because of practical difficulties. The search for a progressive yet practical form of native taxation still goes on.

21   (☼)   GOLD-COASTING*

United Africa Company

The African trader rarely keeps books of account, and most of his accounting records are inscribed on the tablets of his memory. Besides memory he acquires a considerable skill in turning a small profit not only by bridging the geographical gap between the place where he buys and the market where he sells but also by linking two markets in *time*. In other words, he has learned to take a view, and to profit by changes in market prices during the course of a season.

There is an excellent and oft-quoted example of this financial aptitude. It is referred to in Nigeria as "Gold-Coasting." Lest the reader should gather that this is an expression of contempt, it should be explained that it is a technical term used to describe a particular operation. It is no more derisory than reference to the frugality of a Scot.

The operation is as follows:

1. The trader, who has an account with the United Africa Company, takes up some easily saleable goods *on credit*. A typical example would be a case of cigarettes, which in some areas can almost be regarded as currency.

2. He then sells these goods at once for cash, thereby, if necessary,

* From "Merchandise Trading in West Africa," The United Africa Company Limited, *Statistical and Economic Review*, No. 6, September 1950, pp. 39–40. Reprinted by permission.

underselling the Company's retail stores in the district, and disturbing the market in cigarettes.

3. Having obtained cash, he may either—

    (*a*) employ it by buying produce, in the hope that produce prices will subsequently rise; or

    (*b*) lend the money at usurious rates of interest to persons with fixed monthly incomes who require temporary accommodation until the end of the month. When the borrower receives his salary he repays the loan with interest, and the trader then settles his account with the Company.

In either case the profit arising from the use of the money is calculated to exceed the loss on selling the cigarettes.

It will be noticed that the trader, in this example, is virtually borrowing money from the Company for use in a field which the Company does not enter. The Company will not lend actual cash for such a purpose, but is prepared to deliver goods on credit to a skilled trader, who can turn the goods into cash, albeit at a temporary loss.

It should not be supposed that operations of the kind just described are universally practised. Only the skilful traders would attempt this sort of business, and then only when market conditions were appropriate. Nevertheless, even an occasional example of this kind affords some evidence of the unsuspected financial skill of the experienced African trader.

22   A CHANGING AFRICAN ECONOMY*

C. W. Barwell

In recent years a remarkable change has come about in the economy and the mode of life of the Kipsigis tribe of Kenya. The object of this note is to describe the nature of this change by com-

* From C. W. Barwell, "A Note on Some Changes in the Economy of the Kipsigis Tribe," *Journal of African Administration*, Vol. VIII, No. 2, April 1956, pp. 95–100. Reprinted by permission of the Controller of Her Britannic Majesty's Stationery Office.

paring the lot of the Kipsigis of yesterday with that of the tribes-men of today, and to explain, very briefly, the manner in which the significant changes which are indicated by this comparison have come about since the end of the Second World War.

The Kipsigis inhabit part of the Nyanza Province of Kenya. The tribe is not a large one and at the last census, taken in 1948, it numbered only 143,000 persons. Like many African tribes it is, however, increasing rapidly in numbers. The Kipsigis are a Nilo-Hamitic people who migrated from their original habitat some-where in the north many years ago, although the actual time of this migration has never been established. The pioneer Kipsigis appear to have had a good eye for the land since they selected for them-selves an excellent area in their new homeland in Nyanza. Their country today covers about 1,000 square miles and is bounded to the north by the lands of the Luo and to the south by those of the Masai. On the west the Kipsigis are separated from the more docile Kisii tribe by the European farming area which centres on Sotik. This land was, indeed, alienated for European settlement in order to keep the two tribes separated. Before the European areas were developed, the Kipsigis and Kisii lived in a state of endemic warfare and inter-tribal raiding and at this time the favourite occu-pation of the Kipsigis appears to have been the stealing of Kisii cattle. This tendency has now, however, been brought under effec-tive control but this was not accomplished before the early Euro-pean settlers in the neighbourhood had experienced some very stirring times. In the south, on the Masai border, cattle raiding was also a popular pastime, but here the Kipsigis were apt to get as good as they gave from their warlike neighbours. This border has now very largely been brought under control, but continuous vigi-lance is necessary on the part of the police and the administration in order to prevent minor incidents from developing into small-scale inter-tribal wars. Indeed, in this area an alarm system is still in force among the Kipsigis. The writer has seen one of the emer-gency "mobilisations" which result from a warning of a raid, dur-ing which several hundred warriors were assembled in a matter of twenty minutes or so.

THE TRADITIONAL ECONOMY

Before the [Second World War] the Kipsigis lived a very primi-tive life, supported by cattle herding and by a crude form of shift-ing cultivation which produced the only crop which was grown to any extent—*wimbi* or finger millet. In addition to the large numbers of cattle which the tribe possessed, very many sheep and goats were herded by the children.

The basic diet of the people consisted of milk and blood, both of which were obtained from the cattle. Such meat as was eaten was supplied by the sheep and goats. The children were fed on *wimbi* but the greater part of the graincrop was used for beer making. Apart from food, the needs of the people were very few and extremely simple. The men usually dressed in skins or in a single piece of trade cloth. This *shuka,* or trade cloth, gradually gave way to the trade blanket worn as the only garment and knotted over one shoulder. This garment was, however, usually removed and hung on the man's spear if he wished to do any manual work, such as hut building or bush clearing. The women dressed equally simply in the hides and skins of cattle, sheep and goats, and to this day about half of the female population continues to dress in this manner. The garment consists of a hide skirt and a skin cape worn over one shoulder. The cape is usually removed when the woman is working. Cooking and water pots, made of baked clay, were usually obtained by barter from the neighbouring Luo tribe. The homestead consisted of one or more circular huts constructed of mud and wattle with a thatch roof. Furniture was virtually non-existent and utensils and personal possessions were kept on the floor around a central fireplace of stones. Beds were made in the form of crude hammocks of ox hide. The goats and sheep usually shared the hut with the family at night, and since the dwelling had no chimney the smoke had to find its way out through the thatch. Insanitary as it may have been this system of living in a "kippered" atmosphere had, nevertheless, the great advantage of keeping down mosquitos, vermin and white ants.

The economy of the people and their occupations were as simple as their mode of life. The men herded the cattle, assisted by the older boys, and the women were responsible for milking the cows and tending the calves. The men helped to clear the bush from new land for agriculture but the women undertook all the actual processes of cultivating, from planting and weeding to harvesting. It was the men, however, who drank the larger part of the resulting crop in the form of beer. The male children graduated from tending the poultry to minding the sheep and goats and eventually to herding the cattle. The girls helped about the house and were given an early training in weeding, wood-gathering and drawing water. Such excitement as existed in the life of the tribesmen was provided by the frequent raiding parties which were sent against neighbouring tribes and by the many and varied local customs, such as initiations and marriages, all of which involved celebrations and dances. At all these ceremonies, and whenever a decision had to be made, nothing was done until large quantities of beer had been consumed, principally by the elders.

All land was traditionally considered as belonging to the tribe as a whole and this has been, as so often elsewhere, the root of the trouble as far as the encouragement of agricultural progress is concerned. A man and his family customarily held agricultural land by right of user only, and all grazing land was owned and used communally. Of course under such a system no attempt was ever made to curtail the numbers of stock and the only solution open to the individual herdsman when grazing became scarce in his area was to migrate to a less heavily populated area where conditions were more favourable. This process led to the tribe becoming very widely dispersed, so that even today there are no real villages in the district. Nor was an attempt ever made to cut down the bush or to improve the pasturage, other than by burning the whole country-side in the dry season. The idea of improving the land for personal gain or profit was naturally completely foreign to a people who had no concept of property. If a man wished to cultivate he had to ob-tain the consent of the appropriate elders and this involved the provision of large quantities of beer if the applicant hoped for a decision within a reasonable time. Once the area to be cultivated had been decided, it "belonged" to the cultivator and his family for as long as they made use of it. In the days before the introduction of maize this would generally be for one year only, because *wimbi*, the staple crop, was always planted in new land. Agriculture as a means of profit or gain was, as we have seen, completely foreign to the tribe and the Kipsigis consequently lived entirely within the limits of a purely subsistence economy. This was perhaps a matter of good fortune for the present day Kipsigis since the fertility of the land was in the past continually being built up rather than be-coming progressively more exhausted, as was so often the case, and the evils of soil erosion were, as a result, almost unknown.

The traditional economy, as in so many other areas, was based on a cycle of activity involving marriage and agriculture. As soon as a man had sufficient cattle, sheep or goats for the brideprice he acquired a wife. Having done so it became the wife's job to assist her husband in accumulating sufficient wealth in cattle to buy a second wife and at the same time to produce sons and daughters by him. Daughters were very popular acquisitions to the family be-cause, in their teens, they could be disposed of as brides and the family herds of cattle and small stock augmented as a result of the acquisition of the brideprice stock accruing to the bride's father. Indeed the whole life and economy of the tribe hinged upon stock, as has been shown, and the very acme of contentment and satisfaction to a Kipsigis was to watch his large herds grazing. In these circumstances rinderpest or the outbreak of a similar disease occasioned absolute disaster and involved the breakdown of the whole economy, in no small part because of the lack of cattle with which to pay brideprice in such times of crisis.

THE MODERN ECONOMY

Such was the economy and manner of life of the tribe in the past. Today, however, the scene is very different and some most significant changes have taken place. Perhaps the first and most impressive thing that strikes a visitor to the Kipsigis tribal area today is its resemblance, in many ways, to certain parts of England. This resemblance is largely due to the existence of the many small enclosed fields which are demarcated with hedgerows and are interspersed with small plantations of trees. Almost every square inch of land is now individually, as opposed to communally, owned and in 75 per cent of the district these individual holdings have been enclosed by hedges of either Mauritius thorn or a species of euphorbia. In some places stick or barbed wire and cedar-post fences are erected round the fields but these are not being encouraged because of their high cost and the demands which they make on the available timber. Within the many small and fenced farms crops of maize, English potatoes, millet, beans, wheat and onions are now grown and above all each farm includes an area of bush-free grazing land. Plantations of wattle trees line the roads and produce a saleable bark, the proceeds of which add to the economic well being of the people. Stock has now been reduced to reasonable numbers by what is sometimes referred to as the "squeeze method." This virtually painless system of stock limitation and redistribution is itself a product of individual ownership, since with only a limited grazing area available the family is, of necessity, forced to sell, or to pass on to relatives in less enclosed areas, the surplus stock which its own limited paddocks will not accommodate.

Owing to the difficulty of keeping goats in restricted spaces, very few of these are seen in the areas where enclosure has progressed, although small flocks of sheep are very common. Donkeys—which appeared in Kipsigis as a means of transport with the introduction of maize growing for the market during the last war—are now the chief means of transport to and from market and almost every

tribesman possesses one or more. Except for the small hand-culti-
vated millet plots of the women, all the land is now ploughed along
the contour with ox-drawn ploughs. The ox plough is, however,
already beginning to give way to the small tractor and there are
now about 20 tractor companies operating locally. The soil under
the plough is protected from erosion by a simple soil conservation
system involving the use of uncultivated grass strips of a minimum
width of five feet. These strips are marked out by use of the line
level on steeper land and by eye on the more gentle slopes. This
simple system of restricting run-off produces, over a number of
years, a "benching" effect and the grass banks, or "stop-washes,"
can easily be seen even when the fields are put down to grass. Much
work on the cultivation of grasses, and on grassland ecology in
general, is being carried out in the district as an adjunct to the soil
conservation measures in use.

A comparison of the pre-war economy of the Kipsigis with that
of the tribesman today illustrates clearly the changes which have
taken place. The modern tribesman conducts a cash economy rather
than exists on a subsistence one, as in the past. From the sale of his
crops and his stock he has been able to produce a steady cash income since the war. Whereas, as has been seen, at one time the only
outlet for stock was in the payment of brideprice, today both male
and female stock are sold on the open market and cattle are at last
acquiring an individual value rather than being regarded merely
as units in a large, but uneconomic, herd. As an indication of the
care which is given today to the now valued beasts it is of interest
to note that over 1,000 stirrup pumps have been sold in one year
alone to Kipsigis farmers who wish to undertake weekly spraying
of their stock in order to keep them tick free.

Pride of ownership is evident in the houses and homesteads
which are now to be seen scattered over the Kipsigis area. Sound
square-built houses with permanent, rather than thatched, roofs
have fast become the fashion and these are surrounded in some
areas by orchards, vegetable gardens and even small decorative
flower beds.

The Kipsigis family today lives in a much better constructed and
more hygienic home than that of the past. Ventilation has been introduced and living conditions have been improved out of all recognition, with the result that airy houses, equipped with well constructed furniture, are rapidly becoming the fashion. Separate
bedrooms allow more privacy within the family and natural mod-
esty has led to the construction of pit latrines near most homesteads. Aluminium cooking utensils and china pottery are preferred

to the traditional Luo earthen cooking pots. Pictures are sometimes seen on the walls and there is a most refreshing attitude of "pride in the home" among the womenfolk. Bicycles are now in general use and lightweight motor cycles and even cars have also made their appearance. The Kipsigis family today dresses in good European clothes and the younger women are fast becoming fashion conscious. The children go to school at an early age and this in turn is in part due to the fact that with the establishment of enclosed paddocks, the younger members of the family are no longer required to act as herdboys and are, therefore, free to attend classes.

The good farmer realises that he must alternate his crops with grass and elementary forms of crop rotation are being followed. Largely as a result of reduced numbers the stock are improving and are receiving reasonable treatment for the first time in Kipsigis history. At one time, for example, all Kipsigis cattle were herded into a small enclosure near to the house. This enclosure was usually a morass, knee deep in mud and dung, so that if a beast lay down it would be most likely to get stuck in the mire. Fodder and water were not provided for the cattle within these cattle-pens. Under present day conditions, in contrast, the stock are allowed to graze-out in a paddock at night. This means that they can lie in comfort and are able to graze the fresh dewy grass in the cool of the morning. It also enables the stock to seek shade in the heat of the day instead of having to move constantly in search of food. The making of silage and the planting of green crops for dry season supplementary feeding is also starting in many areas. The provision of adequate water supplies on or near the farm holdings is, however, still a major problem, but this large issue is slowly being resolved by making loans available to individual stockholders, and to groups of farmers, for the construction of tanks and other water installations.

The modern Kipsigis farmer is encouraged to plant trees for fuel and shade and to cultivate fruit trees in order to augment his and his family's diet. Maize monoculture, which resulted largely from the government maize planting campaigns during the last war, is now gradually giving way to a more balanced cropping system. Cash crops, such as coffee and pyrethrum, have been introduced and a small pilot scheme for growing tea has also been started. The whole economy of Kipsigis is still, however, and must always essentially remain, based on the cattle and so the several departments of government are working together towards the improvement of this mainstay of the tribal well-being. To this end a stock breeding station has been established and an ever increasing number of improved bulls are going out to the more progressive farmers and stock-owners.

The Kipsigis African District Council, on the advice of its energetic president and of the various government officers stationed in the district, has introduced a set of comprehensive land usage and veterinary bye-laws. These bye-laws and the support of the local authority council are of great value to the African staff since the field instructor now feels that he has the backing of the tribal elders in carrying out his work of promoting better methods of farming.

SOME REASONS FOR THE CHANGE

It remains to indicate how this very great change in the Kipsigis economy has come about in the space of so short a number of years. One clue is to be found in the character of the average Kipsigis. The tribesman is a frank and cheerful individual who is always ready to laugh, even at himself. His processes of reasoning appear to be far more similar to those of the European than is the case in many other African tribes. He will turn over new ideas in his mind for an extended period, but when once convinced of their advantages he will adopt them and will willingly accept the work involved in putting them into effect. He is inclined to treat the European as being but little superior to himself, and, since he does not have too high an opinion even of himself, he is more often than not prepared to take, and to understand, European advice.

Even before the last war the younger and more enlightened members of the tribe were, no doubt, struck by the fact that their traditional way of life did not provide the purchasing power with which to acquire the luxuries which they were both seeing and hearing about. Early in the last war the government introduced a policy of increasing the maize acreage in Kenya as a contribution to the war effort and, after a slow start, the Kipsigis readily accepted this food production drive and co-operated willingly in its application in their area. As we have seen, the traditional Kipsigis methods of land use were not designed to cope with large acreages of arable and so the younger generation, amongst whom were the maize growers, were forced by circumstances to fence their maize fields in order to protect their crops against neighbours' stock, which, by tradition, were allowed to graze indiscriminately. Hence a tendency began to be apparent, about halfway through the war, for individual farmers to enclose portions of land for their own use. The tribal elders were at first somewhat perturbed by this development and consequently an African district council resolution was passed which banned the enclosure of land until the end of the war. This resolution was, however, merely the dying gesture of the old system and enclosure gradually became a general practice in some areas. With but little opposition from members of the older age grades, the younger generation began a process of systematic land grabbing, accompanied by a mutual respect for each others' boundaries. This led to a spate of land cases which served to focus the attention of the agricultural, and other departments, on the trend and so led to its eventual control. It is interesting to note that although initially enclosure was practised with the sole idea of bringing about the permanent demarcation of the individual holdings, as the practice gradually became more general it was not difficult to persuade the more intelligent landholders that sub-division of their farms into areas of arable and pasture was needed in order to afford protection to the crops.

From this small beginning, and on this foundation, it has been possible to build up the present and widespread system of small holdings. Very much still remains to be done but in the Kipsigis area agricultural development has a sound foundation upon which to build and one which will be hard to equal in Kenya. Both the Kipsigis and officers who have been concerned with the changes which have taken place have been fortunate in that for 15 years the agriculture of the district has been under the direction of only two agricultural officers. This continuity has enabled the officials concerned to get to know both the people of the district and their problems, and has made it possible to establish the personal relationships with many hundreds of Kipsigis farmers which form one of the bases upon which the changes which have been described in this note have been built.

Part Three

SOCIAL CHANGE

A common thread throughout the political and economic sections of this book is the change that has come about under the impact of markedly different cultures each with their own ways and values. This thread must be followed still further into the area of social change that is so intimately bound up with the political and economic forces at work in contemporary Africa. Few are better qualified to set the stage than Dr. K. A. Busia, Professor of Sociology and former leader of the Opposition in Ghana now in exile, who points out some of the many areas of social change brought about by the impact of Western culture upon indigenous African ways. In a sense, the social changes are a bit more subtle and rather more difficult to perceive than the political and economic changes that are so often obvious in the speeches of political figures and, indeed, in the very landscape. They are no less important. Attitudes to kinfolk alter, the concept of the family changes, marriage systems evolve, new classes arise and old authorities decline—all these developments are tightly interwoven and affect each other. A man goes to school and to the university and becomes one of the elite; his respect for the traditional authority of his father and the elders of the family diminishes; he marries a woman of his own choice outside his own people; his feeling of obligation to his relatives when they come to see him in the city is half-hearted at best— the changes cannot be separated, all are bound together and a change in one person under the impact of an alien culture is reflected in the others.

As Daniel McCall, of the African Research and Study Program at Boston University, points out, the cultural conflict is nowhere more apparent than in the towns, for "the town is the door through which Africa is entering the modern world." Although a few towns did exist historically, many new towns have mushroomed from small villages and trading centers during the past one hundred years. Most of them are ports and cities based upon mining, a few are inland centers of trade and communications; but, no matter what their function, their influence extends far beyond their own boundaries. Walk with the colorful, jostling crowd in the market-places of Kumasi and Kano and you will see cattle, cloth and fish traders who have traveled six hundred miles to these ancient trading centers; go down into the gold mines of the Rand that form the roots of Johannesburg and meet the miners who have been drawn to the city from a thousand miles away; go into the locomotive shops of Nairobi and see men who have had no previous experience with machinery learning the complexities of diesel maintenance, and you will begin to understand the tremendous power of the cities of Africa to draw people to them and bring them face to face with ways of life totally different from their own. More than any other feature, the town is a source and transmitter of social change, a vital and integral part of the rapidly evolving scene.

But the rapid growth of a town also brings a host of problems in its wake, and one of the most serious is the growth of slums as people from the rural areas pour in and settle down. In some of the slums the people have retained, with few alterations, the old social ties and obligations. Now the older slums are being cleared away, but the results of slum clearance are not always foreseen. What happened in Lagos is described by Mr. Peter Marris, Research Officer of the Institute of Community Studies, London. For all the squalor of central Lagos with its shabby, neglected houses, the area cleared represented for the people who lived there a familiar, comfortable home with well-established social ties. Now they have been removed to new clean suburbs, and the well-meant schemes that have broken the old ties have unwittingly shattered the lives of the people. In the United States we have seen the same thing happen in New York when the small community, with the familiar faces greeted each day in the local drug and grocery stores, is destroyed by removal to the scientifically planned and designed housing project. So, too, in Lagos, Nigeria: no longer is there the central location upon which so many depended for their livelihood; no longer the strong family ties when sisters and brothers are dispersed; and no longer the income to buy those happy unnecessary things when bus fares eat away the small wage packet.

Moving to a town means tearing oneself away from the security and familiarity of the village with its ordered ways and comfortable, known routines. To cushion the feeling of social isolation many a man and woman feels in the town, organizations have sprung up to provide town dwellers with the opportunities to meet others and to give them a sense of belonging. Some of the most prominent organizations, which in a sense take the place of the activities left behind in the village, are the churches of both the Christian and schismatic variety. Professor Busia, in one of the first sociological studies of an African town, shows how the churches of Takoradi, a bustling West African seaport, cut across tribal and occupational lines to bring some comfort to the lives of their members. Making one's way in a new and alien town is not an easy business, and judicious observance of both Christian and traditional fetish beliefs offers some hope that the forces influencing one's prosperity will be kind.

We have previously noted the way in which the political, economic and social changes are intimately related to one another. To illustrate the point vividly, Dr. Pius Okigbo, Economic Adviser to the Prime Minister of the Eastern Region of Nigeria, traces the social impact of a recently introduced economic innovation. The people of the Eastern Region depend upon the sale of palm oil for their cash income. Formerly, oil was extracted by pounding and boiling the palm nuts and kernels, an inefficient process that did not produce a high grade oil. After the Second World War, hand presses and then pioneer oil mills were introduced with the result that yields of oil nearly quadrupled. It was as though a stone had been dropped into a quiet pond—the ripples of suddenly increased income spread and influenced nearly every aspect of the society. Children obtained paid employment in the mills and began to depend far less upon their families; the traditional rights of the wives to the palm kernels were threatened and literally caused rioting in some areas; some people achieved new status through their increased wealth and threatened the authority of the elders. By the time the ripples lost their force the old equilibrium had been upset to the point where the society could never be the same again.

The introduction of an oil mill obviously represents only a tiny portion of the process of mechanization and industrialization that is taking place all over Africa. In essence, industrialization introduced into a society from the outside represents a sudden alternative way of working and living, and two immediate results are large-scale migration from an increasingly deserted countryside and the creation of a class of wage earners. The social problems arising from large migratory movements are posed in a general study by Mr. Paul de Briey, a former staff member of the International Labour Office, and in a case study on Nyasaland by an anthropologist, Dr. Margaret Read of the University of London. The main export of Nyasaland for over fifty years has been the labor of its men. For generations, therefore, villages have had a large proportion of their male population away, and the result is an increasingly gloomy picture of deserted wives, children growing without paternal guidance and authority, and steadily loosening moral and social ties. The men who return to the villages after their work in the mines tend to reject the old ways, although they are unable to accept completely, or to be accepted by, the new. In more senses than one they are called the *machona* by their people—the "lost ones."

If we were to try to single out one thing more closely tied to the social and cultural values of the people of Africa than any other, that thing would be the land and the systems of tenure under which the land is held. Thus, changes in land tenure become a measure of the social and economic forces at work. Mr. H. A. Oluwasanmi, Lecturer in Agricultural Economics at the University College of Ibadan, describes what the traditional systems of land tenure have been, and how they are changing under the impact of an increasingly commercialized agriculture, the introduction of new crops and an increasing population. The traditional communal land tenure system, under which the land was worked on a shifting basis, represented a binding force in societies mainly composed of cultivators. Today, in many areas, the land tenure system is changing as a direct reaction to new social values, and there is an increasing willingness to examine the problem of land tenure in the light of new goals and values that have supplanted the old.

All too often, when we examine the ways in which social change is taking place in Africa, we are left with an impression of malleable societies upon which new cultural ways and innovations may easily be pressed. Change is certainly taking place, but new ways, that appear to have been absorbed, sometimes turn out on a closer examination to be only skin deep. An excellent example of the apparent acceptance of a new feature in a culture is provided by the Anchau Scheme, a health and resettlement project designed to combat sleeping sickness in Northern Nigeria. The disease is carried by the tsetse fly, which inhabits the thick bush growing along streams. Clearing the bush, therefore, could eradicate the fly, and treating the people could gradually stamp out the disease. By forcing a new pattern of behavior upon the people, the Anchau Scheme succeeded in having the area cleared, but the remarkable thing is that while the brush along the streams has been destroyed regularly for twenty years, no one in the area accepts the explanation that stream clearing eliminates sleeping sickness. In no sense has the forced pattern of behavior been accepted into the culture of the people. This can provide a lesson for us, for as we examine the changing scene and note the adoption of new political, economic and social ways we should be ever hesitant to accept the changes at face value—sometimes they merely represent a veneer under which the old is slowly evolving.

24 ☸ THE CONFLICT OF CULTURES*

K. A. Busia

Culture, as the anthropologist and sociologist conceive it, is cumulative. It embraces all the modes of thought and behavior handed down by communication and interaction; it is the social heritage acquired through the learning process rather than through inheritance. The cultural anthropologist or sociologist does find differences in culture, but the differences are not racial differences. Cultures are cumulative, based on experience and learning. It is important to emphasize this point because the belief in a pacific and workable adjustment of social situations created by cultural differences depends on the fact that culture can be learned. The problems of social change in West Africa, as elsewhere, arising from the impact of peoples possessing different cultures, do arise precisely because men aspire to assimilate cultures different from their own.

The impact of Europe and America upon West Africa is most obvious in economic life. The houses in which people live, the clothes they wear, and the ways in which they earn their living, the shops and factories, motor roads and railways, all testify to the changes that this impact has wrought. All over West Africa, a large number of men and women earn their living by selling and distributing the manufactured products of Europe and America, from canned foods to luxury cars and radio sets. There are now many ways in which people earn their living, from unskilled labor on the roads, on cocoa, rice, and cotton farms, or in the mines to the work of the highly skilled technician, engineer, barrister, or doctor. The self-sufficient economies of small African communities

* From K. A. Busia, "The Conflict of Cultures: A Plea for Patience," *The Atlantic,* Vol. 203, No. 4, April 1959. Reprinted by permission.

have been displaced by a money economy and dependence on international trade.

There have also been changes in the physical environments. Forests have been cleared to make room for cocoa farms or new towns, some villages have disappeared while new ones have sprung up along newly built roads, and large towns have grown near mines or factories.

With all this have gone a redistribution of population and new social patterns. Workers who have acquired new skills play new roles. The traditional social structure is changed. No longer does the network of kinship encompass all the activities of social life, and relationships, obligations, and reciprocities are changed or are expressed in new ways.

Illustrations of this may be found in the kinship and marriage systems, which are an essential part of the social structure. In West Africa, as in other African communities, the network of kinship embraces all the needs and activities of life. One's duties and behavior toward one's kinsfolk are clearly defined and taught. Included in the kinship structure is the domestic group, which is variously composed: there may be the monogamous household, consisting of parents and their unmarried children; or the polygamous family of one father and two or more mothers, in which the mother and her children constitute a separate unit of the group; or the extended parental family, in which a man lives in the same household with his married sons and their wives; or the domestic group consisting of a man and his wife and their daughters and their husbands.

Though in rural areas these patterns of residence remain, in many new towns and cities the housing situation makes the maintenance of the old traditional patterns difficult. The domestic group is divided. In many rented houses, members of different tribes and classes share the same dwelling, and so the old structure has been destroyed and new ways have to be found to fulfill the ties and obligations of kinship.

Whatever the size of the domestic group in West Africa, the range of relationships recognized for social purposes extends beyond it to the larger kinship group, the lineage, which is a group of relations descended from a common ancestor or ancestress. One owes duties and may expect help from this larger group at certain crises of life. The kinship system provides security.

But marriage and kinship systems are products of evolution. They are affected by the change from a subsistence economy to one based on acquired skills in a money economy. They are also affected by modern systems of communication and mobility, by industrial agriculture and mining, and by the impersonal relations in large towns and cities. Traditional forms of behavior, old sanctions of morality and conduct, the reciprocities and security of the large kinship group, all tend to change. The isolation of the family unit in the town, the splitting up of domestic groups of kinsfolk between urban and rural communities, the new social contacts and relationships in a competitive capitalistic economy, all compel changes in the established ways.

The encounter between Europe and West Africa has also led to profound changes in political and administrative structures. Colonizing countries, such as Britain and France, have brought together tribes and chiefdoms that were once separate or at war with one another and have administered them as one territory. Out of alien rule and administration the concepts of nationhood and nationalism have been learned, and nationalist Africans have challenged imperialism by using the political philosophies and arguments employed by their imperial rulers. The administrative structures built by imperial officials laid the foundation for nation states. Where opportunities have been given to Africans, they have learned new ideas and skills and have accepted and incorporated changes in their culture to meet the new situation. So, in West Africa traditional chiefs play new roles alongside elected African cabinet ministers and African administrative officers.

The false racial theories by which some have sought to justify imperialism and segregation have been disproved by the successful assimilation of alien political institutions and culture, as exemplified in West Africa. The independent states of Liberia, Ghana, and Guinea—and the approaching independence of Nigeria, the Cameroons, and Togoland—all testify that, given adequate opportunity, contemporary man can master highly developed cultures whatever the color of his skin. The parliamentary institutions of European democracies and the techniques and machinery of government have been successfully adapted in West Africa.

Europe brought to West Africa its own system of education through formal schooling. In West Africa today, there are primary schools, high schools, teacher-training colleges, technical institutes, and universities, all on the French, British, or American model. Those who receive instruction at these seats of learning are prepared for service and leadership in their own countries. They encounter the culture of Europe through what they learn at school, but they live in their own traditional culture, which is undergoing rapid social change.

Education in school or college has been based on the requirements of the European ruler, missionary, or businessman, and it
has taught more about Europe and its culture than about Africa.
Today in some of the best schools this is being remedied; there is
an increasing awareness that the school must be rooted in the culture of the society it seeks to serve. But reading and writing were
taught, and some Africans were given the opportunity to share in
contemporary European culture.

Those who learned to read and write acquired a new status and
prestige. They became clerks, teachers, skilled artisans, or professional men. They became leaders in political life, displacing the
chief and the traditional councils from political leadership. The
birth of West African nationalism and the agitation for independence are the direct result of education as introduced from Europe
and America.

The assimilation of European education and the adaptation to
the social changes it has brought about are another proof that
pacific and workable adjustments can be made to changes in culture,
under favorable circumstances. In West Africa, where the opportunities for education have been given to Africans, even if on a
small scale in relation to the total population, those who have bene-
fited have shown that cultural differences are not due to differences
in capabilities, as is maintained by scientifically unsupported racial-
ists, but to differences in experience which can be eliminated through
the learning process.

There is plenty of evidence from the writings of cultural anthro-
pologists and sociologists to show that differences of culture do not
support policies of segregation and separation, for cultures can be
and are learned. Every people wants to preserve some aspect of
culture which is peculiarly its own and which continues to serve
desired purposes in its society. These cherished traditions are not
signs of inferiority but of differences in experience.

For every people has its own reflections on the nature and purpose of life and its own beliefs concerning the supernatural, to
which its religious rites give expression. In West Africa generally,
there is the belief in a Supreme Being who is the Creator of man
and the universe, and also in other gods, and in the ancestors who
continue to guard and guide the present generation. To peoples
holding these beliefs of polytheism and ancestor worship, European
missionaries brought the Christian gospel of one God, of salvation
through Christ, and of universal brotherhood. Christianity is one
of the factors of social change that the impact with Europe has
introduced into West Africa.

As an institution, the church has provided fellowship among different tribes, education through the Bible and the hymnbook and through reading and writing, and opportunities for new types of associations that help to provide some of the services and security that the all-embracing kinship groups once provided but no longer adequately do. Christianity has also offered cultural challenges. It has insisted on monogamy in societies whose customs permit polygamy. It has challenged ancestor worship and polytheism, which provided some of the sanctions of conformity to social norms and usages. It has taught new songs and music and frowned on our traditional forms. It has made converts refrain from joining in some tribal rites and religious ceremonies and necessitated their rejection of some cultural patterns. But within the church there is a growing awareness of the problems of social change, and a concerted effort is being made through research and exchange of views at conferences to meet and resolve the new challenges in the light of Christian teaching and insight. The church recognizes the need for every Christian, white or black, to belong to his social group and share its life as fully as possible.

This approach itself expresses belief in the fact that the problems arising from the conflict of cultures can be solved in a pacific way. The spread of the Christian church in West Africa and the prominent part it has played in social advancement give proof that people from different cultural backgrounds share certain values and that fellowship is possible on the basis of intellectual and spiritual communion.

The impact of Europe on West Africa has often been destructive of social, economic, political, and religious systems. Cultural changes carry some problems of maladjustment in their wake. The obligation to share scientific, technical, and material resources requires a sensitivity to cultural and social values. Money values have often replaced the personal values of the traditional system. In the place of the desire to maintain harmonious human relationships has grown the insatiate acquisitiveness for material things. It is true that the standards of living in West Africa are, by comparison with those of Europe or America, low, and men need material things to live with; but even more, they need an adequate system of values to live by.

A study of the social and political institutions of West African peoples will show that a great deal of emphasis is laid on personal relations and that the quest for a harmonious and peaceful society is basic to all their social practices and institutions. This quest for a humane society is not confined to West Africa, but in industrialized countries like those of Europe and America it has tended to be obscured by the quest for power. At any rate, in the encounter between Africa and Europe, it is Europe's power that has most impressed the African and stimulated his quest. Europe's power over nature, conferred by science and technology—its power to produce more things to enrich the life of man, to build roads and railways, to overcome the barriers of space, or to prolong life by successfully combating illness—has expressed the superiority of Europe and has made the African want to learn European ways. For it is clear to Africans, too, that African cultures are less efficient than those of Europe or America for bending nature to serve the needs of man.

Large buildings are being constructed and harbors, roads, railways and airfields, hospitals and dispensaries, schools and colleges; and the trained African personnel that man these services testify to the fact that science and technology can be learned. They cannot be acquired without changes in other aspects of culture and without social problems and maladjustments, but social change in Europe and America has been attended by similar problems.

Contrasts between the cultures of Europe and West Africa are everywhere manifest. Yet even in the remotest village, with its narrow streets and simple mud houses, some product of Western technology will be found in the shop or the home.

The impact with Europe is seen in the clothes that people wear, which may be the latest fashion in New York, London, or Paris or the traditional robes made to suit local tastes and style from materials manufactured in Europe; in the churches, where Christians sing tunes and recite creeds familiar to European congregations; in the schools and colleges, where the language spoken or the ideas examined may be the same as in any European school or college; in the courts, where barristers in wig and gown cite European law before judges dispensing justice according to European traditions. Yet beside all this are the traditional religious ceremonies; the local courts settling disputes according to native law and custom; the old African world of song and dance and rhythm, of family ties and relationships, of chiefs resplendent in traditional regalia. The old herbalist tries out his cures alongside the trained African medical specialist equipped with the latest instruments and knowledge of European medical science. It is in this amalgam of life that cultural adjustment goes on; new ideas being learned or rejected, old ones being discarded or retained or modified.

In the encounter between peoples there is an interchange of experience, and folkways change. In spite of the superiority of Europe in science and technology Europeans have changed in response to the encounter with Africa. West African communities are already evolving cultures that testify both to their encounter with Europe and America and to their own genius and heritage. Under conditions of favorable opportunity and freedom, the process of growth and social change will continue without friction.

25 ⚘ THE DYNAMICS OF URBANIZATION IN AFRICA*

Daniel F. McCall

Town life, and a constantly increasing movement of people to the expanding towns, is one of the most striking characteristics of present-day Africa. Town life, in itself, is not new to the continent. An early Dutch merchant was surprised at the size and orderliness of Benin City and compared it favorably with the Amsterdam of his time; Diogo Cam was impressed by the efficient organization of the capital of the Bakongo kingdom; Arabic writers testify to an extensive development of urban centers in the medieval Sudanic Empires; and there are the immense ruins of stone towers and walls of Zimbabwe in Central Africa. The Yoruba people are particularly noted for their propensity to build large towns; Ibadan, the third largest town in Africa, has often elicited surprise that it could survive on an essentially indigenous basis.

These old towns, however, were different from modern African towns in several ways: they were different in structure in that they were organized on the basis of kinship, and power and commerce were channeled through that form of organization; they were different in scale in two ways, in actual size and in extent of outside contact; and they were parochial in culture.

Many of these older towns have disappeared and those which remain, like Kano, have been modified and are being further transformed. The new cities and towns are the result of contact with the

* From Daniel F. McCall, "The Dynamics of Urbanization in Africa," *Annals of the American Academy of Political and Social Science*, March 1955. Reprinted by permission. Vol. 298, pp. 151–160.

West; one writer says that the cities are a colonial creation, and another, that the city is the creation of the whites and peopled by blacks. The old towns grew out of, and maintained, their distinctive cultures; in the new towns, Africans who are being urbanized are also, to some extent, being westernized. The old towns had trade with some other areas, but the new towns are an integral part of the network of world trade. This paper is concerned only with the new type of town.

The proportion of people living under urban conditions is already significant, but it is not possible to give exact figures for the whole area because of the inadequacy of available statistics. However, in the Union of South Africa, where the process of town growth has gone farthest, approximately 25 per cent of Africans are living in towns, but in some territories, particularly in East Africa, the number may fall below 5 per cent. North and West Africa come next after the Union in the matter of urban growth, and Central Africa has shown a considerable recent growth.

FACTORS IN URBAN DEVELOPMENT

The towns are administrative and commercial centers; they are therefore the nexus between Africa and Europe. As investments increase, urban growth accelerates. Towns are a symbol and an index of economic development. The rate of growth of African towns in this century has been rapid but this pace has accelerated astonishingly during World War II, owing largely to the need of the West for strategic materials and bases. In the postwar period a number of factors, such as the desire of the European powers to meet the threat of anticolonialism, the acceptance of the doctrine that rich countries should help poor countries, increased knowledge of African economic problems, the generally increased scope of government activity in business, and a feeling that the African people should be rewarded for their loyalty during the war, combined to encourage the public sector of investment which it is hoped will stimulate private investment. All of the territories have development plans envisaging extension of transportation and communication systems, education and medical programs, and electrification and industrialization which, if successful, will undoubtedly contribute to urban growth.

The harnessing of hydroelectric power, of which Africa has an enormous potential, is now in varying stages of planning or realization in various parts of the continent. The utilization of this power will necessitate new industries which will require labor, and since the only reservoir of labor is the subsistence sector, more and more people will be drawn out of the tribal villages to build new towns and to enlarge the old ones.

This period has already witnessed the development of some secondary industry which, outside the Union of South Africa, is relatively insignificant in the total economy but is important in regard to urban growth. Some production for the local market has begun. Furniture, cement, bread, beer and cigarettes are now being made, and textiles are being machine woven from local cotton.

A favorable world market has furthered the increase of cash crops; and finally, in certain areas, there has been a transfer of some capital from Asia. Such developments help to explain the fact that several towns have doubled their populations in the last decade.

It should be recognized that the economy of an African territory is a fragile one. It is an adjunct of the economy of the metropolitan power and would be the first to be affected in the event of a slump. The emphasis on mining, and the tendency toward monoculture with the consequent dependence on a single export, or at best on a small number of exports, make an African economy extremely vulnerable.

A fragile economy. The modern African town did not grow out of the needs of, and in service to, its own hinterland; its primary relationship is to Europe. In many cases it has grown beyond the capacity of its hinterland to support it without radical agricultural reform, which has not been achieved anywhere as yet, so that some of the food for townsmen has to be imported from overseas. Even so, some of the towns are a burden upon the land; wood and charcoal are brought to the town, where people can afford higher prices, and fuel becomes scarce in villages at considerable distances from the urban market.

In any economy there is an exodus from the towns when commerce declines, but in Africa a slump not only would mean an abrupt halt in town growth and a dispersal of urbanites but the villages probably could not absorb them. The land under the present methods of farming could not tolerate a return of the urban population to agriculture.

African territories, like other places, cannot hope to achieve autarchy, but an increase in food production and the production of more industrial goods for local consumption would make the economy healthier and the basis of town growth more secure. For the most part, industry means processing for export. The oil from peanuts and palm nuts is being extracted; logs are being sawed into

boards; some ores are smelted into ingots. This reduces the shipping space needed, thereby lowering transport costs, creates more
jobs, which require more training for new skills, and increases the
amount of money in local circulation; the result is an increase in
urban activity but not in economic stability.

THE TOWN AND ITS HINTERLAND

The towns and the countryside are inseparably interrelated; in
truth, they are different aspects of the same reality—like the two
faces of a coin. The character of the town is determined, among
other things, by the nature of the hinterland from which it draws its
labor force and for which it acts as an emporium. But rural life has
been transmuted by the same forces that have given rise to the
towns. Money transactions are replacing traditional exchanges of
gifts in kind and service. Crops are grown for export now as well
as to fill compound storage bins. Much of the money in circulation in the villages has been remitted to rural families by absent
members working in the towns, mines and plantations.

African society has been affected to such an extent by the impact
of the West that the tribe is a sick institution even in the rural
areas. The superimposition of outside authority, the intrusion of
proselytizing religions which attack the ideological foundations of
tribal authority, the values of the market place superseding the
values of the kinship system and allowing commoners to become
richer than the chief, all contributed to the decline in effectiveness
of tribal organization. The necessity of meeting new situations for
which there were no tribal precedents, the temporary or permanent
loss of much tribal manpower to outside employment, the corruption of chiefs in their role of custodian of land, and the venality of
many of them in spending such profits for personal use have further
reduced the capacity of tribal organization to function.

The social disorganization of the countryside further contributes
to the growth of the towns, which, to a greater extent, are able to
provide the basis for the synthesis of a new society.

DIVERSITY AND SIMILARITY OF TOWNS

In a continent as large as Africa, one would expect some regional variation, and, of course, these differences are felt in the
structure and life of the towns. National differences among Europeans as well as the diversity of tribal cultures, length of contact,
religion, availability of education and the type offered, altitude,
latitude, and climate contrive to give different towns different char-

acteristics, but all are undergoing more or less identical processes although the outcome may vary from place to place because of different combinations of such factors.

Given this range of variation, it is difficult to make any generalization on the characteristics of urban centers that would be true of the whole continent. The fact that we are dealing mainly with the process of urbanization allows us to consider some details as irrelevant, but even in the realm of process there are variations. Only the central tendencies can be indicated.

All Africans living in, or moving into, towns find their customs affected by the fact that town relationships are predominately universalistic rather than particularistic; all statuses, except racial, are achieved rather than ascribed; and kinsmen make up only a small part of the people with whom they daily interact. Contacts are numerous but casual; relationships involve segmental roles rather than the whole personality; ethnic and cultural heterogeneity, mobility, the impersonal nature of commercial contracts, and the mere numbers of the community combine to give the individual an anonymity which lessens the effectiveness of approval and derision of others in control of behavior, so that law enforcement agencies become indispensable. The division of labor has antisocial forms and crime is a profession.

The conditions of employment entail the necessity of regularity and punctuality, forcing change from habits based on rural seasonal patterns. Training on the job gives new motor habits and skills. Common experience encourages organization for common interests. A greater variety of goods are available, and new standards of living can be aspired to, even if they are not always reached.

The town is a source of social change because it has its own necessities of organization, arising out of its economic functions and the ethnic diversity of its population, but it is also a transmitter of other forces, such as education and commerce, which also make for a social change. The town is both a response to forces of change and a focus for them, a place where they operate more intensively.

SEQUENCES OF URBAN GROWTH

The following outline of urban growth is an abstraction which applies, within limits, to most African towns. Although only a few have yet completed the process, they generally can be placed somewhere along this line of development.

Before the town is founded, there is a tribal population, probably sparsely settled and living by subsistence farming. A few intruding

Europeans select a site suitable for mining, or for a port, a trading station, or a headquarters for regional administration.

There might already have been a village at the spot; in fact, that might have been one of the reasons for choosing the site. A certain amount of labor is needed for the activities which Europeans have begun, and this is hired from the village and the surrounding countryside. As the enterprise expands, labor is drawn from greater distances, and as the number of people increases, it becomes necessary for the supply of food and other necessities to be organized, and for the community to be governed. This, in turn, means additional employment and adds to the growth of the town.

At first tribesmen come into the town to earn money for a specific purpose, such as to pay taxes or to buy a bicycle, and consider their stay in town as a temporary sojourn. They may return when other needs arise; in fact, the desires and necessities for which money is required tend to become recurrent and the habit is formed of spending a certain number of months each year in town.

Some skills as well as muscle power are needed; tallying and keeping records requires schooling, and certain manual operations require training. Clerks and experienced workmen may be brought in from older towns, or even from Europe, but eventually a school is indispensable for the continuance of the commercial and governmental functions of the town. When a school is established, it may be under the auspices of a religious mission and dedicated to other purposes, but most of its graduates will generally find employment as clerks. Manual training is often furnished by the employing company on an apprenticeship basis.

The kinds of tasks performed in the town will multiply; agricultural products that in the beginning were merely collected for export may now be processed first. Even services necessary to the town itself contribute to specialization. As the complexity of labor requirement increases, employers encourage workers to stay on the jobs for which they have been trained. For the employees, a rise in income makes it feasible to keep a family in town.

At this point, the town has a few permanent residents who are outnumbered by the temporary residents, and in addition there are always some visitors who come for various reasons. This majority of temporary residents are semiurban, semirural, spending part of their time in town and part on their farms. Of them, one might say that, in general, the child grows up in the village, the young man comes into the town to earn a living, and, when aged, returns to the village. This type of town dweller is tied to his rural relatives and they to him; they send him food from time to time and he sends money home, and they cultivate the fields which will support him in his old age.

There is a great deal of movement back and forth between the country and the town at this stage; relatives may come to visit a man and crowd into his quarters while they sample the excitements of the town or look for work; and he fairly regularly goes home to rest and to display his acquisition of goods and to distribute some of them to kin and relatives by marriage. To the degree that this situation obtains, it minimizes the development of distinctive contrasts in urban and rural traits. As long as these ties last, a villager has somewhere to stay in the town and someone to show him around the pitfalls and through the intricacies of the maze of urban relationships; the villager is abashed at the strangeness and the complexity of the town but does not feel completely solitary and lost. Equally important, the townsman avoids making changes in habits that will alienate his rural kinsmen to whom he will return.

During this period, country patterns tend to persist in the town, but town ideas also get disseminated to the villages, and the difference in the rate of change between the two is thus lessened.

The demographic structure of an African town, during this phase, is different from, and inverse to, that of the rural areas. The town has a preponderance of males and youth. There are comparatively few children in the towns and very few of the aged, but between the ages of seventeen and fifty, that is, the employable years, an individual has a greater chance of survival in the town. The number of females, smaller in total than that of the males, shows the same bell-shaped distribution in ages. The newer the town, the greater the unbalance in the demographic structure; the older the town, other things (such as the government's urban policy) being equal, the greater the approach to demographic stability.

Toward demographic stability. The subsequent developments in town growth are largely measures tending toward demographic stability, that is, to a lessening of the disproportion in the sex and age ratios. One important prerequisite for stabilization of town populations is housing. African townsmen, primarily, are a labor force, and it is cheaper for employers to provide housing for a single man than for a family. If a married man is hired, he is frequently given the same-sized quarters as a single man; when the married man later wants to visit his family, he may quit his job and hope to find another when he returns. This means high turnover of labor, which in turn contributes to keeping low the level of skill, so that the employer is constrained to offer inducements, at least to his more skilled workers, to remain; better housing is often provided for this reason. Skilled workers tend to change jobs less often than the unskilled.

Another prerequisite for demographic stability of the towns is a larger income for the urban family. In the country, the wife supplements the husband's income by her labor on the farm; in the town there are usually few opportunities for her to contribute to the family income. In the Union of South Africa, an increasing number of urban African women are employed in domestic service and other occupations. Many, however, are dependent on earnings from illicit beer brewing; income from this traffic is curtailed by frequent police raids. In West Africa, women are petty traders who sell food, cloth, cigarettes, and many other things; and some earn more—a few, much more—than their husbands. This economic opportunity, as well as the age of the towns, explains the more nearly normal sex ratio found there.

A further prerequisite for stabilization is a system of social services. Kin groups, due to dispersal, can no longer fulfill their mutual obligations to help an individual in distress. Welfare costs have to be borne by the governments, and this helps to account for administrative ambivalence towards urban stabilization.

In South Africa, a further factor slows down but does not reverse the tendency towards stabilization. The philosophy of *apartheid* designates the African as essentially a rural being, and the town is considered as belonging to the white men. The African can come to the town on sufferance when the purpose is for the service of the white man, but it is thought proper that the African's wife should stay on the reserve and keep a farm; economic development, however, has made this impossible, and cities are building housing for African families despite the contradiction of this action with the prevailing ideology.

In spite of these obstacles, the growth of commerce and industry with its division of labor and specialization and the fight against high rates of labor turnover, constantly force increased stabilization.

As long as an unbalanced sex ratio continues it has serious implications in regard to family life, birth rate, and mobility. Many of the men in the towns are bachelors, but those who are married may keep their wives in the country to cultivate the farms, although a wife sometimes joins her husband in the town. If a man is a polygynist, he is able to achieve both ends of having a wife with him and one tending the distant farm.

The scarcity of women in towns militates against the fidelity of a town wife, who is unceasingly importuned during her husband's absence at work by numerous womanless men. A husband sometimes sends his wife back to the village, where his relatives can guard her chastity, and then, perhaps, he begins to prey upon some other man's wife, or forms a liaison with an unmarried woman, or consorts with prostitutes. Sexual infidelity is a frequent source of friction and a significant factor in the brittleness of urban marriage.

This separation of many of the men in the towns from the women in the villages has a depressing effect upon the birth rate and population growth. In comparison with the rest of the world, Africa appears sparsely populated, and many development plans hinge upon availability of labor supply. Population has increased owing to suppression of warfare, improvement of sanitation and health facilities, and rising levels of living, but a continuation of the unbalanced sex ratio in both towns and rural areas may slow down the rate of increase.

Beginnings of classes. As the urban population progresses toward stabilization and tends to become distinct from the rural population, further divisions in the urban population take place. An incipient class structure appears. Wealth, education, and occupation set some apart from others less favored or gifted, or perhaps merely newcomers, and doing the less remunerative work.

Differences in fortune, training, and ability in the competitive towns give rise to a number of stations, or statuses, which approximate classes, whose members influence each other in evolving group mores which are a departure from the past.

Several factors hinder the solidification of classes in urban Africa. One such factor is the continuation of kin obligations, which drain the resources of the successful individual to aid his less fortunate relatives. Another is that trade is dominated by European, Asian, and Levantine merchants, and a large, well-to-do African middle class based on commerce is prevented from arising. Discrimination, which varies in degree (and in the rationalization for it) in different territories but is never absent, puts all Africans in one category and all Europeans in another. As long as the European fills the dominant role and is exclusive, the emergent upper group of Africans will feel psychologically bound to the lower group. And frequently housing shortages prevent the rising elite from separating itself residentially from the other elements.

The lesser differentiation of women also retards class formation. Women receive less education than men and although more urban women than rural women are literate, still the number is small. The occupational opportunities for a woman are limited and in some places absent, so that she is less affected by these modifying influences than the man, and because she is not employed, she is free to visit the country relatives and may keep up the contact with her husband's kin as well as with her own. Therefore, the woman, generally, is more conservative, more apt to preserve the traditional customs, and less likely to take up town ways that are glaringly different. To some extent illiterate wives slow the rate of internalization of urban attitudes by the husband and are not able to identify themselves on his level of the class structure.

Children also are often not able to identify with the father's status because of the common practice of sending children to grow up in the country with relatives; accordingly, adjustments to urban and class attitudes have to be made as adults, after rural patterns have been set. Thus men show the marks of class more than their wives and children, a fact which raises the question whether class exists, since class is usually considered as being composed of families. Among the elite especially, where families tend to be stabilized, this less often applies.

Class formation tolls the knell of tribalism in the urban environment. The marks of class are independent of the marks of tribal membership; classes comprise people of various tribes. A European language is not only a means of communication but a symbol of status (like European clothes) for the elite. For other levels, a vernacular lingua franca usually serves the multitribal population. The lines are still fluid and the word "class" should be used with care, but we are not dealing with a static situation and it is necessary to indicate the trend.

Old and new overlapping. The processes outlined above are operative simultaneously and are interrelated. In the towns we see the old and the new, the contrasts and conflicts of Africa, the past refusing to die and the future struggling to be born. Nowhere has the town completely sloughed off its tribal background; nowhere has the urban synthesis finally jelled; but everywhere change is moving in that direction. It is not implied here that there is a renunciation of all African cultural features but merely of traditional organization.

URBAN SOCIAL STRUCTURE

The feeling of ethnic solidarity carries over into the town and is especially important for new arrivals. Some sections of towns tend toward a tribal or language homogeneity. Even when this is not possible, some form of organization is usually felt necessary for the protection of the members of a common ethnic group in the strange environment of the town. Each "strangers' community" may elect a headman to represent it, and town authorities sometimes find it convenient to deal with certain matters through the several headmen of the various tribal elements. Or a Tribal Union may be formed for mutual aid.

On the other hand, mutual sharing groups in which each contributing member takes the "kitty" in rotation exclude kinsmen, since custom frowns on exactness in exchanges between kinsmen. Other collectivities which have begun to knit the disparate tribal elements into common units are schools, churches, trade unions, political parties, nationalist movements, and public places of recreation such as beer halls and football fields. The more that Africans identify themselves with these groups, the less important tribal affiliation becomes; these associations perform services, or create outlets for emotions and energy, that formerly were found in the tribal organization.

Classes. The upper stratum of African society, which one could logically term a middle class, keeping in mind that the European forms the upper class, includes the most educated, who in some places may be university graduates trained in Europe or America, and in other places locally educated persons of lower level; the upper ranks of government service, which may mean Senior Civil Service, or merely chief clerks; the most responsible employees of commercial firms, which may be managerial staff or only storekeepers or cashiers; perhaps teachers, headmasters of schools, and ministers of religion; and sometimes privately established professional men, or traders successful enough to survive the non-African competition. The actual composition varies with the occupational opportunities in the territory, which in turn depend upon economic, educational and administrative conditions.

Between the elite and the laborers are an artisan group—tailors, shoemakers, goldsmiths, masons, carpenters and other skilled workers. Even where the level of skill is low and the craft could be learned in a few months, the apprenticeship is for a number of years, so that ordinarily anyone out of his teens would be discouraged from beginning, but there is nothing actually to prevent anyone from moving from the category of laborer to that of artisan or even to the elite, if he can acquire the education and the income.

Family. The above positions and institutions in the social structure are innovations, but previously existing institutions, such as the family are modified in the new milieu. An African who ventures into a town is an offshoot of a kin group, and others may follow to the extent that they can be supported; but those who cluster around the man who has gained a foothold in the town are only a fragment of his primary group. The family in the town exists under difficulties and tends to approximate the nuclear family in form, that is, a husband, wife, and children. Other relatives found in the compound of the extended family in the country are found more rarely in town dwellings.

When a crisis arises and the members of the nuclear family want to discuss it with others, being habituated to the extended family of the villages, they call in whatever kinsman, no matter how distant, who happens to be in the town. Proximity in space takes the place of closeness of relationship in the town.

Marriage. In most areas, there are three kinds of marriage which are recognized as legal: civil, church and customary. The first two are on the Western model and the latter is supposed to be according to tribal customs. In fact, however, customary law cannot operate effectively to attain traditional goals in the towns because a marriage is a contract between families and not merely between individuals, and it often happens that both of the families are not in the town and may even be unknown to each other. Traditional gifts are usually commuted to money, and labor services, if observed, are shortened in time. Furthermore, customary law marriage between members of different tribes is an anomaly unless, as sometimes happens, both agree to accept one of the tribal forms. If a man is an immigrant into a town where one tribe is dominant he may do this. In addition to legal marriage, there are casual unions which break up when either party so desires.

OUTLOOK

The towns and cities will play an increasingly vital part in the life of Africa. The town is the door through which Africa is entering the modern world. Civilization in the twentieth century is an urban civilization. "The influences which cities exert upon the social life of man are greater than the ratio of the urban population would indicate, for the city . . . is the initiating and controlling center of economic, political and cultural life that has drawn the most remote parts of the world into its orbit and woven diverse areas, peoples and activities into a cosmos." In Africa cultural groups are beginning to appear in the cities; nationalist movements get rural support but have their headquarters in the towns. Nations are in the process of formation in Africa and the towns are the crucible. The towns today give us an insight into the future. "As the city is, so will the nation be."

26   SLUM CLEARANCE AND FAMILY LIFE IN LAGOS*

Peter Marris

Slums are amongst the most obtrusive of social evils. Physical squalor catches the eye; the degradation of human dignity shocks the social reformer, civic pride is outraged, the privileged are uncomfortably reminded of the circumstances in which their fellow countrymen must live. To people who do not live in slums, their demolition seems self-evidently desirable. Yet the slum dwellers themselves often bitterly resent being displaced. Where, as in South Africa, slum clearance is openly undertaken for the protection of the privileged, such a conflict of interests is not surprising. But the conflict also arises where the welfare of the people to be rehoused is the principal aim of policy.

In Africa, the initiative in slum clearance usually comes from public agencies, which are run by aliens, or the most privileged members of society. They tend to assume that physical squalor must be associated with moral degradation: the slums must be riven with crime, ill-health, a demoralized irresponsibility in family life. But this need not be so. The slum may be merely the longest-settled neighbourhood, grown shabby with age, which yet enjoys the most integrated social life of any in the city. The people who live there are not necessarily all impoverished, or humiliated, by their surroundings. Even if they are, they probably cannot afford to live otherwise, and, unless the underlying causes of their poverty are first removed, the attempt to rehouse them at a standard beyond their means will only make them destitute. There is a danger, therefore, that slum clearance schemes will be based on arbitrary assump-

* From Peter Marris, "Slum Clearance and Family Life in Lagos." Reprinted by permission from *Human Organization*, Vol. 19, No. 3 (Fall 1960). Published by the Society for Applied Anthropology. Subscription is by membership in the Society.

tions as to how slum-dwellers live, and ought to live; and that they will set standards related more to the social values of the leaders of society, than to the needs and resources of the people to be re-housed. But the more realistically the difficulties are assessed, the more intractable they are likely to appear.

The part of Central Lagos to be cleared as slums has been settled for two or more generations. The streets are shown in their present form on a map of 1885. The houses would have been built originally by families for their own use, although many have later been divided, or let to tenants. A few still standing follow the de-sign of a traditional Yoruba compound, the rooms surrounding an open courtyard on four sides. But, in more recent building, the courtyard has dwindled to a passage leading from the street to a yard, often with rooms opening onto it from one or two sides, and lavatories and washplaces at the back. In these yards, or on a verandah overlooking the street, the women do most of their housework. The rooms are sometimes so full of bed and baggage that there is hardly space to put a chair. But such cramped quarters are manageable because the occupants do little but sleep and make love there.

The houses are shabby—the walls patched, the roofs leaky, the ceilings blackened with smoke. But some have solid walls, well-made doors and windows, and a concrete floor raised above the ground. They have suffered as much from neglect as from dilapi-dation.

According to Yoruba custom, the children of the founder of a family property occupy it, together with their wives and children, and their descendants after them. The daughters have much the same rights as the sons, except that they would be expected to live with their husband in his family house. In fact, there seem to be only a few family properties still occupied in this way in Lagos. Usually some rooms are let, some are occupied by the descendants of the founder, and others by more distant relatives, for whom those with rights in the house are responsible.

About two-thirds of the residents of central Lagos now are tenants, but they are long settled there. In one neighbourhood I in-vestigated, more than half the tenants interviewed had lived in Lagos for over twenty years, and nearly half had been in the same room for ten years or longer. Even the more recent arrivals had mostly held their tenancies at least six years. Nine-tenths of the owners and their relatives were born in Lagos, half of them in the house in which they still live. The population is the most stable in Lagos.

The slum clearance area is at the heart of Lagos commercial life. It lies between the two main shopping streets; surrounded by the largest markets in cloth, vegetables, meat and poultry, enamel and earthenware, herbs, fancy goods and fruit; and within a few minutes of the great importing houses. Much of the working population of Lagos passes every day by its narrow lanes. The people of the neighbourhood earn their living by the commerce of the city. The men are traders, importers and exporters, shopkeepers, dockers and market porters; drivers, watchmen, clerks or mechanics for the foreign firms; or craftsmen who often deal in goods on the side—bicycle repairers selling secondhand machines and tyres, spray painters selling paint, blacksmiths buying up used tins and making them into cheap oil lamps. The women nearly all trade.

Traders and many of the craftsmen work on their own account, and depend for their livelihood on attracting a group of regular customers to whom they are readily available. Some of the labourers, too, are only casually employed, and must be in easy reach of employers who may be hiring men for the day. So, more than half the working population are likely to earn less, at least for awhile, if they are moved from the neighbourhood where they have established themselves.

The people of central Lagos are, therefore, largely dependent upon their location at the centre of commerce for their livelihood. And because they have, on the whole, been long settled there, an integrated pattern of social and family life has grown up. The affection and sense of mutual obligation of the family group is the outstanding loyalty of Lagos social life.

Nigerians are brought up to regard the needs of their kinfolk as their first responsibility; they support their mothers and fathers in their old age, and often elderly aunts or cousins as well. They contribute to the marriage payment of a younger brother, bring up their nephews and nieces, help out their married sisters. More than half the people interviewed in central Lagos were spending at least a tenth of their income on help to their relatives. Without this family loyalty, there would be no one to care for the old, the sick, the widows and orphans, no one to set men on their feet when they were out of work, or to pass on to younger brothers and sisters the advantages of an education for which, as likely as not, the family has paid. For, as yet, public social services in Nigeria are few. The family group collects its dues, and distributes its funds to those in need; it gives its members at least an ultimate security against the misfortunes of life.

Besides these personal obligations, the family displays its unity in frequent celebrations—naming ceremonies for a newborn child, marriages, funerals, anniversaries, a sendoff for a brother going overseas—and to these each branch of the family will contribute its share. A group of relatives will often choose a costume for the occasion, and symbolise their unity by appearing in this uniform—a pretty but expensive custom. There are also regular meetings— sometimes weekly, or on a Sunday of each month—when the difficulties of members are discussed, disputes settled, and the progress of the family reviewed. Many meetings raise a small subscription, minutes are taken, and officers elected from time to time; they are, therefore, formal gatherings, comprising from half-a-dozen to fifty people or more. In some families, the subscription will be put aside toward the building or repair of the family house, or even the running of a corporate business in the name of the founder. Two-thirds of the men and women interviewed in central Lagos belonged to families which held such meetings regularly in the course of a year.

But the day-to-day visits exchanged by relatives strengthen the unity of the family group more than do these formal meetings. News is passed on, problems discussed as they arise, and the old people are able to live comfortably on the small presents of cash or kind brought for them by the kinsfolk who call during the day. Although it is less common now for all a man's descendants to be together in one house, the families of central Lagos live, for the most part, no more than ten or fifteen minutes walk from each other. Tenants tend to have fewer kin near them than owners, but the longer they have lived in Lagos, the more likely that they will have attracted other members of their family to the town.

Most of the people in this part of Lagos, therefore, have many relatives nearby. They may also be members of mutual benefit societies, Bible study classes, Moslem organisations, or associations of people from their town or village of origin—all of which flourish. Everyone who belongs to such a group has a status, rights and obligations, and enjoys the sense of security which comes from these.

All Nigerians, I think, are very loyal to their family group— they regard their membership in it with pride and affection, and derive a deep sense of emotional security from it. I believe that some of the emotional security which a European would look for in marriage, a Nigerian expects to find rather in a more generalised relationship with his kin.

Because of this emotional and economic dependence upon the kin group, there is less emphasis on loyalty between husbands and wives. Marriage is more of a contract, with limited obligations.

Husband and wife, recognising the attachment of the other to his own relatives, tend to trust each other less, and share less in common. Feelings are not deeply committed. The marriage may break down when money problems or the claims of other loyalties press upon it, especially in a polygamous household. When a man has to share his income amongst several wives, the place of any one of them is less secure. Jealousies and rivalries may lead to irreconcilable quarrels. A woman may prefer to return to her own people, rather than suffer the introduction of a new wife into the household—particularly if her husband did not consult her beforehand.

A woman cannot allow her own and her children's welfare to rest only on what her husband can provide. Wages are low, employment insecure, traders are at the mercy of fluctuations in the market; illness, for lack of medical care, may be serious and protracted. There is no guarantee that her husband will always be able to support her. He may—with her consent or not—take other wives, and his resources will have to go all the further. So every woman tries to secure an independent income from a shop, or dressmaking, or, most commonly, from trade. Unless her parents have provided for her, she will expect a sum of money from her husband to buy a stock in trade, from which she may make anything from a few shillings to fifty pounds or more a month. Her profit is her own, an independent income which protects her against losing her husband, and enables her to fulfill her obligations to her own family. Her husband is saved responsibility for her personal expenses, and she may be able to help him out of her earnings if he finds himself in difficulties. The trading of women is, therefore, an essential part of the household economy and, but for it, she would be an unequal and vulnerable partner in marriage, and would have nothing to contribute to her own kin. A woman may be at her market stall from early morning until dusk, and this, rather than her home, gets her best attention.

The slum clearance scheme requires the wholesale demolition of the neighbourhoods of central Lagos whose way of life has been described. Families are offered tenancies in a rehousing estate, at Suru Lere in the suburbs, in terraced cottages of one to four rooms. The owners of the property are compensated and have the opportunity to repurchase plots in central Lagos as they are developed, but the price considerably exceeds the amount of compensation. At present, it seems unlikely that any of the owners formerly resident in central Lagos will be able to afford to return there. The population of central Lagos will probably be premanently dispersed by the scheme. Their rehabilitation presents serious difficulties, both for their family life and their livelihood.

The rehousing estate provides well-built and well-spaced houses, with gardens, quiet, running water and proper sanitation. But it is five miles from the centre of Lagos, at the end of an uncomfortable sixpenny bus ride. So those who moved to the estate were much further from their relatives in central Lagos. Also many of those whose houses have been pulled down have not gone to the estate at all, preferring to rent cheaper accommodation on the outskirts of the town; or they have gone to stay with relatives, or have evicted tenants from other property which they own. A young clerk, who had been moved from a large family house, told me:

> When we were about to come here, most of our people didn't want to come to this bush—they call this place bush—they think there are bad spirits here. So the proportion of us who came here, in short, was only two of us out of twenty. The rest went to rent places in E. B. or Idi Oro [suburbs of Lagos]. They think these houses here are not the kind of houses in which we Africans live—you know we live in groups, not one here, one there. So I have only one relative here. She is a woman selling cloth, and since she came here, the trade has flopped. This woman is too fat, she can't be going to Lagos every time on the bus, so she had to give up. She is even thinking of quitting because of the rent. They have a family house in E. B., and they have just quitted the tenant, who has been there a long time. Now she has to leave this place and go to live there. She has a brother too; that one did not come here. He could not afford the rentage in E. B., not to think of Lagos, and has to go to Agege [a town fifteen miles distant]. He is a pensioner, and if you see his condition now you will pity him.

Because they live at a greater distance, the residents on the re-housing estate also see their relatives less often. They pay fewer visits: leaving early and returning late, they make as many calls as they can on their way to and from work. Once home, they are usually too tired to go out again, even if they could afford it. And they receive few visitors. Many I interviewed explained that their relatives found Suru Lere too isolated: fares were too expensive, they lacked time for the journey, tired of waiting for the bus, or were even unable to find the address when they arrived.

> In Lagos you'd have your supper, and you'd think, I'd like to go and see my sister. And you'd come back in an hour's time and tell your wife, I've been to see my sister, see my aunt, see my brother . . . now sometimes for a month I don't see them.

> When I was in Lagos they were with me. We live in the same street. Old wife's family, new wife's family, we see each other every day. In

Lagos you see everybody nearly every day. Do you see any of my family visiting me here?

On Saturday I made 5 shillings gain, and I ran to see my mother. I've not seen her since Saturday and God knows when I shall see her again. She wept when I was to leave, because she didn't want to leave me, and she is afraid to come here. When I was in Lagos there was not a day I don't see her—if I couldn't go in the morning I go at night.

The more formal cohesion of the family also suffered. Sixty-one percent of those interviewed in central Lagos were members of a regular family meeting, but only twenty-seven percent at Suru Lere —either because they no longer attended, or because the meetings had been abandoned with the demolition of the family property. Even where the meeting was still held, fewer came. One man remarked:

All these meetings I told you of were when we were in Lagos; when the slum came, it scattered us. [He was the most senior of his family, and the meeting was still held, at his home on the Estate. But it was now fortnightly instead of weekly, and attendance had dropped from thirty to five.] When we came here, you only get those of the same father. Last Saturday we had a meeting, there were only five. But before there would be my aunt, her children, my brother's children. . . . This place is far, number one. Money to come, number two.

Slum clearance, therefore, means that family groups tend to be disrupted. This can be especially hard for old people who had lived in family property and been cared for by relatives around them. Their relatives elsewhere are no longer so aware of their needs, and they themselves cannot afford the fare to go and ask them for help. The system of mutual support begins to break down. Many of the people on the estate, who were used to giving regular help to their relatives, could no longer afford it. Although rents on the estate are subsidised, they are still, on the whole, more than was being paid before, partly because in central Lagos, where tenancies are of long standing, rents are exceptionally low; and partly because households occupy more space on the estate than they had before. The former owners are usually paying rent for the first time in their lives. In central Lagos the average rent of the accommodation occupied by the tenants interviewed was £2. 1s. 6d., on the rehousing estate £2. 7s. 9d. But the cost of transport worried them even more than the rent. It was the most universal complaint—fares to work, to get their children to school, their wives to market. It also raised their expenses indirectly: the men had to buy a midday meal at work, since they could not afford to come home, and prices in the local shops were higher because of transport charges. Apart from the shops, where prices were high, there was no market. Fifty-seven percent of those interviewed were spending upwards of £1 a month on fares—a tenth of the income of over half the sample. Some of the men who worked late into the night, and had to depend on taxis, spent over £5 a month on fares.

To make ends meet, they could no longer be so generous in helping their kin. In central Lagos, thirty-five percent of the household heads made regular monthly allotments of at least £2 to relatives apart from their immediate family, but at Suru Lere only thirteen percent could do as much. Because they could no longer contribute, they were sometimes shy of visiting relatives whom they had been used to helping. One woman, for instance, told me she had an especially affectionate relationship with a young half-sister, who was still at school.

> She treats me like a father, she asks me for anything she wants—school books, money, clothes. I don't go to see her now—she's sure to ask me for something, and I can't afford it. Once in a month or two months perhaps I go, when I can scrape together five or ten shillings.

Their families apart, they also tended to give up entertainment and their membership of benefit societies, church groups and social clubs, because they could no longer afford either the fare or the subscription. One young man, a salesman who was earning a better income than most, remarked:

> I was a member of four clubs when I was in Lagos. I used to attend the functions regularly, almost every night. I've never been again since I came here. Even table tennis—I don't think I could hold a bat now. And cinema—I used to go to the cinema every night with my wife. But even if we could get transport, I don't think we have enough allowance for the pictures again. We used to attend dances in Lagos too, but we don't do it now. And I went to church every Sunday in Lagos too, every day in the Lenten season. Since we've been here, I don't think I've been to church more than twice.

The higher cost of living in the rehousing estate is much more difficult to meet, because so many of the households earn less as well. Traders and independent craftsmen lose most of their business when they move. Few if any of their former customers are willing to lose time and money on a long bus ride, when they can take their orders more conveniently elsewhere. The population of the estate itself is too small and too dispersed to support many traders or craftsmen, especially as most people go into central Lagos every day and continue to buy there, where the choice is wider and prices lower. The estate lies off the main roads and attracts few outsiders. Moreover, the people already established in the neighbourhood have pre-empted the best sites for market stalls along the road to the city centre. Even those on the estate who still work from a shop or stall in central Lagos find that business suffers. They are no longer accessible to customers at home; lose time in travelling and cannot supervise their apprentices so thoroughly; and since they cannot carry their stock home every night, have now expenses in storage or guards.

Most of the people interviewed on the estate who had been traders or independent craftsmen were therefore in real difficulties, some destitute. A shoemaker I went to interview greeted me with the comment,

> I am alone working. Alone "playing" I should say. When I was in Lagos I would reluctantly give you half an hour. Now, if you want five hours. . . . Before I moved here, I was first class shoemaker having shoemaking machine. I had a shop—that was Broad Street—and if you see the condition of my shop in Lagos you will like to repair your shoes there. It was my father's occupation so I have sufficient tools. When I was there, I had a certain contract with the Police force, and another from the Elder Dempster Company for the crews' shoes. And the crews themselves when they came from England, they bring their shoe for repair. Broad Street is not far from the Customs. Murray Street [where he lived] is even nearer, only one street cross us. All now—nothing from there now. [He used to make £200 or £300 a year.] Since I came here, not sufficient money to rent a shop here, let alone work there. This is what I have since Monday—it is 4s.6d., and when I took it to the owner he said, "Didn't you know? This is not like Lagos, I will come for it when I have got to have money." From Monday now, I've got one threepence, this morning. If you look at the street now, you will not see a single man. They have all gone to Lagos, and take their shoes there for repair. . . . This is not a place, but a punishment from God.

A butcher who had made 20s. to 30s. a day in Lagos, selling from a market stall, had used up all his capital on fares and meeting the higher cost of living, and his trade declined until he was virtually destitute.

> Everything has changed against me. I've never had anything like this happen to me since I was born. It seems like being taken from happiness to misery.

A dressmaker had been almost as unfortunate:

I printed cards out and gave them, but they say they can't come the long journey, there are so many tailors in Lagos. All these people here, they go to Lagos to buy, give all their business to traders in Lagos. They only come here to sleep. There's nothing at all here. They say we should take one of the shops here—but there's no one to patronise. I cut out paper patterns for the girls here sometimes, and that's all, except baby dresses occasionally—two or three shillings. Business is paralyzed.

Some of the skilled workers had given up working on their own account since they moved to the estate; and many of the traders and craftsmen probably avoided the estate in the first place. Nearly half the men interviewed in central Lagos were self-employed, but only a quarter at Suru Lere—and most of these were earning less. As a whole, the income of self-employed men had fallen by an average of £8 a month since their move to the estate. Since it is more difficult for a woman to find a paid job, they suffered even more; the income of the women interviewed fell by an average of £10.

The wives of the men interviewed were equally affected. A quarter had given up any attempt to trade, while as many had lost most of their business but still struggled, rather hopelessly, to scrape together a few shillings in the month. There were four times as many wives earning nothing on the estate, as in the households interviewed in central Lagos. They had to depend more on their husbands, and the men at Suru Lere did, in fact, give more substantial allowances to their wives—mostly at the expense of other family obligations.

The rehousing estate had, therefore, all the disadvantages to a trader that its isolation and dispersed population would suggest. Central Lagos is the hub of the city, alive from early morning until late at night: "It is Canaan to us," said a woman trader, "a land of milk and honey." Suru Lere is deserted for most of the day, and its only thoroughfare skirts rather than crosses the Estate. So there were fewer traders at Suru Lere, and more women not working at all, and those who still traded much made less by it. In central Lagos, the average profit of all the traders in the households interviewed was £11. 12s. 4d.: on the rehousing estate it was £4. 1s. 9d. As one old lady was driven to exclaim: "May God deliver me out of this place."

As a whole, therefore, the tenants on the Estate earned less and paid out more than before they were moved. The amenities of the estate, its gardens and peace, sanitation and piped water, were luxuries they could not appreciate. Many of the families had got into debt since they arrived, especially in arrears of rent, and were haunted by the fear of eviction. Harassed by financial worries, some households disintegrated.

Life on the estate, with fewer wives at work, husbands paying them more generous allowances, and interfering relatives at a distance, ought to have encouraged marriage: and there were several young couples who enjoyed their new independence and privacy. But more often, far from husband and wife drawing closer together, they were forced to separate. Unable to meet the expenses of suburban life, some of the husbands sent their wives home to their families and distributed their children amongst relatives who could care for them. Wives, finding no opportunity for trade, left to live with their own relatives nearer the centre of the city; others simply deserted when their husbands could no longer support them. One man, who had been particularly unlucky, said of his junior wife, "I hadn't a penny to put down for her, so she had to desert me, she said she couldn't stay here to starve." Another man had sent his wife to her mother on Lagos Island. "I can't keep her here when I can't maintain her." He went to see her once a month. "It's no use going when you can only put your hand in an empty pocket." A van driver said:

> When I was in Lagos, I never pay for house, I had money. I could have financed my wife with something to sell. Now the house is pulled down it change everything. She is every time crying, fighting, worrying me for money. Even yesterday I told her to quit if she kept on worrying me for money. I can't steal.

Of the married men twenty-seven percent had been divorced at some time, an appreciably higher proportion than in the central Lagos sample, and at least in some cases the quarrel had arisen out of the difficulties they experienced since they were moved.

Even when there had been no quarrel, husbands and wives spent more time apart. In central Lagos eighty-one percent of the married people saw their husband or wife daily; at Suru Lere only sixty-four percent. More of the young children, too, were living outside the household. The more scattered the family group, the more difficult it is to fulfil obligations without absence from home. And the poorer people are, the greater the strain on the loyalty of husband or wife, and the competing claims of marriage and kin are less easily reconciled.

It would be wrong to imply, however, that all the families in the estate were either miserable, or in danger of disintegration. A third of those I interviewed preferred it on the whole to where they had lived before. They liked the houses, the quiet in which to study, it gave some of the young couples the chance of a private life out of reach of interfering neighbours and relatives. But those who were best pleased with their new surroundings were least characteristic of the people of central Lagos for whom the Estate was planned: they tended to be immigrants from distant parts of Nigeria, and in the more senior clerical posts. For the rest, the people of the Estate felt they had acquired the amenities of a modern house at a sacrifice of their family life and livelihood, a change which had been forced upon them and one which they would not have made from choice.

Slum clearance raises the fundamental problem: how can you destroy a neighbourhood physically, without destroying at the same time the livelihood and way of life of the people who have settled there? If these are destroyed, the clearance of slums is likely to do more harm than good.

If compulsory rehousing is to be just, and a benefit to those rehoused, it must, I believe, fulfil two conditions:

1) The people must be able to afford it. In Africa, this must mean that it will cost them no more to live in their new houses than their old, since very few people have money enough to pay for better housing. Those who can afford it and want to spend their money in this way will have already provided for themselves. If people are forced to pay for housing they cannot afford, their poverty will oblige them to restrict their participation in social life. Above all, it will withdraw them from their family, and this, in Africa especially, can cause great unhappiness.

2) They must be able to re-establish their pattern of life in the new surroundings. They must not be too far distant from their kin, nor their work, and the same range of economic activities must be open to them. And their new homes must be so designed that they can be adapted to their way of life. That is to say, if they have depended for their livelihood on being at the centre of trade, they must be rehoused where they have the same chances of custom, or where there are alternative ways of earning a living open to them.

These two conditions are likely to be very difficult to fulfil in practice. The second condition can most easily be realised by rehousing the people on the site which has been cleared, but if they are to be less crowded than before, the buildings will have to be of several storeys. In Lagos, at least, this would have been very expensive indeed and the cost could not have been recovered in rents. To provide for the people in the suburbs, as in Lagos, brings down the cost of housing only to increase the cost of fares, and makes it very much more difficult to prevent the disruption of family groups and economic relationships. New markets must be developed, new opportunities of employment provided; and the new estate must be able to absorb not only those removed from the slums, but relatives who wish to settle with them or near them.

Lastly, however the problem is tackled, it is likely to cost a lot of public money. The tendency is therefore to make the people who are rehoused pay for some of the cost themselves, on the grounds that they are, after all, enjoying a higher standard of housing, and the scheme is for their benefit. I believe this to be unjust: if they have to pay for it, it will not be to their benefit, for the reasons I have given. If their interests only are to be considerd, it would be better not to rehouse them at all. If slums are to be cleared for reasons of national prestige, the cost is a fair charge on the public purse.

But if slum clearance is costly, difficult to achieve without hardship and cannot fairly be charged to the people rehoused, then is it perhaps better to concentrate first on other equally urgent problems? Where the population of a town is growing so fast, overcrowding may well be more effectively stopped by building up new neighbourhoods as yet underdeveloped, than by displacing those already settled. The worst housing can meanwhile be gradually improved and rebuilt as opportunity arises. After all, it will be some while before the people of Africa can afford what to us seems a minimum standard of housing. Meanwhile, I think they value more the social amenities of their lives.

27 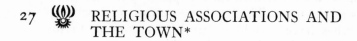 RELIGIOUS ASSOCIATIONS AND
THE TOWN*

K. A. Busia

In addition to the occupational and tribal associations there are other associations of many different kinds which cut across occupational or tribal classifications. The multiplicity of such associations is a prominent feature of the social life of the town. Promi-

* Excerpts from K. A. Busia, *Report on a Social Survey of Sekondi-Takoradi* (London: Crown Agents for the Colonies, 1950). Reprinted by the permission of the author.

nent amongst them are the Religious Groups, each representing some branch of the Christian Faith, and centering its worship in a separate building. It should be explained that the definition of membership varies in the different Churches, and may not imply the same degree of attachment. Besides those whose names appear on the Roll Books of the Churches, there are many more who would claim membership, though they do not fulfill all the obligations required of them, and are consequently not included in the lists of active members. Within each Church are various associations providing not only for religious, but also for educational and social interests. It is through these associations that the cultural and social influence of the Churches is asserted.

The population of the town consists of many different tribes, all gathered here for the purpose of making a living. There is little consciousness of civic responsibility, and no one is his brother's keeper. In such circumstances, the Churches become important social agencies. The various Church Associations, Singing Bands and Choral Societies, Class Meetings and Sunday Schools and Youth Associations attract many members and bring together people of different tribes who share the same faith; in this way they act as social agencies acquainting members of the community with each other. This makes up for the social isolation which some of the members would otherwise feel. It is in the religious associations too that the Churches fulfill educational functions by teaching singing, reading, sewing and knitting, cleanliness, etc.; they also fulfill social functions by encouraging and sponsoring service to the sick and needy members of the community.

Attendance at Church Services and the meetings of the various associations connected with them is prominent amongst the leisure activities of the town. The Sunday aspect of the town suggests that the Churches have a hold on its life; according to the answers given to a Questionnaire on the subject, an average of 70% of those on the active membership lists attend services regularly. In addition to the weekly meetings and services, there are special celebrations like annual harvests or picnics to which members pay no little attention. So much enjoyment is derived from them that there is usually a great deal of money expended on clothing and bands in preparation for the celebrations and outings.

One of the most popular criticisms advanced against the Churches is that they encourage extravagance by providing a regular forum for competitive dress display, especially by the women. It is a fact that the women provide themselves with many changes of dress for the purpose of attending Church Services, and that there are some whose attendances fall off, if they are unable to have frequent changes of dress. In this sense, the Churches influence the standards and cost of living. Although there is some rivalry amongst the different denominations, two interdenominational societies both with large memberships have been formed. They are both of local origin. These are the "Hope Society" and the "Honesty Society." The former has 888 members and the latter 500 members in the town. There are junior and senior members of each society, and the membership is open to both sexes, literates, and illiterates alike. There are branches of these societies in other towns in the Colony and Ashanti. Junior members pay an entrance fee of 5s.6d. and a monthly contribution of 1½d. and seniors an entrance fee of 10s.6d. and a monthly contribution of 3d. Both have distinctive uniforms, worn at meetings. Their popularity is due to the fact that when a member dies, a donation, usually £3, is made to the bereaved family, and the Society turns out for the funeral. They are thus Burial Insurance Societies, guaranteeing a decent burial on which the community places a very high value. In addition to this prime function, the Societies hold regular weekly meetings in which they have prayers, scripture readings and hymns, encourage friendships and settle disputes amongst the members. Their annual picnics and church parades are also extremely popular, and a chief source of attraction to many members.

These associations fulfill two socially significant functions. In the first place, like the Churches, they bring together both literate and illiterate members of the community; in the second place they offer some sort of security from the hardships and isolation of town life to those who seek it, in Christian Associations founded on Christian Teaching. Another interdenominational association is the branch of the YMCA at Takoradi. Its membership is open to Africans and Europeans and it stood at 80 at the beginning of the year. The Association has a centre where a canteen is run; and for recreation, it provides Table Tennis, Billiards, and a Reading room. There is also an orchestra composed of members interested in music. There are services on Sunday evenings. As in other countries, the YMCA caters for religious and social interests, and promotes Christian friendships.

Taken together, the activities of Christian Churches and Associations pervade in a significant way the life of the community. But as one watches the daily lives and activities of the people, and takes account of the rites connected with marriage, birth, death, widowhood, harvests, or installations to traditional offices, one learns that a great deal of the normal communal activities of the converts lie outside their Christian activities, and that for all their influence, the Christian Churches are still alien institutions, intruding upon, but not integrated with indigenous social institutions.

In this connection, the influence of the cult of Tigare should be noted. It has been established here recently as a rival Religious Association which has gained many adherents. Earning a living in the town is, as has been shown, a precarious business. Prosperity is dependent upon forces over which a worker has no control. A sense of insecurity enters where a situation gets beyond control, and some seek security from traditional practices and beliefs. Accordingly the cult of Tigare, which is a form of dynamism expressing the traditional belief in magic or an all pervading potency, has gained many votaries. It was established at the village of Ngyeresia, one mile from Sekondi. Its devotees include Pagans and Christians of all denominations. It is believed that the fetish helps in child-bearing, cures diseases, and protects against envy and evil spirits. Accordingly, people go to it to seek protection from sickness and witchcraft, or from failure in business, or for help to bear children, or to gain wealth or promotion.

Tigare has been introduced from the Northern Territories. Its earlier home was in the Ivory Coast. In the South, it has acquired so many accretions from adaptation to the beliefs and practices of the people that its origin would be hardly recognizable, but for the toga worn by the priests, and the cowries and the kola attached to the fetish. This consists of a black bag containing cowries and kola. The latter is offered to devotees who seek its aid. The Tigare fetish at Ngyeresia has the following commandments which devotees must promise to keep:

(1) Thou shalt not steal.
(2) Thou shalt not covet thy neighbour's wife.
(3) Honour thy father and mother.
(4) Thou shalt not bear false witness against thy neighbour.
(5) Love thy neighbour as thyself.
(6) Thou shalt not administer medicine of noxious or poisonous nature.

Devotees are also enjoined not to practice witchcraft, or cherish evil thoughts about others, or speak ill of them, or take the life of another. If a devotee breaks any of these commands, he has to make full confession, do penance, and pay the necessary fee in order to be "sanctified." There are regular celebrations on Sundays when the fetish may be consulted, and, after the traditional Akan religious practice, there are special forty-day festivals on the "Akwasidae" and "Wukudae" or "Anwonada." Many of the townspeople flock to Ngyeresia to participate in the singing and drumming connected with the rites of the fetish, and Tigare is one of the agencies through which some of the people seek protection from the hardships of town life.

28   SOCIAL CONSEQUENCES OF ECONOMIC DEVELOPMENT IN WEST AFRICA*

Pius Okigbo

The interaction of several economic changes in the first half of the twentieth century has transformed the economic structure of West Africa. Railroad construction undertaken in the late nineteenth and early twentieth century links the northern and southern regions and enables the agricultural and mineral resources of the interior to be brought down to the coast for export. Trade and commerce have been developed within the territories and with the metropolitan powers, and the foundation of financial institutions has been laid. A few industries have been developed: first, mineral and extractive industries, and recently, light industries—soap, beer, textiles, shoes, tobacco, dairy and timber. These developments have had tremendous consequences on the society and on the modes of living of the West African. We shall trace these consequences through the following indices of social change: family and kinship relationships, class and status relationships, social mobility, indigenous institutions for the maintenance of social cohesion. To simplify the analysis, we shall select a particular economic innovation and by working out its consequences show how it has affected the social structure of the region.

An innovation introduces new factors into the social ecology. The society will adopt some of these factors and, in doing so, adapt itself both structurally and operationally in order either to resist the innovation or to accept its consequences. Social resistance may

* From Pius Okigbo, "Social Consequences of Economic Development in West Africa," *Annals of the American Academy of Political and Social Science,* Vol. 305, May 1956, pp. 125–133. Reprinted by permission.

arise at the initial stage, giving rise to a re-evaluation of the economic change. The process involved will be seen clearly if we select the introduction of a new technique which is clearly a breach with tradition.

CHANGES IN PRODUCTION TECHNIQUE

Let us start with an example which has served to transform the peasant production of palm oil and kernels. All along the coastal belt of West Africa, the production of palm oil and kernels is one of the major sources of revenue and one of the main pillars of external trade. For the family, it constitutes a direct source of cash income. Since the family grows practically all its food, the fruits of the palm tree provide a cash income which helps the family to defray some of its cash expenses—school fees for the children, medical fees, other household expenses, and—most of all—the taxes collected by the government.

The method of production had, until just before World War II, been largely traditional. The trees grew wild. Because of the diffuse and dispersed nature of land tenure, the family's palm trees were invariably scattered over wide areas. Collection of palm fruit thus consumed a lot of time and effort. The fruit was allowed to ripen for a time, then it was boiled and pounded with pestles in a wooden mortar. The oil was extracted by hand and so much of it was lost in the pulp.

The changes in the technique of production came in two stages. First, manually operated presses were sold to peasant proprietors. Normally, by traditional methods, from a hundred-pound weight of fruit thirteen pounds of oil had been extracted. The manual presses raised the oil yield from thirteen pounds to sixteen pounds and enhanced the quality of the oil by reducing the free fatty acid content. Introduced in the war years, by 1953 no less than three thousand of these presses were in use in the Eastern Region of Nigeria alone. Each press could, however, handle only a small quantity of fruit at a time. The family organization of production was not disturbed by the manual presses. The husband continued to collect the fruit, and the wife took it to the press for extraction of oil. She continued to retain her interest in the kernels but turned over to the husband the proceeds of the sale of the oil.

The second stage came with the introduction of what were called Pioneer Oil Mills. These mechanized all the processes of extraction of oil and cracking of kernels and handled very large quantities of fruit. The early success which they received in Eastern Nigeria led to their rapid extension in Nigeria. They raised efficiency and nearly quadrupled the oil yield from a given weight of fruit as compared to the efficiency of traditional methods.

Increasing monetization. The economic consequences are easy to follow. With the increase in output made possible by the mechanized mills, economic activity would be more highly monetized in the area where this innovation was introduced. The traditional pattern whereby the husband collects the fruit and the wife takes it to the manual presses has now to be changed. The fruit is now sold in the market place where the agents of the oil mill purchase in small lots and then bulk the purchases for the mill, to ensure the mill's operating at near capacity for most of the time and not lying idle for inadequate supply of fruit. Purchasers, therefore, go far into the remoter areas and villages in order to maintain a steady supply line. In effect, the logistic problem of maintaining a regular flow of fruits to the mill means that an increasingly large part of the village's palm fruit will be bought for the mill. In this way, the erosion of the subsistence sector of the economy has been accelerated.

Extended economic opportunities. In addition to the enlargement of the exchange economy, the increase in output may be expected to lead to the extension of economic opportunities, assuming that there are individuals who recognize the wider opportunities offered by the operation of the mills and who are willing to seize them in order to make a profit. In other words, it is assumed that there will be people (1) who will imitate the innovation by introducing similar mills in other areas, and (2) who will seek to make a profit by undertaking ancillary functions connected with, and widened by, the initial investment. That both processes are at work can be seen from the progress made by the mills in Nigeria.

SOCIAL CONSEQUENCES: THE FAMILY

The impact of the introduction of this new technique of production on the indigenous society can be seen from the effect it has had on family and kinship structure. The family system in Eastern Nigeria where pioneer oil mills were introduced, can be readily described as patriarchal. The father is the breadwinner and head of the household. The family's income is derived from three sources: (1) agriculture—the production of food crops either for subsistence or for sale; (2) forest products—mainly palm fruit for oil and kernels; (3) home industry—the making of cloth, baskets, pots, household utensils, either for domestic use or for sale. In some families, these sources are supplemented by income from the retail of imported merchandise brought in from the neighboring towns and sold in very small lots in the villages.

Production of food is undertaken by the family as a unit. The father does most of the heavy work, which includes tilling the ground and preparing the mounds. He is assisted by the wife and the children. The wife's function is to help in the planting. She attends to the weeding, and in addition to the work on the family farm, which is often far from their dwelling place, she may cultivate entirely on her own the little family plot adjacent to their dwelling. After harvesting the fruit of the season's labor, the family has clear rights to the harvest. The forest products require no cultivation. No effort is called for other than that spent in collection of the fruit. The wife arranges for the extraction of the oil and sells the oil, but retains a right to the kernels. The division of function is thus clearly defined. The wife's title to the kernels, the auxiliary benefits which she derives from the traditional methods of production, the satisfaction that she derives from her independent income—these are some of the advantages that the indigenous and traditional form of production confers on the woman.

Consumption also involves the family as a unit. Most of the food is grown on the family farm. The surplus, where there is one, is sold for cash to meet the family's cash expenses. The sale of the forest products provides a ready source of income for contingencies. Children are entirely dependent on the family for their needs, but when they attain adulthood they help the family to maintain their consumption level by periodic contributions.

Such division of labor and function as existed under the traditional system of cultivation gave a stability to the family structure. The children were brought up within this system and taught the functions and the rights of the two sexes in the family. With the introduction of pioneer oil mills, new opportunities were opened for the children. They could obtain some form of paid employment at the mill; they could sell some of the family's fruit to the mill; or they could engage in petty trade in imported merchandise in the village, where money incomes were now rising. The dependence of the child on the family was beginning to weaken. The wife's position was threatened by the potential loss of an independent source of income. When the fruit was sold to the mill, the right to the kernels did not revert to the wife. More often than not, the proceeds of the sale would go to the husband. When the erection of a pioneer oil mill was mooted in the Ibibio area of Nigeria in 1951–52, the women led a violent demonstration that threatened order and peace in the area for several months. The vehemence of their resistance was a magistral demonstration of the lengths to which a society can go in resisting a change that fundamentally threatens the stability of the family. Such resistance cannot be explained purely on grounds of negative opposition to change. The mills may raise the family's income, but they disrupt the family organization. It may be remarked that in the controversy the resistance came only from the women, a fact suggesting that it was the woman's role and position, not the man's, that was threatened.

CLASS AND STATUS RELATIONSHIPS

Innovations that give rise to new opportunities are likely to give rise to a new plutocracy. If this happens, the innovation may be accompanied by a re-evaluation of the traditional basis of authority. In most parts of West Africa, authority in the family is vested in the father; in the kin it rests with the elders; in the village and larger communities it is vested in the elders or some variant of such gerontocracy. Prior to the twentieth century, when land was the most important economic asset, the power to dispose of the land carried with it a power to impose sanctions against the infringement of local custom. Since the disposition of land was invalid without the positive consent of the elders of the community, authority was conferred by virtue of age. In the family, children were taught to respect their elders, and the sign of good breeding was the extent to which a child showed deference to his elders within and outside his family. Family disputes and marriage disputes were settled by the older members of the families concerned. Village disputes were settled by the elders of the village. Where chieftaincy existed, the chief was assisted in the execution of his office by the old men of the community, who were supposed to have acquired wisdom through long experience.

New statuses arise with the emergence of a new class, the rich who have made their fortune in trade either by selling the raw produce of the land or by retailing imported articles manufactured abroad. In social relations money talks. The growth of this new class of rich, divorced from the land that was so important a link in the chain that bound the society to the elders, has weakened the authority of the elders, especially if they happen to be, as is often the case, impecunious. The new generation that made its money in trade has challenged the traditional basis of obedience. Where the traditional authority of the elders is set against the intrusion of new ideas from the younger generation, the conflict has been characterized by an extraordinary degree of vehemence.

The new plutocrat is likely to have traveled outside the village more frequently than the elders. He has been exposed to the influence of new ideas, and tries to bring them to the village. The old statuses based on age are giving way to new statuses based on education and affluence. The chiefs still retain, and continue to exert, considerable influence over their subjects, but their position is becoming more honorific than functional. The local councils in which the chiefs and the elders controlled administration are now diluted with younger members of the society thrown up from the educated and wealthy groups, whose success in life gives them the ready ear of their fellow citizens. The chiefs themselves have found that, to retain their prestige and their influence, they will have to march with the times by identifying themselves with the aspirations of the younger members. This situation is clearly a symptom, not a cause, of the social decay which is occurring in the region as a whole.

OTHER INDIGENOUS INSTITUTIONS

When economic changes are occurring in many areas and in several spheres, the total impact on the society is greater. The disorganization of the family structure is but the beginning of a larger story. Sex roles have been upset, the division of functions has been disturbed, and the equilibrium of the family pattern has been superseded by a situation in which new balances have to be struck with the emergence of a vigorous individualism. The institutions that previously derived their strength from family and kinship relationships now have to find new bases. West African society had formerly been developed on the basis of a strong family link. Some of this link remains. The basis has not been static but it has been stable. The changes introduced into the social ecology by the changes in techniques and the accompanying attitudes call for a readjustment of social institutions and the development of those institutions which will minimize the cost of transfer to the new order.

The questions which we take up on this section are wider than the issues that arise with a single innovation. Not all the changes in the social structure can be attributed to a single technological change. Several economic changes have taken place in the economy, and these have repercussions on the indigenous institutions of socio-economic security. The aged, the infirm and the disabled, the unemployed—these did not present special problems in the traditional society of West Africa. Most African peoples in the various regions had evolved their own peculiar systems of poor relief, old-age pensions, welfare schemes, all of which were operated through some social unit. Where this unit was the family, the income of the family was spread out to take care of its unemployed members, of the old, and of the disabled. Those who had an income just adequate to support themselves found that they had to maintain their less fortunate relatives, the number of whom grew as incomes rose. In some areas, the social unit was larger than the family, increasing the burden of the richer members of the unit by widening the circle of obligations. As [the economist] Pedler so well put it: "A poor man may lose track of his brothers and cousins: a rich man is constantly reminded of their existence."

Economic development means extension of the means of production and increase in the level of living. So long as the socioeconomic goals were designed to meet the requirements of mere subsistence, the demands of the aged, the poor, and the infirm were rudimentary. The social unit could, without gravely depressing the consumption level, meet this requirement. But the level of living has been rising steadily. The needs of the unemployed, the disabled, and the old have risen with the needs of the wealthy, and the obligation to meet the needs of the indigent and nonproductive members of the household has become increasingly onerous. Even the expense of feeding the unemployed has become burdensome. Evasions of responsibility are, therefore, more frequent now than they were two decades ago. It would appear that indigenous institutions for the maintenance of social cohesion are breaking down and that something ought to be done to replace them if the social disorganization that is thus exposed is to be remedied. The more economic activity has become individualized, the more the institutions based on communal activity are likely to show signs of stress.

Should social security functions be transferred? A fundamental question is at once raised by this situation. Should the indigenous institutions of socioeconomic security be used in this period of economic development, or should the function be transferred to the state? It must be realized that the concept of the welfare state is here to stay. In most African areas it is received as a fact. The question cannot, therefore, be framed as a choice between indigenous institutions or none at all. If the indigenous institutions are not suitable for the transition from the old to the new order, then the responsibility must be taken over by the state or some other agency. If the state is to take over, increasingly larger public expenditures will come to be devoted to social welfare.

It may be pointed out that one of the reasons why the level of

private savings is low in most African areas is that the rich have
to finance the consumption of the poor. The level of consumption
is thus maintained by the traditional system, while a large measure
of "disguised" unemployment exists. It is often argued that if the
functions of the indigenous social security institutions were transferred to the state, the unemployment would become overt and
might shock the government into taking appropriate monetary and
fiscal measures to combat it. So long as the unemployment remains
disguised, it may tend to perpetuate itself. Since government relief
is likely to be more stringently distributed than that under the pre-
existing system, those persons who now maintain themselves on the
largesse of their wealthy relatives but who would not qualify for
government relief would be compelled to seek productive employment. No matter how little they contribute to production, it is
argued, the system would be better than that in which they contribute nothing but live on the charity of the working members of the
social unit.

Those who argue in favor of the indigenous system seem to
share a mystical faith in the system of indirect rule, that is, they
believe that the existing institutions must be used as a vehicle of
change in order to minimize the social cost of change. These institutions must be used unless it is unmistakably clear that they stand
in the way of progress. If we do not share this mystical faith, it is
difficult not to insist that these institutions constitute a serious gap
in the capital formation process. The indigenous institutions are
cracking. If so, a transfer of the welfare function to the state or
some such agency would unquestionably accelerate their disintegration, and as disintegration proceeds, further state responsibility
would become necessary. What is clearly called for is that social
policy should be thought out carefully and unambiguously, so as
to be able to take on the fresh problems that will inevitably arise
as the old order breaks down at an increasing rate.

SOCIAL MOBILITY

Economic development in West Africa has shown how interdependent the various geographic sections are for the maintenance
of a stable standard of living. Trade has grown between the seg-
ments of the region. Rail travel has linked up various parts of each
country, and the demand for labor for several purposes has driven
peoples that hitherto never left their home towns to distant parts
of the region in search of paid employment. Nigerians are to be
found in large numbers in [Ghana], Sierra Leone, and Liberia.
[Ghanaians] fill the ranks of the Nigerian civil service. Laborers

are recruited from Nigeria and the Cameroons for the Spanish territory of Fernando Po. Such voluntary spatial mobility was a thing unknown in the nineteenth century and is likely to grow in size as communication improves and trade develops.

Vertical mobility within the geographical areas did not raise serious problems. With the disintegration of the class groupings based on age, the society acquired a fluidity which made it easy for an individual to move up from the peasant status by acquiring some wealth or education. While job opportunities were restricted by the low level of income and by administrative fiat, these obstacles have gradually been swept away. In postwar West Africa, especially in the British territories, the artificial obstacles to vertical mobility appear non-existent; within the ambit allowed by the facilities for self-improvement, the individual seems to have boundless opportunities of moving to the top.

A discussion of the changes in class structure and class mobility is inadequate if it fails to touch on the development of a middle class. Discussions of this subject often postulate that the economic development of West Africa will proceed faster if a middle class is developed. The suggestion seems to be that a middle class has to be created independently of economic development, a position that is difficult to maintain in the light of either logic or history. It must be emphasized that the process of economic development by itself engenders the emergence of new classes in society. If the primary income-generating asset is land, as it was in the early part of the twentieth century, the disorganization of the social order may give rise to a new class divorced from the land. If the catalyst is derived from the development of trade, as is the case in West Africa, then the disintegration of the social structure may be accompanied by the emergence of a new commercial plutocracy. The accumulation of wealth in the first fifty years of this century in West Africa has come through trade, both in local materials and in internationally traded commodities. The new commercial classes that emerged as a result have given rise to a substantial measure of economic development which has only recently come to be recognized. As West African development follows the path of industrialization, it is to be expected that an industrial middle class will develop. Though it has its origin outside the industrialization process, industrial development is the soil necessary to maintain it.

CONCLUSION

If we were asked what has been the most significant change in West African society in the twentieth century, the answer would readily be found in the individualization of activity which seems to have taken firm root in most sections of African society. The production and consumption units in West Africa have traditionally been much wider than the European concept of family would suggest. In the fifty-five years of this century, the social unit in West Africa has been shrinking because of emergent individualism, a shrinkage revealed in production and consumption no less than in marriage and other social relationships. Europeans commonly think of the family as consisting of a man, his wife, and their children. In West Africa, the concept has included the relatives of the man and the relatives of his wife, several branches up the genealogical tree on both sides. The shrinking of the social unit has led to the shrinking of the wide circle of obligations that bound the individual to the family.

With the family structure showing signs of instability, other associations and relationships based on the family have shown signs of breaking down. Kinship structures have felt the impact of the growing individualism, and new alignments are springing up in the form of associations in which the base is similarity of outlook and education rather than age.

Some observers have viewed the social change with alarm. It has been described as an unhappy development leading to social disintegration and chaos. Underneath this alarmist note is a nostalgic cry for a return to the good old days and a belief that the social cost of economic development has been exorbitant. The implication is that it is unfortunate that the pre-existing social system should be allowed to break down. It is easily forgotten that no social system is invariant in the face of external influences. At the other extreme is the view represented by Lord Hailey in a recent paper in which he asserts:

> That the modernist urge has led many African leaders to discard some of the most typical institutions of traditional origin, such as the chiefdom or the rule of tribal elders, is today a matter of no great importance.

Lord Hailey argues that most African peoples have adjusted themselves to a change from barter economy to exchange economy.

Unquestionably, further development in the second half of the twentieth century will place greater strain on the indigenous institutions. The problem that will be faced will call for more than a mere lament over the disappearance of pre-existing institutions. What is required is that the emergent individual find in the new society some of what he has lost from the old. This requires, as Alport [author of *Hope in Africa*, London, 1952] has pointed out, that the individual be given those opportunities whereby he can re-establish some communion with his surroundings, find a status in his new position as a wage earner, and find some room for his ambition in politics. Social policy has, therefore, to assure that the individual in losing both the benefits and the burdens of the old society acquire no weightier burdens and at least as many benefits as he had in his previous station. If this assurance can be given through the development of private institutions, so much the better; if not, the emergence of a positive welfare state in the various West African areas will be inescapable.

29 ⚜ INDUSTRIALISATION AND SOCIAL PROBLEMS IN AFRICA*

P. de Briey

The economy of a territory is determined by the very nature of the soil and of the people who inhabit it. While a single territory may sometimes include areas with different economies, there are also cases where similar physical conditions and standards of living are to be found over considerable areas of neighbouring territories, despite great differences in climate, geographical position and density of population. The territories of Central Africa are an example of such a natural unit.

With the exception of Nigeria, where fairly dense clusters of population still remain, Central Africa is a very thinly inhabited region. Yet even this scanty population is unable to obtain the necessary means of subsistence from the soil. Before the coming of the Europeans, the native peoples were just able to maintain themselves with the absolute minimum as regards clothing, housing and food. The introduction of Western civilisation destroyed this delicate balance, for some of its products corresponded to hitherto unconscious needs and have now become indispensable to the African. Unfortunately, the people are too poor to be able to satisfy these

* From P. de Briey, "Industrialisation and Social Problems in Africa," *International Labour Review*, May 1951. Reprinted by permission.

elementary needs. In the country districts, where the vast majority of the population live, the natives cannot afford to buy clothing and have no means of building houses. They seldom receive any medical attention and are undernourished. There is the vicious circle mentioned by a former Governor of the Belgian Congo: "The people are poor because they produce little, and they produce little because they are too poor to pay for the means of producing more."

The only solution therefore is to "prime the pump" by investing the capital that will enable productivity to be increased. This is the essence of the whole matter. Only increased productivity can provide the means for a general improvement in the standard of life of the African and give him better housing, better food, and a higher wage. Only increased productivity can slow down or stop the migration of workers, which threatens to destroy the structure of the native tribe and family, and to undermine their economic basis. In the territories where extreme poverty prevails, increased productivity means that a larger number of persons will remain alive. An increase of productivity enables hospitals to be built, the infantile mortality rate to be reduced, epidemics to be combated, food industries to be created, etc.

Increased productivity is normally thought of in terms of industrialisation of production, and in fact the beginnings that have been made in Africa have taken this form. Nevertheless, there is a vast difference between high productivity and industrialisation, not only because industrialisation implies a particular form of productivity, but also because, while the former need only mean an increase in the pool of goods to be shared, the introduction of industry into a society transforms the social structure itself. The need to increase the productivity of the African worker is self-evident; the need for a certain degree of industrialisation is also clear. But industrialisation is not without its drawbacks. The upheaval which follows shakes the foundations of the community in which the process takes place.

The territories selected for study here are those of British East Africa (Kenya, Uganda, Tanganyika), Northern and Southern Rhodesia, Nyasaland, Mozambique and Angola, the Belgian Congo, a large part of French Africa, the British territories in West Africa and the territories subject to the British High Commissioner (Bechuanaland, Swaziland, Basutoland).

In all [the territories of Central Africa], a rural native population of agriculturalists, pastoralists, hunters or fishermen, who had hitherto only known small, isolated groups of Europeans (explorers, missionaries, traders), suddenly came into contact towards the end of the nineteenth century and at the beginning of the twentieth with a stable and organised immigrant population from Europe, bringing to Africa the commercial and industrial methods of the countries of Western Europe. One of the elements of this new civilisation was the existence of industries based on the employment of a hired labour force. This was an important new factor. It enabled the native population to increase their resources, if they wished, by entering paid employment. It offered an alternative to agricultural labour and the traditional way of life in the tribe. In the long run this fact had a revolutionary effect on the native communities. It is impossible to say whether the introduction of industrial undertakings in a primitive country would have been enough by itself to transform the population. And in any case, in most of the territories where colonisation took place, the trader was the first to arrive. He offered the natives clothes, blankets, tools, candles, sugar, fuel and many of the other adjuncts of civilisation. What could the African give in exchange? He was poor and had only his labour to offer. He therefore sold his labour in exchange for wages with which to buy these novel products of western civilisation. He ceased to be a tiller of the soil and became a wage-earner, when part of the population enrolled as employees of European undertakings and the development of the territory began. Can it be said that the new balance which began to be established between needs and resources has proved a satisfactory solution? Before answering this question, it should be noted that the offer of European products in itself constituted an unbalancing factor. Whereas in the primitive society before the arrival of the European a balance between income and expenditure was laboriously maintained, a new liability now arose in the new society as a result of the development of new needs.

It is not easy to determine the present standard of life of the African after a number of years of contact with western civilisation. A comparative study of the living standards prevailing among the peoples of Central Africa has not yet been undertaken. There are no statistics which can be quoted to show the precise balance between their earnings and expenditure and to indicate their level of existence. All that can be done is to make use of the work of the isolated investigators in various territories who have attempted to find out whether the native cultivators, who form the vast majority of the population, can adequately maintain themselves by their labour now that contact with the European has created new needs.

The general conclusion to be drawn from these investigations is that there is a state of disequilibrium in Central Africa. Now that the needs of the natives have increased, the means of production and subsistence are no longer adequate for the population. A single crop of manioc could formerly satisfy a whole community; today the people also want clothing, tools, soap, tobacco and sugar. The richest of them look forward to owning a bicycle or a sewing-machine. Yet the manioc harvest is no larger; consumption has increased, but productivity has remained stationary.

The immediate result of the growth of needs was migration towards industrial centres and towns. The large-scale migration, which is of course not only due to economic necessity, is one of the most striking characteristics of Central Africa today. It is not universal, but the areas where it does not take place are precisely those in which industry is lacking and there is no possibility of obtaining work by emigrating.

In certain respects emigration appears to offer a solution to the problem facing the people of Central Africa. Since income from the land does not cover the needs of those living on it, a reduction in their number might leave a larger share of the common income for those who remain. In practice, however, the contrary takes place. Those who leave the villages to work in industrial centres are youths or men in their prime. When the fittest of the men have gone, the crops suffer from neglect and the number of fields under cultivation falls. But food requirements remain unaltered, for the town dwellers have to be supplied with produce from the country. In addition, migration has disastrous social consequences for the migrant workers themselves, who have not the advantages enjoyed by a stable labour force. The village is still their home; but their families are dispersed, the birthrate is threatened, and the social authority of the tribal community is weakened or lost. Wages are low, because the worker does not stay long enough in the same place to become skilled. Housing in the labour centres is inadequate, because it is intended only as temporary accommodation.

In some respects a still more sweeping migration would be more to the advantage of the population than the present migration of adults only. If part of the countryside were completely deserted in favour of the centres, a stable labour force with an organised social life could be established in the centres, which would become a market for agricultural produce. A revolution would have to take place in farming technique; agriculture would become industrialised and mechanised, and a new balance would be achieved on the basis of greater productivity. But, before a system of this kind can be established, a higher degree of development in the main industries of these territories would be required and a still greater demand for labour. A solution on these lines has been advocated on several occasions. A Belgian Government agricultural expert has written as follows:

> In the Congo, with nine-tenths of the population belonging to the rural class, it is clear that there is only a very restricted market for agricultural produce. This is a very great obstacle to the improvement of agriculture. . . . The essential purpose of our programmes of soil conservation and agricultural improvement is to raise the material and moral level of the rural class, which means making ever increasing wealth available and, therefore, more productive work over a wider area. . . . If he is to clothe himself and his family, build and maintain a house worthy of the name, buy some furniture and household equipment, improve his diet, and simultaneously contribute more in taxes for improved social services, the native will have to adopt more modern agricultural methods and increase the area of land cultivated by at least ten times. If the number of cultivators remains constant, a double problem will arise: how to dispose of the vastly increased production and how to find the necessary land?
>
> The answer can only be found if an increasing proportion of the population is impelled into the ranks of the wage-earning or artisan class. . . . The improvement of agriculture (in which I include not only technical improvement but also social progress and soil conservation) *demands* the creation of a stable working class. By stable, I mean a class separated from the land for good and living permanently in industrial centres—the contrary of what happens at present. Today the large majority of paid workers only remain in employment for a period varying from a few months to a few years. They still have their huts, fields and cattle at the native village, and often their wives and children too. Later they return to take their place in the general rural population. This process is clearly an obstacle both to the training of the skilled working class which modern industry needs, and to the evolution of the peasant class in the desired direction. Working efficiency suffers—in industry and on the plantations, because the labour force is continually replaced by illiterate savages; and in native agriculture, because individual enterprise is restricted within limits incompatible with any sort of rational organisation of production. This restriction is the result either of a lack of land or of a lack of markets, and is highly prejudicial to the improvement of agriculture. The development of a working class presupposes a development of industry; hence the general conclusion, which may have appeared absurd at first sight, that *the preservation of the soil depends on industrial development.*

These far-reaching conclusions are not, however, universally accepted. One thing that is proved by the phenomenon of migration is that the standard of life of the African cultivator must be raised. It is not merely a question of averting famine; the African peasant must be enabled to obtain from cultivation of the soil an income sufficient to provide ample subsistence for himself and his family. Migration must not be allowed to be the only means of escaping from want. No one will deny that a certain degree of industrialisation may be essential to ensure the development of the territories; but those who have experienced the distress into which sudden proletarianisation has plunged thousands of African homes will hesitate to extend still further a social revolution of this kind.

The three problems which will now be discussed are in reality only three aspects of a single problem, three aspects of a society in transition.

The first problem arises out of the creation of a class of wage-earners, who still have a hard struggle for existence. The second problem is due to the migratory movements of workers, which threaten social stability. The third problem results from the desertion of the countryside and the deterioration of the soil.

The way in which a class of wage-earners came into being has been briefly indicated above. Driven by economic necessity and a desire to escape from the atmosphere of poverty and monotony in their traditional surroundings, a constant flow of native cultivators are leaving their homes to obtain new resources by employment in industry. These workers generally return to their villages after a longer or shorter period of employment. A certain proportion, however, remain in the industrial centres and gradually become urbanised. In this way, an African proletariat is being created, and is growing in size every day.

The circumstances in which these workers live are not easy. Up to the present the supply of labour has in most areas exceeded the demand. Industrial undertakings have therefore always had an abundant supply of labour, though the level of efficiency is low.

Consequently, in many undertakings where it would have been possible to make use of improved machinery operated by a small number of skilled workers, it has been considered more economical to employ a large number of unskilled workers. Moreover, it must not be forgotten that many Africans regard employment in industry as the only possible means of improving their lot. They are therefore the first to want the present system continued since, if firms were to improve their equipment and employ only a small number of skilled workers, most of the present workmen would be left without a job and might be obliged to return to their villages.

This competitive labour force with a low rate of output is normally ill-paid. Only a few years ago it was impossible for a worker to keep and house himself on his wages. The fact that he usually maintained contact with his native village, where his wife and relations continued the traditional forms of cultivation, was felt by the employer as a justification for this state of affairs. The position has now changed. In the territories of British East and Central Africa, there is legislation on minimum wages, which guarantees the African worker a wage based on the cost of living for an unmarried man.

For so long as employment in industry remains temporary and periodic, this legislation may be enough, since it is assumed that the worker's family will remain in his native village and be self-supporting. However, in all the African territories, industrial employment is steadily growing and a class of permanent wage-earners is coming into being. The position of the worker's family is consequently becoming a social problem. If serious disturbance of the native communities and the creation of a dissatisfied proletarian class are to be avoided, the worker's family must be settled at the place where he works, and his remuneration fixed at a rate enabling him to support his family. But any increase in wages is made difficult by the extremely low output of the African workman.

The social evils which ensue [from migration] can be summed up as follows. Migration tends to perpetuate the low conditions of remuneration and output among the workers; it is impossible to improve the output and, in consequence, to increase the pay of a man who only spends a few months at his place of work.

Secondly, the migrant workers compete with other workers and often prevent them from obtaining the employment they need. The system of migration hinders the development of trade unionism, which demands a certain permanence in employment. The movements of workers are at the expense of the agricultural population and make it more difficult for the work required for soil conservation to be carried out.

Lastly, the social disorder created in the villages and tribal communities by periodic migrations cannot be over-emphasised; neither the family unit nor the wider group (clan, tribe, etc.) can remain intact under the impact of such continual disruption.

The effect of the return of the emigrant to the tribal community is described in the following passage:

> A primitive and self-contained community will be exposed to an influx of returning travellers who have experienced entirely novel methods of life; new ideas will be imported, and old observances will be criticised; tribal law and authority, formerly unquestioned, will be disputed or ignored.

It cannot be expected that the elders, accustomed to be regarded as the exponents of the ancient and infallible rules, will not resent such an attitude; the subversive element will be regarded with extreme hostility, as being disruptive of all moral standards, and the offenders will be subjected to marked disapproval. The fact that tribal law derives its authority so largely from the support of supernatural penalties for infringement renders it very vulnerable to the attacks of the sceptic, and the community is thus divided into two hostile elements with irreconcilable views.

The desertion of the countryside is the immediate consequence of migration. The serious aspect of this process is that it tends to become more and more rapid. The villages are impoverished as a result of the exodus of men towards the industrial centres. The impoverishment of the village results in new emigration, which in its turn gives rise to further impoverishment. Thus the gap which separates the emigrant from tribal life continually grows.

The harmful effects of the desertion of the countryside are unfortunately aggravated by some of the characteristics of the native farming methods, and by erosion. Native cultivators, living in almost complete destitution, are obviously driven to obtain the maximum yield from the land. They are naturally inclined to open up virgin soil each year—if they tried to preserve and enrich the land already cultivated, they would have to put in twice as much work. They are encouraged in their methods by the fact that individual ownership of the soil is unheard of and that they are able, as a rule, to change the area under cultivation each year, the soil not being regarded as a thing of value. This manner of cultivation is described in the following passage:

> An area of trees which may be as great as twelve acres, and is probably nowhere less than two and a half acres, is cut to provide branches to be burnt on each acre of land. An enquiry made during a recent locust campaign showed that the average area of a man's millet garden was about one and one eighth acres. As a rule a new garden is cut each year. It takes some twenty years for the trees to recover. Thus a man requires some two to three hundred acres of woodland to keep himself and his family alive. A village works out all the land within a radius of some three miles in about five years and it must then move. Consequently, permanent improvements, satisfactory buildings, the planting of fruit-trees, are all impossible. . . . A system that depends upon an area of two hundred acres or more of woodland for each family cannot endure indefinitely with a growing population and declining woodlands.

In the Congo a similar process takes place.

> The native agricultural system is semi-nomad. The natives only stay for a few years in a given area, and regularly move their village in search of new and fertile land. The layer of humus is very thin in the Congo, and the action of the sun and torrential rain continually threatens to destroy it and wash away the basic elements. Bush fires scorch the land every dry season and indirectly help to make it barren. . . . In short, the native system of cultivation is a system of rotation, but on such a scale and covering such distances that not only are the fields moved but also the village. It is easy to see that in such circumstances no tendency towards progress and civilisation is possible.

> As a result, the native will make no effort to improve his land. Here, as elsewhere, the path of evolution is from hunting, through nomad agriculture, towards a fixed and settled type of agriculture in which the same land is continually cultivated and improved by the cultivation.

The system just described is customary in most of the territories of Central Africa, though there are slight differences in the methods employed. Thus, in a large part of the continent, the fertile land tends to disappear, as the soil is never enriched by the work of man. The land is impoverished and the scanty resources of the native grow even less.

The attempts to reintegrate detribalised workers in their habitual surroundings seem, on the whole, certain to fail. It must be accepted that a very large proportion of the urbanised population will never again submit to the traditional discipline of clan and village. In attempting to raise the standard of the mass of unskilled workers, the principal task is one of education and vocational training. These labourers need to be given a trade. This is one of the chief means of raising their efficiency; and the standard of life depends above all on productivity.

The task to be accomplished is far from easy. Illiteracy must be overcome, new apprenticeship centres established, training in industry encouraged and technical instruction made general. Once the teaching has been given, it will be necessary to see that adequate remuneration is given in exchange for the work done. Finally, the general living conditions of the workers must be improved.

There is no fear that the number of jobs to be filled will prove insufficient. Secondary industries are still at an early stage of development in the territories of Central Africa, and many new industries may come into being. An example of rapid development may be found in a Far Eastern country, Indonesia, where, at the time when that territory was still dependent on the Netherlands, the textile industry made an astonishing advance in ten years. In

1930 there were only 500 modern handlooms and 40 power looms in Java. In 1941, there were 49,000 handlooms and 9,800 power looms. If one considers that in several areas of Central Africa hand-weaving has continued to be practised for generations with primitive methods, the full significance of this example becomes apparent. It is probable that Governments could introduce new crafts in their territories after a few instructors had been trained.

In conclusion, it may be said that the Governments of most of the territories of Central Africa are moving towards a dual series of measures (a) to stabilise the industrial workers at the place of employment, and (b) to stabilise the rural communities.

If these measures are successful, society will tend to divide itself into two clearly differentiated communities: a rural class whose position will progressively improve, and an industrial proletariat which will no longer have any link with the original tribal life. Living conditions for the wage-earners will of necessity approach more and more closely to the living conditions of European wage-earners. However long this may take, it is in this direction that the path of normal development for the African community must be sought.

30   MIGRANT LABOUR IN AFRICA AND ITS EFFECTS UPON TRIBAL LIFE*

Margaret Read

"The migration of large numbers of the male population from their homes to distant places of work is one of the characteristic features of the labour question in Africa." In these words [Lord Hailey's *An African Survey*] describes the outstanding feature of economic development in Africa—namely, the necessity for assembling large numbers of Africans in labour centres, such as towns, mines or plantations, and therefore denuding village areas of equally large numbers of their male inhabitants. One of the most common mistakes made is to assume that the migration of African

* From Margaret Read, "Migrant Labour in Africa and Its Effects upon Tribal Life," *International Labour Review*, June 1942. Reprinted by permission.

peoples is a new phenomenon. As far as we can tell from tribal traditions, archaeological evidence, and early European observations, the movement of peoples in Africa has been a feature of its history from earliest times. Though those former movements of whole populations seeking new homes in more fertile areas were of a different nature from the modern emigration of male Africans to supply labour for European economic enterprises, they have more than one common characteristic. What we refer to nowadays as the "African's love of adventure" or the "African's desire to travel" is part of his traditional urge to seek a new and more propitious environment when impoverished soil and successive bad seasons made him leave his home village. His proved ability to adapt his life and activities to new conditions is another common feature of past and present migrations. Possibly also, though the analogy should not be pressed too far, there is some connection between the independence and initiative which drove him in the past to uproot himself and his family and his clan from poor lands, and take the risk of finding better elsewhere, and the evident preference for free and voluntary forms of labour in spite of all their risks and insecurity, instead of the binding, though possibly more secure, forms of contract and recruited labour.

Statistics show that the modern phenomenon of migration to labour centres in East, Central, and South Africa, where European settlement and large-scale industries, such as mining, depend entirely on African labour, has assumed proportions which threaten the basis of village life.

The chief export of Nyasaland in the past fifty years has been men. Male labour began to emigrate in the 'nineties to the port of Beira, to the Rhodesian Railway, to the Belgian copper mines and the Rand Gold Mines, to farms and plantations from Tanganyika to the Cape, and even, as soldiers in the King's African Rifles, to Mauritius, Ashanti, and Somaliland. Early Government and mission reports show that, already in 1902, 3,000 to 4,000 Nyasaland Africans were going annually to Southern Rhodesia and Portuguese East Africa to work in the ports and on the railways, and by 1904 the number was said to be over 10,000. In 1903 recruitment began for the Rand Mines, and in that year just under 1,000 went, and in the two following years over 1,700. In 1920 it was estimated that 20,000 Nyasaland men were employed annually outside the Protectorate, 14,000 on the mines in Southern Rhodesia. In 1935, at the time of the Emigrant Labour Committee in Nyasaland, it was estimated that 120,000 men were at work abroad, and this was calculated to be over a quarter of the total male adult population.

Before we go on to discuss the Nyasaland situation it will be useful to indicate certain problems arising from the transference of large numbers of males from the villages to the labour centres.

The major question which arrests attention is: are these labour centres becoming the permanent homes of African workers, or are they destined to be centres of *migrant* labour whence the workers return periodically to their village homes? White employers on the whole are ready to put up with migrant labour provided the supply is constant, for the important reason that migrant labour is likely to be cheaper in the long run than permanent labour. Apart from a rising scale of wages, a permanent labour force would require social amenities, such as housing and recreation, of a more extensive and costly type than the migrant labourer will accept. Even more costly, whether at the employers' or the Governments' expense, would be the necessary provision for old age and unemployment. The white employers, provided they can get their labour at what they consider to be "reasonable wages," do not, naturally, concern themselves with the problem of whether the African by working for them is undermining the economic life of his own village. A common assumption by European employers in this part of Africa is that village economic life entails for men only a few weeks' work in the year, alternating with long periods of sitting in the sun and beer-swilling.

It is extremely difficult to get data on the extent to which labour can be considered as permanent in towns and industrial centres in Central and South Africa. "Northern Natives," recruited for the Rand mines by the Witwatersrand Native Labour Association since 1935, have the option of returning home after a year's work, and must be repatriated after two years, though there is nothing to prevent them joining up again after they have been at home either for a few months or for a longer period. The labour figures for the Copperbelt do not show how long the labourers have been at work —only the annual turnover. Labour in Southern Rhodesia, whether on mines, farms or in towns, is so constantly moving and changing employment that there is a chronic shortage. The only Government which has taken deliberate measures to stabilise a permanent labour force is the administration in the Katanga Province of the Congo. The *Union Minière* has pursued a consistent policy of attracting permanent mine workers, and has accordingly built up social services and urban amenities to meet this need.

Although there are few statistics available, I think anyone who has had first-hand contact with industrial centres would support [the] assertion that the tendency is towards the development of "temporary urbanised" labour. This has progressed farthest in South Africa, but there is evidence of it in the towns and labour centres of Southern and Northern Rhodesia and Nyasaland. The use of this phrase implies the maintenance of some ties between the migrant worker and his place of origin, and is certainly preferable to the rather loosely used term "detribalised Native." When Africans have become really detribalised, to the extent of cutting off *all* their connections with their original villages and of regarding the town or labour centre as their permanent home and that of their children, their residence in the town and their employment and their manner of livelihood no longer affect their home village. In course of time the villagers cease to regard them as part of the home circle, and the gap they left at first gradually closes up, and it is accepted that they have gone for good even though they are not forgotten. But this stage of detribalisation has been reached in only comparatively rare instances in Central and East Africa as yet. The great majority even of "temporarily urbanised" Africans maintain some links with their villages of origin, and this is the outstanding sociological phenomenon in the African labour situation to-day. While migrant labour profoundly affects the social and economic life of the villages by denuding them of adult males for long periods, these villages in turn exercise a deep influence on the men who return to them periodically. It is true that the gap between the economic life of the towns and that of the villages grows wider every year. But life in the villages is not static. It is changing all the time as the men return and leave again. The gulf between urban and rural standards makes for a profound malaise in the villages, while the claims of relatives and others in the villages to financial help prevents the achieving of satisfactory standards of living in the towns on present urban wages.

The Nyasaland Committee, appointed to investigate the problems of emigrant labour, consisted of officials, settlers and missionaries. Their chief difficulty was the absence of any reliable statistics on the exodus of men from the villages. The only check on the numbers emigrating is the issue of passes or passports at the district headquarters which have to be shown at the "port of entry," and even then there are many ways of crossing a frontier other than through the recognised port of entry.

In addition to the lack of statistics, the members of the Committee admitted that they were ignorant about the details of village life under tribal conditions, and therefore were not in a position to estimate the changes due to labour migration. They took evidence from local officials, settlers, missionaries, and Africans. The result

was an almost consistently gloomy picture of deserted wives, un-
disciplined children, uncultivated fields. It is clear on reading the
Report that the members of the Committee were deeply concerned
with the problem of the *machona*. The term, which means literally
"the lost ones," is used for those men who have been away without
maintaining any links with their families for so long that no one
knows where they are, and they are written off as "lost" to the village. In 1935 a belief was gaining ground in the villages that the
machona were being deliberatedly held back by the Governments of
the territories where they were working. The Africans giving evidence therefore painted the picture as black as they could in the
hope that the Nyasaland Government would do something to find
and repatriate the *machona*.

Labour migration and its effect on tribal life is an important
aspect of culture contact, [and] the disintegrating effect on tribal
life and village economy is obvious and does not need an anthropologist to demonstrate it.

In the migrant labour situation as I found it in Nyasaland it
would be inaccurate as well as an over-simplification to regard the
tribal villages as primitive and untouched. They have been profoundly influenced for fifty years by several agents of change,
among which the labour recruiter is only one. Men going to work
in the mines have already known European administrations with
their different Native policies, missions with their various ideas
about education and vocational training, traders with their chains
of stores and their straight or crooked ways of dealing. Culture
contact is everywhere—not only on the mines and plantations and
townships, but on the roads and railways, round the district office
and the local store, and even in remote villages.

With these facts before him the anthropologist is aware that
labour migration cannot be isolated as a factor of change in tribal
society, and anyone who has had first-hand contact with tribal areas
affected by emigration will agree with him. The problem, in fact,
of the changing tribal life in the villages is immensely complicated,
even more intricate than the study of an urban location or a mining
compound. There, on a mine compound, the Europeans are very
much in evidence with their elaborate machinery and their planned
organisation of labour, above and below ground, their wage tickets,
their food canteens, their football ground and cinema and beer hall.
The African arriving from his tribal village is brought into immediate contact with all these new phenomena. We can study how
he is conditioned by them to mine copper or gold for a fixed period
of each twenty-four hours, while in his leisure time in the compound

and beer hall he builds up new forms of social and economic activities which have some African and some European features.

In the villages, on the other hand, where the men come and go from the mines and other employment, there may be at first sight almost no outward and obvious evidences of European contact. The thatched mud huts, the circular cattle kraal fenced with poles, the cultivated fields, the village paths, all *look* wholly African at first glance. Yet the old headman who tells you of his exploits in past tribal fights may proudly display two khaki shirts sent him by a son in South Africa; bicycles, sewing machines, books and oil lamps may be found in the huts in varying numbers according to the degree of education reached; a cook on leave from Johannesburg may discuss the relation of wages to hours of work; women may bemoan the fact that their husbands have left the village long ago and yet it is not easy for them to get a divorce because their husbands' families do not want to return the bride-price; a note of rage may break out when the older men and women ask why the Government does not take active steps to find and repatriate the *machona* who have been away for years and lost all touch with their families.

The African, therefore, who arrives at the mines or other labour centres is the product of a gradual transformation of standards of living and of ideas which is going on all the time in the villages. In the township or mining compound he mixes with other men from slightly or totally different village backgrounds, and takes every opportunity in the course of his work and social contacts to examine what he hears and sees. When he returns to his village again on leave with altered ambitions and ideas he tries them out and discusses them in company with his friends and relatives, and they in turn have been influenced by what they have heard and seen. The current conception that an African worker returns to his village with only a box of trashy trade goods, and after giving them away right and left sinks back easily into his old village ways is very far from the truth. It is only when you live in the villages and observe men on their return that the true nature of the changes taking place becomes clear, and also the fact that this alteration of standards and ideas is not a one-way traffic. If the mining compounds and townships by drawing men away from their homes drastically affect the life of the villages, so also do changing conditions in the villages affect the labour force on mines and plantations. Proof of this is available in Southern Nyasaland, where the European tea estates have to rely largely on immigrant labour from Portuguese

East Africa, because the standard of living in Nyasaland villages is such that the wages offered do not attract local labour.

It has been more or less taken for granted that village social and economic life will go on in its traditional manner in spite of the emigration of men, [but] the disproportion in standards of living between urban and rural areas, [creates] what Dr. Wilson calls an "economic disequilibrium." Urban areas grow richer, rural areas grow poorer, but *the same Africans have a footing in both,* and the increasing maladjustment is only too obvious. The second reason is that the villages are the real laboratories where new standards and ideas are being tested. In the relative leisure of their homes men from north, south, east and west discuss the assimilation or rejection of new elements in culture, and African standards and values are altered and crystallised.

It is evident throughout the villages under investigation that standards of living are changing rapidly, and that emigration on the whole is making them rise rather than fall. In the old days a household was considered "wealthy" if it had large gardens and plenty of cattle, and so was free from fear of a food shortage. A high standard of living in the old days therefore meant abundant food resources, while in terms of housing and possessions there was little differentiation between one household and another. Exactly the opposite is the case to-day. Households are "wealthy" if they have good houses and furniture and other goods, while the contrast in food consumption in general is much less marked.

It is obvious that the absence of a third to a half of the male population creates abnormal conditions for family and village life. I found two schools of thought about this in Nyasaland. One, the advocates of controlled migration, asserted that as long as men were repatriated at regular intervals, from one to two years, the women were more or less content, and the birth rate could be maintained, since as a rule two years was the normal interval between births. This school of thought placed more emphasis on the women as mothers than as wives, and said that if a man came home regularly, bringing presents and clothes for his wife, and, in the vernacular phrase, "put a baby in the village," there could be little objection to controlled migration.

The other school was more realistic. One old chief put the position bluntly by saying: "a woman wants a man to live with more than the presents he gives her." The Africans and the missionaries were mainly of this school and pointed to the broken marriages and slacker moral standards as a result of men being away. They also recognised the joint responsibility of husband and wife for the economic life of the household and the social upbringing of children. "I must have a man to help me," was the constantly reiterated cry of the women whose husbands were away, and the poignant refrains of the songs they sang about their absent husbands were more on the theme of their having to live alone than of their wanting more children.

It is not easy to produce satisfactory figures on a large scale to illustrate the effects of migration on marriage and family life. One statistical way in which to assess it is on matrimonial cases decided in the courts. On the basis of some sample villages it appeared that the highest rate of divorce and of adultery cases was in [an] area which had 43 per cent. of the men away, and the lowest rate was in [another] area where 41 per cent. of the men were away. The reason for this sharp contrast lies in the difference between the two tribal organisations, and illustrates the importance of the anthropological aspect of this investigation. The Ngoni patrilineal society stands the strain of the absence of many men from the villages much better than the Chewa matrilineal society.

During my two previous years of field work it became increasingly a matter of surprise to me how the official policy could go on supporting and encouraging the old chiefs while at the same time allowing and encouraging recruitment for the Rand mines and for other enterprises. Two results of these irreconcilable policies became more evident the longer I stayed in the villages. One was that unless the chiefs "modernised" their outlook and their methods, unless in fact they made very rapid strides in this direction, they could not hope to hold the allegiance and active support of the younger men whose views and ambitions had been radically changed by education and emigration. The other obvious result was that the lure of wages and a higher standard of living was enticing away the most ambitious and energetic of the younger men, and leaving village affairs to the dullards and the lazy ones, and village welfare could not be be expected to prosper under such conditions.

The Ngoni chiefs and their headmen had on the whole succeeded in maintaining their traditional authority and adding to it new powers conferred by the Europeans. For the most part the Chewa chiefs and village headmen were only just holding their own, and coping with difficulty with modern conditions. The outstanding exception among the Chewa was in [an] area where a progressive chief was all the time increasing his authority and effectiveness as a ruler. Since the areas where the chiefs' authority was strongest were also those where emigration was heaviest, it might be deduced that emigration was partly in order to avoid submitting to this authority. This, however, was not the case. It is more likely that progressive chiefs encouraged higher standards of living which made emigration inevitable under present conditions.

It should be clear that there is a close correlation between education, a rising standard of living, and emigration. It would be impossible to find in the Northern Province of Nyasaland to-day a village where a number of inhabitants had good houses, furniture and clothes, and other goods, and where none of them had been away to work. Wherever men have been to school, they want, sooner or later, these goods which denote to them a higher standard of living, and they tend on the whole to seek employment where wages are highest.

I had abundant proof of this when discussing emigration in the village meetings. The men, and not a few women too, made constant comparisons between living conditions in the villages and in the towns or mines where they had worked. Clean and tidy houses, well-kept furniture, clothes washed and mended, plenty of water and soap, varied and well-cooked food, facilities for buying food, opportunities for recreation—these were the desirable features of town life to them, and their absence was bitterly lamented in the villages. They put their finger shrewdly on two important reasons for the comparative squalor of the rural areas. One was that the women had so much hard physical labour to do in the daily round of hoeing, fetching fire-wood and water, pounding grain, that they had little time or energy left to be house-proud according to town standards. The second was that when women were left for long periods without a husband to keep house for, they became careless cooks and made no efforts to maintain their household and children on the level which their husbands expected.

I would not hesitate to say that the material economic changes in the villages already indicated are the most obvious and the most widespread effects of emigration. In other words, money, the earning of wages and the spending of them on personal and household goods, is the dominant factor in Nyasaland village life wherever it has been touched by education and emigration. For two generations the schools have trained men to work for wages. These men know now that the higher their level of education, the more wages they can command. To earn high wages they must go south, and in the towns of the south they see the standard of living they want. But when they return to the villages, they do not achieve a uniform change in their surroundings. The standard of food has not gone up as a result of emigration to the same degree as that of housing and clothing. You find households eating much the same food though the inhabitants of one may live in a many-roomed brick house with beds, chairs and tables, and those of another in a round mud hut with only reed mats on the floor. Why has the earning of wages and the use of money not been devoted to an improved dietary when we know that the satisfaction of the food instinct is a primary human need? Why do we not find anywhere that as a result of education and emigration the standard of food and of cooking has gone up proportionately to housing and clothing? I suggest here that part of the answer is to be found in the universal custom on mines and plantations of giving food rations as well as wages. It is true that a little money is often spent in industrial areas to supplement the basic food ration, and that in a few forms of employment in towns a food allowance is not given. But the Nyasaland African has been trained since the earliest days of wage earning to regard his wages as something *additional* to his board and lodging. The "carry-over" of this attitude is seen to-day in the villages. Money brought home or sent home from the south is not spent on more and better food but on things like clothes and houses which are by comparison lasting.

The inevitable consequence of this is that emigration and education are making subsistence farming less and less popular. Among the Chewa, the young bridegroom used to be expected to work for his wife's parents, hoeing their land as well as his own in company with his wife, to add to the parents' food supply. To-day he gets out of this obligation whenever he possibly can by going off to work on the mines or farms. "Our son-in-law used to be our servant," the old Chewa say. "Now he goes away to the south and never even sends money to help us. It is we who are his servants, looking after our daughter, his wife."

The women left behind in the villages, who continue to grow their food, want money for their other domestic needs—clothes, hoes, baskets, mats, apart from any luxuries. Household requirements as well as the food supply used to be the joint concern of husband and wife, who made some things and bought others for cash or barter. To-day, unless the husband sends money regularly, the wife has to beg from her or his relatives for a few coppers, the alternative being to find money herself. In most Nyasaland villages the women have very few opportunities of earning spare cash. Beer making and selling is the most profitable form of trading, but it uses grain and may encroach on the food supply. They sell foodstuffs to Indian storekeepers, but often come away with a handful of salt for a basket of flour, and seldom get anything near an economic price for their produce. There is therefore, as a result of emigration, an increasing need for women to achieve more economic independence.

Men who go away, leaving a wife behind, expect on their return to find a welcome, and food, and a chance to rest and enjoy themselves. The fact that women in matrilineal tribes tend to cultivate less land and depend on their mother's food supplies is the main reason for an increase in a modified patrilocal form of marriage among the matrilineal Chewa. The husband takes his wife to live in his village, though the children are usually sent back to the wife's mother. Emigration is speeding up this change for two reasons. The first is that during the husband's absence the wife's morals can be better watched over, from his point of view, by his own relatives, and they in turn are under an obligation to help her with cultivating, house repairing, etc. The second is that the husband on his return home is fairly sure of finding enough food in his own household, so that he can enjoy himself and entertain his friends, whereas his wife in her village might have grown lazy and ceased to cultivate her own land at all and he would be dependent on the charity of his mother-in-law.

Evidences such as these of social maladjustments and tension meet one on every hand in Nyasaland villages. The anthropologist is constantly reminded that he is not in the midst of untouched tribal areas. Men on their return are constantly comparing what they have seen and experienced—Native housing in locations, educational facilities, wages and working conditions—reflecting on these things, wondering how soon these changes will destroy the last remnants of the tribal life of their ancestors. The women on the other hand, with certain exceptions, have had no opportunity of seeing standards of living different from those of their own neighbourhood, nor are they educated yet, for the most part, to the point of making an effort to improve their surroundings. The women who are educated, or who have travelled, do sometimes make such an effort, and one sees it occasionally in their well-kept households and clean, well-dressed children attending school regularly. But many of them are too isolated in their villages and too dependent on their families to dare to be very different from their fellows. They are afraid of meeting social disapproval which would make life miserable for them and might even lead to accusations of magic and witchcraft.

The situation then is one where many of the men are definitely aiming at a higher standard of living, but the dead weight of the women is pulling them back. This makes for friction in families, and the men's escape is to emigrate frequently. Another inducement to go off again is the malaise felt by the men who return with money and want to use it profitably and intelligently. There is a constant conflict between their reputation among their friends and relatives for generosity and their common sense about the use of their new-found wealth. In the more backward areas I found the majority of returned emigrants pessimistic and despondent about their economic future. Many of them had sent money home and it had been distributed in small doles to a number of people, and no result was to be seen from it but a number of stretching hands. If these men want to improve their houses and surroundings instead of giving away their money, they are often suspected of aiming at un-authorised leadership, and they can seldom be a constructive force in village life because there is nothing to build on.

On the other hand, the educational level of a village can be a definite inducement to return and contribute to village life. In the more highly educated areas where some degree of emigration is inevitable because the people have established a standard of living which cannot be maintained except by money earned abroad, the men who return do so with some satisfaction, and the money which they bring or send back is used to some extent "productively" in buying milk separators, paying school fees and building good houses.

Briefly, what has happened in Nyasaland in the last fifty years is that the labour demands of an alien economic enterprise have completely undermined the old economic life of the country, and are going far to undermine its social life as well. What is going to be the future of Nyasaland village life? Studies in other areas would show the relative importance of distinctive Nyasaland features such as the high density of population and the long established primary school system. But in all East and South African territories, with the possible exception of Uganda, the economic future of the Africans in their villages depends upon the policy followed for meeting the European demand for labour. Nor is it only the economic progress in rural areas which is threatened. The future of "indirect rule," which can only be built on stable social life in the villages, is at stake. For these reasons I hope that it will be possible to view migrant labour problems from the point of view of the tribal villages and their future, as well as from the point of view of labour engaged in industry.

31 ⁂ LAND TENURE AND AGRICULTURAL
IMPROVEMENT IN TROPICAL
AFRICA*

H. A. Oluwasanmi

During the past fifty years most of the old assumptions underlying indigenous social and economic institutions in tropical Africa
have undergone radical and fundamental changes. This is the inevitable and logical result of the contact of two cultures. In many
respects the changes are of such magnitude that old nomenclatures
fail to describe adequately the resultant institutions. This observa-
tion is particularly true of tropical land tenure. New economic and
social forces have registered themselves on the age-old system of
tenure with a greater impact than elsewhere in the social system,
partly because land is basic to the procurement of the elementary
needs of life, and partly because land is more closely tied to the
social and cultural values of the people.

Communal land tenure, still the predominant form of land
holding in tropical Africa, and the system of shifting cultivation
commonly associated with it developed under conditions in which
there was an abundant supply of land and the man-land ratio was
relatively low. So long as these situations existed the only serious
problem confronting the cultivator was that of the periodic selection of new sites for cultivation. This situation is, however, no
longer static. We will examine briefly the economic and social forces
at work in the changing pattern of tenure.

The partial commercialization of agriculture with its implication of conscious production of surpluses for the market—more
especially production for the export market—introduced new elements into the traditional system of tenure. The cultivation of
cocoa may be cited as an instance where production for exchange
has modified customary land tenure. As a perennial, cocoa ties up
land for a longer period than do the crops typical of subsistence

* From H. A. Oluwasanmi, "Land Tenure and Agricultural Improvement in Tropical
Africa," *Journal of Farm Economics*, No. 39, August 1957. Reprinted by permission.

farming. Since the right of the cultivator over trees planted by him is recognized under the traditional system of tenure, cocoa plantation means an indefinite interest on the part of the peasant in a plot of land and the abrogation of shifting cultivation.

Furthermore, the cultivator has the right to mortgage his crops (although not the land), or pledge them against indebtedness. At death the cultivator can also transfer the right over these cultivated trees to his heirs, thus indirectly impinging, or limiting the reversionary land rights to the community.

The growth of population in recent years has also affected old conceptions of land tenure. In Nigeria the population was calculated at roughly twenty million in 1931. Twenty years later the population reached the thirty million mark. This unprecedented upsurge in population means a drastic reduction in the period of bush fallow, and consequently, the deterioration of soil fertility. In some divisions of Owerri, Onitsha and Calabar Provinces of Eastern Nigeria where the density of population varies from 300 to 800 or more persons to the square mile, increased population has led to extreme fragmentation of holdings and the emergence of a quasi-individualization of tenure. In the circumstances, the cultivator not unnaturally regards his uneconomic holding as his absolute possession. The reversionary right of the community to this patch of land is however unimpaired by the process of fragmentation. In the event of death, or in cases where the cultivator and his family or their heirs fail to cultivate the land or use it in a manner beneficial to society, the right of the land-holding group to arrogate to itself rights of ownership remains unquestioned. This fact remains the true test of ownership in commonalty.

Social forces also combine with the purely economic forces to influence tenure practices in tropical Africa. The term "commune" in the indigenous society, especially as it relates to land matters, is coterminous with the extended family or the clan. The chief of the clan, or the head of the family was the sole authority in all matters pertaining to the administration of land. The emergence of new economic and social classes deriving their power and prestige from such unorthodox sources as material wealth and formal Western education has made a deep inroad in the authority of the tribal chieftain over land matters. As the traditional and narrower concept of "community" acquires greater flexibility in interpretation so also has the power of the tribal chieftain diminished. This breakdown in traditional loyalties reflects itself inevitably in the administration of land.

There are numerous cases in Nigeria in which one branch of an extended family, or a division of a land-holding group has alienated portions of communal land without reference to other interested parties, and usually in defiance of customary usage and authority. Avaricious chiefs, rich and educated individuals of land-holding communities have been quick in grasping the changed economic conditions that are fast turning land into an economic good. Such individuals have in some cases used their superior knowledge and resources to acquire communal property for their private use. This tendency to private appropriation of communal property is more widespread in the urban areas where the impact of trade and commerce has resulted in increased land values, and in the more densely populated areas where increasing population is slowly conferring upon land a scarcity value that it never possessed in the traditional system. Also English and other European legal ideas have intruded upon the traditional tenure system. In many urban areas in Nigeria, notably Lagos, Port Harcourt, Ibadan, Aba and Onitsha, the English concept of individual ownership in land has become the rule rather than the exception. In these urban areas land is freely transferred by sale, mortgage or lease. This practice is slowly extending to the rural areas.

It is clear from the foregoing that the growth of an exchange economy, pressure of population, foreign legal ideas and the introduction of new types of crops constitute the major influences in the changing pattern of African land tenure. Whatever influence the slave trade, the two World Wars, the infiltration of Americanism, monotheism, adult suffrage and fiscal policy might have exerted in the growth of individualism in tropical Africa, a closer examination of the facts compels us to conclude that the effects of these forces on land tenure have been peripheral and indirect. The changes in land tenure, especially the tendency towards individual holding, are direct and spontaneous reactions to new economic and social forces. These changes, together with the incipient growth in certain areas of the country of capitalist land-owners, call for a thorough appraisal of present land policy to determine its adequacy for agricultural and economic development.

In Nigeria and in other parts of British tropical Africa official policy has long reconciled itself to the Lugardian theory that economic progress, more especially agricultural improvement, is synonymous with the progressive individualization of tenure. Freehold right in land was and is still considered a natural evolution from primitive collectivism to individual enterprise; in addition, it is believed that individual right in land "would so effectively tend to emancipate the peasant class from the servile attitude of mind which long generations of slavery had induced in them . . ."

The assumed superiority of individual right in land over communal ownership can be validated only when it can be conclusively demonstrated that the former has superior economic and social advantages that are lacking in the latter. Such conclusive proof of superiority is yet to be advanced by the advocates of individual rights in land. Instead, it must be observed that communal tenure enjoys certain inherent social advantages that are absent from the individual forms of tenure.

From the purely social standpoint communal tenure acts as a strong cohesive force in an agrarian society. The system affords the cultivator a stake in the major assets of the community and assures him a secure place in society. By banning sale of land the system precludes the rise of a landed aristocracy and thereby removes much of the source of social unrest inherent in the landlord-tenant relations elsewhere. In India and most Middle East countries a system of peasant proprietorship has been in operation for many years. The heavy indebtedness of the peasantry to middle-men and money-lenders in these countries raises doubt as to the ability of individual tenure with its unbridled freedom of transfer by sale to emancipate the peasant from serfdom.

To determine how efficiently a given system of tenure performs its economic functions it is necessary to know whether under that system land is utilized in such a way as to give maximum yield and maintain the soil in "good heart." Given an abundant supply of land, sparse population and subsistence farming, communal tenure constitutes no insurmountable hindrance to the attainment of sustained maximum yield. The system recognizes the need for maintaining fertility and assures this by providing for a long period of fallow during which the soil regains its fertility through the process of natural regeneration. But as we have already seen these assumptions are undergoing tremendous changes. For instance, increases in population have introduced some of the worst defects of any agricultural organization, notably soil mining and excessive sub-division. Soil mining is not confined to communal forms of land holding; but the process is accelerated in a communal system where as a result of population pressures the period of fallow is considerably reduced.

As a result in the change in the economy of Nigeria the old system of tenure has become a slow, ineffectual, and inadequate vehicle of effecting fundamental changes in agricultural practices. It is therefore vitally important to evolve a system of tenure that will preserve all that is best in the old system and permit at the same time the introduction of innovating techniques in agriculture. As a prerequisite to evolving a more satisfactory system of tenure the concept of ownership and control needs to be re-examined in the light of changing social conditions. This is particularly true of the ownership and control of uncultivated bushland.

Within the traditional framework of tenure the responsibility of the community over land is clear and unmistakable. In the "tribe-state," authority in land matters is vested in the head of the family or in the chief of the clan. One of the most significant facts in tropical Africa today is the rapidity with which larger territorial aggregates are supplanting tribal units. These new entities are acquiring the political and social functions once performed by the tribal authority. It follows inevitably that for an orderly economic development the "nation-state," as the logical heir to the fast-disappearing tribal order, should acquire one of the latter's most potent responsibilities—responsibility over land matters. The state as the communal landlord should be vested with authority over uncultivated bush and waste. It should be in a position to utilize the uncultivated bushland in much the same manner as the tribal authority disposed of virgin land.

The system of ownership advocated here will preserve in the larger social aggregate the beneficial features of the communal system; in addition, it will enable the government to "enclose" large areas of unused land for resettlement and other agricultural projects without paying the heavy compensations now required under existing legislation. Lugard's argument in favor of government control of uncultivated bushland still constitutes the most eloquent statement of the problem extant:

> "It is not necessary to demonstrate that the development and the assignment of such lands should be controlled by Government. It often happens that a Village Community, or even a whole tribe, dwindles in population while its neighbour may be rapidly increasing till there is not enough land to provide for its actual food requirements. The necessary adjustments were in former times made by inter-tribal war, accompanied by the extermination and enslavement of the weaker. Under British rule such arbitrament has ceased, and it follows that the Suzerain power must in such cases exercise supreme control over land, which has become waste, even though it may disclaim any right to interfere with the titles to occupied land."

"Enclosure" as conceived here differs from compulsory registration of titles to existing holdings. What is intended here is free and unfettered access to the uncultivated bushland by the state which, under the existing economic conditions in the underdeveloped tropics, must continue to be the prime mover of projects of agricultural improvement. Registration of titles to the three-acre peasant holdings, or what is called "enclosure" by certain writers will not of itself compel the peasant producer to adopt improved methods of husbandry. As long as he is free to range over the uncultivated bushland as heretofore, there will hardly be any incentive for him to cultivate grass and legume as fallow crops, or to accept the arduous task of tending livestock. It would indeed be premature "to tie down cultivators to fixed areas until we can indicate to them with confidence agricultural methods which are likely to yield better returns."

But as conscious resettlement schemes and plantation projects encroach on the wild domain and reduce the area within which the shifting cultivator can operate, the peasant farmer will be induced either to leave his land and accept wage employment on the plantations or adopt permanent cultivation. In addition, the superior economic conditions of the farmers in the settlement schemes and on the plantations will act as a powerful incentive to the individual proprietor to emulate the example of his neighbours. Unless the government and enterprising individuals can colonize the bushland without the burden of excessive compensation the process of introducing innovating techniques in agriculture is bound to be slow and socially costly.

32  CULTURE CHANGE UNDER PRESSURE:
A HAUSA CASE*

Horace Miner

The Anchau Scheme [a program of resettlement, health improvement and economic development instituted by the British Colonial government among the Hausa of Northern Nigeria] was

* From Horace Miner, "Culture Change Under Pressure: A Hausa Case." Reprinted by permission from *Human Organization*, Vol. 19, No. 3 (Fall 1960). Published by the Society for Applied Anthropology. Subcription is by membership in the Society.

originally developed to meet a specific problem—the widespread occurrence of sleeping sickness among the Hausa.

The British instituted a special investigation of sleeping sickness in 1921, but it was not until 1928 that they discovered that the disease had reached epidemic proportions and was rapidly decimating the population. Interestingly, the epidemic was an indirect result of the advent of *Pax Britannica*. Before the conquest of northern Nigeria in 1903, the area was in a state of turbulence as a result of incessant slave raids. Towns were heavily walled and the working of fields at any distance from the towns involved considerable risk. Large areas of the countryside were uninhabited and communication was limited. Although there was an area of endemic sleeping sickness to the south and tsetse flies were prevalent all over the North at this time, the disease remained localized. With the establishment of peace, farmers moved out into the bush and mobility increased generally. The increased fly-man contact soon produced the epidemic.

Field surveys showed that in some areas up to forty percent of the people had the disease. The basic problem was that, although there were effective curative drugs, they did little good as long as reinfection from tsetse fly bites was inevitable. The government established a research station to attack the problem and Dr. T. A. M. Nash, the staff entomologist, discovered that the tsetse fly could only live in a microclimate distinctly cooler than the generally prevailing temperatures in sunlight. The fly was therefore confined to the shaded banks of streams, the rest of the country being generally open. It was at fords and water holes that fly-man contact occurred.

Tests revealed that if the brush was cut down along the streams, the fly could not persist in the area. On the basis of these findings the Anchau Scheme was drawn up to initiate control measures in the worst affected region. The proposal was to keep the stream banks clear in an area of 700 square miles within which lived some 50,000 people. In order to accomplish this end, part of the population had to be resettled to create sufficient density to provide the manpower to keep the streams cleared.

In order to understand the Hausa reactions to the program, we must describe those elements of Hausa culture which are immediately relevant.

Important in this regard is their political organization. The Fulani conquest of the ancient Hausa, or Habe, States at the beginning of the nineteenth century resulted in the establishment of a series of feudally organized emirates. Each was autonomous and headed by an emir descended from the Fulani conquerors. The emirates were divided into fiefs, each allocated to a Fulani, commonly a relative of the emir. The fiefs in turn were divided into village areas, each under the control of a Hausa headman, resident in the principal settlement in his area. Even the headmen held their appointments subject to the approval of the emir. The functions of this hierarchy were the maintenance of order, the organization of defensive and offensive forces, and the collection of taxes.

The emirs were all-powerful, even to the extent of interfering with the administration of Moslem justice by the cadis. The emir's position could only be jeopardized by alienating powerful groups of fiefholders. The latter were supreme within their domains as long as they kept the emir satisfied. The village headmen had the support of the fiefholder and his forces but, in the regulation of mundane affairs within the village area, the headman's power derived directly from the support accorded him by his villagers. Being a Hausa, his traditional role depended upon his understanding and manipulation of the local culture.

Even with peers the Hausa peasant adheres to elaborate forms of politeness. The deference shown to superiors is almost oriental in flavor. In the presence of the *hakimi,* or lord of the fief, a peasant removes his sandals, prostrates himself and remains bowed to the ground, keeps his eyes lowered, speaks only when addressed, and employs highly formalized deferential phrases when he does speak. He would never think of expressing a point of view contrary to that of the *hakimi.* Village headmen, although they are peasants themselves, are treated with extreme politeness but the system permits greater freedom of expression with these arbiters of village problems. In summary we may say that Hausa society, including its overlords, is very hierarchically organized. The advent of the British did little to change this except to limit some of the excesses of the emirs and fiefholders. Indirect rule was studiously adhered to. Although British district officers were appointed to oversee colonial administration at the local level, all administrative acts were promulgated by British authorities through the emirs. If problems arose at the local level, recommendations were made upward through the Colonial channels, the emir was persuaded to act, and the directives came down the indigenous lines of power. Because of the powerful position of the British vis-à-vis the emir and because the district officer had access to top colonial officials, a district officer could, if so inclined, wield a considerable amount of derived power in his relation to a *hakimi.*

Another aspect of the Hausa power system involves the cultural devices for holding the power of the overlords within reasonable bounds. One method which the peasants employ in limiting the nominal omnipotence of their rulers is passive resistance. When a headman transmits orders from the *hakimi* which the peasants do not want to follow, they simply fail to comply. The headman can exert his influence to try to secure compliance, but his power in only as strong as his local support. General resistance to repeated orders may be continued until sanctions are applied by the *hakimi*. Such sanctions consist of fines or jail terms and the headman may be replaced if he has been sufficiently noncooperative.

In addition to the political structure, the other aspect of Hausa culture most relevant to the Anchau plan for sleeping sickness control is native belief concerning the nature and cause of the disease. These ideas are best understood in relation to Western concepts. In its most characteristic Nigerian form, sleeping sickness produces sporadic fever, headache, edema of the face and limbs, accompanied by swelling of the cervical glands and persistent weakness. The condition may continue for years but the associated lowered resistance to disease frequently results in death from other causes. Death may even result from a flareup of the toxic effects of sleeping sickness itself, without the central nervous system becoming involved so as to produce the classic condition of continued somnolence and mental disorder. The proportion of patients who show these latter symptoms is always small. This form of the disease is normally fatal and even with treatment the patient may not recover. If he does, he will still show damage to the nervous system. The more prevalent form of sleeping sickness is not easily recognized, even by doctors, unless they have had experience with the disease. On a number of occasions medical officers sent out to investigate epidemics of what later proved to be sleeping sickness failed to diagnose the underlying sickness and reported that the people were dying of pneumonia.

The Hausa recognized only the rarely occurring sleeping and mania symptoms as characterizing the disease *ciwon barci,* a literal translation of "sleeping sickness." They did not recognize the other more prevalent symptoms as characterizing any single disease and, in fact, most of the symptoms occur separately in connection with other maladies. *Ciwon barci* was greatly feared for it was fatal and believed to be highly contagious. Any Hausa so afflicted was completely isolated, even from his family. Although he might be driven from the community, he was more usually fed by a relative who avoided any contact with the patient or his utensils. Not infrequently the mentally deranged invalid would wander off and starve before he died of his disease. When treatment was attempted, it consisted of herbal remedies or written Koranic charms.

Some of the other terms employed to identify sleeping sickness are indicative of Hausa beliefs as to its cause. The disease was also known as *kunturu,* a word which also designates a region which has a reputation of being under evil supernatural influence. *Dudduru* refers to the disease and also means a small stream with wooded banks. Both words refer to the fundamental belief that sleeping sickness is caused by *iska,* or spirits, who live in natural features such as clumps of brush along the streams. The Galma River, which flows to the south of Anchau, is considered to be infested with malevolent spirits and the area is actually still dangerous for sleeping sickness. Because spirits are local, the only way to escape their effects is to leave the region. Whole villages have moved when threatened with epidemic disease. Although such action might remove a population from an area badly infested with tsetse, the insects were ubiquitous and complete escape was impossible. While the Hausa thus recognized the relation between the habitat of the tsetse fly and sleeping sickness, the role of the fly in the transmission of the disease was unknown—the *iska* were the vector.

Against the background just sketched, we are in a position to consider Hausa reactions to the methods of sleeping sickness control instituted by the British. Even before the Anchau Scheme went into operation, medical officers had made an intensive survey of the population to determine the extent of sleeping sickness and to provide treatment. Clinical diagnosis followed by microscopic verification revealed large numbers of cases who showed none of the classic symptoms. Even when tests proved the presence of the infection, the Hausa were very loath to admit that they had the awful disease which previously made them outcasts. Still today, a headman may deny that there is any sleeping sickness in his village, although he knows of cases under treatment. The British interpret these facts as representing a feeling of shame concerning the disease. On the other hand, there is considerable doubt that the Hausa ever accepted the idea that what they and the British called sleeping sickness were really the same thing. None of the old fear of the disease was felt toward medically diagnosed cases which did not fit the Hausa concept of sleeping sickness. The conflicting conceptions need not be resolved now, for advanced cases have disappeared entirely.

When the Anchau Scheme went into operation, the system of indirect rule was adhered to and the necessary orders were issued through the Emir. To strengthen the native authority channel and to reinforce on-the-spot interpretations of the Emir's orders, the Emir was persuaded to send a personal representative to remain in Anchau. Through him the British personnel could put immediate pressure on the *Hakimi,* whose residence was permanently transferred to Anchau. These changes resulted in a concentration of authority previously unknown in the area. The resettlement phase of the Scheme brought together the scattered peasants so that they were under administrative scrutiny of a sort they dearly loved to avoid. The *Hakimi* found he was no longer the highest local official and even the Emir ultimately complained that, as a result of the intense British activity around Anchau, he had been deprived of part of his emirate. In short, while native channels of power were used, everyone along the line felt under unusual adminstrative pressure. This method of administration of the Scheme did have one very important implication for the success of the plan. The specific methods of implementation of many of its aspects were left up to the native authorities and the acculturative adjustments to the changes were as little disruptive to the local culture as they could be.

Before stream clearance was begun, the reasons for it were explained to the Hausa from the Emir to the village elders. They were told that sleeping sickness was common among them, that it was caused by little "fish-like animals" in the blood, that these animals got into the blood when a person was bitten by a tsetse fly, and that the way to get rid of the flies was to cut down the brush along the streams. As we have seen, these statements were in conflict with native beliefs and the explanation of the idea of microörganisms was entirely beyond their experience and comprehension. It is also clear that the Hausa patterns of respect toward superiors made it impossible for them to question openly what they were told. As a result, the British were effectively isolated from any knowledge of their failure to convey to the Hausa any real understanding of what was being done.

Initial stream clearance was carried out with hired native labor. In at least two instances local Hausa refused to cut certain patches of brush because these were sacred and inhabited by spirits. Finally non-Hausa natives from the French Sudan were used to cut the sacred brush. Once the streams were cleared, a plan was drawn up to provide for annual slashing thereafter. Each headman was impressed with his responsibility and the benefits which his village would derive from the elimination of the flies. On a rough average, some two weeks of part-time communal labor would be involved during a period of agricultural inactivity. Orders for the first reslashing went out from the Emir, through the *Hakimi.* The British supervisors and native foremen appeared at the villages to oversee the work but the communal laborers failed to appear. Subsequent attempts to secure cooperation produced only a handful of men and they arrived hours late. Exasperated, the British forced the Emir to stringent action. Headmen were removed from office and fines imposed on the peasants. These methods ultimately produced results. By checking the operations year after year, the pattern of annual stream clearance was finally established.

The result of the disease treatment and the eradication of the fly was the virtual elimination of sleeping sickness. The population began to increase and even migrants came to fill up the land now free from disease. For the past ten years there have been no Scheme personnel at Anchau but a thorough check of the streams showed that the annual orders of the Emir have been carried out in almost all instances and that the area is still virtually free of fly and sleeping sickness. One may well conclude that this, the major phase of the scheme, has been a success. In terms of culture change, the Hausa have for twenty years carried out a new pattern of behavior which is essential for the biological preservation of the group.

It comes as something of a shock, therefore, to discover that stream clearance cannot be said to have been adopted into the culture of the Hausa around Anchau. The basis for such a statement is an exhaustive study of the present attitudes and conceptions of village headmen regarding sleeping sickness and its control. The village leaders were asked why they cleared the streams every year. The common denominator of the responses was that the slashing was carried out because they were forced to do it. A quarter of the headmen literally had no idea why the work was done. All of the others, however, stated that clearing the brush eliminated the tsetse fly, although sometimes this response was added as an afterthought to an initial statement of ignorance of any reason for the task.

Half of those who mentioned flies also stated that they transmitted sleeping sickness. But when one pursued the subject, it became clear that this was a simple repetition of what they had been told. They saw this as the British explanation, but held firmly to their old belief that sleeping sickness was caused by spirits. Elimination of the flies was rationalized by others as desirable because the bite was painful. Still others saw the clearing as a means of driving out crop-destroying monkeys or of improving pasturage for Fulani cattle. Finally, the interviews produced that rarity in social science data, unanimous concurrence. When asked if they would continue to clear the streams if they were not forced to do so, every headman replied, "No."

To recapitulate what happened at Anchua, it is clear that the Hausa experienced no particular need to eliminate sleeping sickness as they knew it. The new culture pattern of stream clearance was adopted and continued solely because of the need to escape administrative sanctions applied in traditional ways. The fact that the new trait was never effectively related to local problems and beliefs produced the anomaly of the adoption of an innovation without its integration into the culture. We find that coercion can produce compliance without any fundamental cultural alteration.

FURTHER READINGS

Bovill, E. W., *The Golden Trade of the Moors,* London: Oxford University Press, 1958. A delightful book that traces the history of the Western Soudan from the time of the earliest Arabic contacts.

Carter, G., *The Politics of Inequality,* New York: Praeger and Co., 1959. A carefully documented study of South African politics since 1948.

Coleman, J. S., and Almond, G. A., *The Politics of the Developing Areas,* Princeton: Princeton University Press, 1960. Written within a highly analytical framework, but most rewarding for its attempt to synthesize and generalize.

Dike, K. O., *Trade and Politics in the Niger Delta 1830–1885,* Oxford: The University Press, 1956. An excellent history by an African historian who is now Principal of the University College, Ibadan, Nigeria. Very readable.

Fortes, M., and Evans-Pritchard, E. E., *African Political Systems,* London: Oxford University Press, 1955. Eight studies of indigenous political systems.

Hailey, Lord, *An African Survey: Revised 1956,* London: Oxford University Press, 1957. A standard general work for nearly two decades, thoroughly revised.

Hance, W., *African Economic Development,* New York: Harper and Brothers for the Council on Foreign Relations, 1958. A series of essays, some of them case studies, on problems of economic development. Readable and penetrating.

Hodgkin, T., *Nationalism in Colonial Africa,* New York: New York University Press, 1957. Draws upon fairly specialized material, especially from French-speaking Africa, but possibly one of the finest and most penetrating books of the many that have been published since the Second World War.

Howard, C., *West African Explorers,* Axelson, E., *South African Explorers,* Richards, C., and Place, J., *East African Explorers,* London: Oxford University Press, 1951–1960. Three books in the *World's Classics Series* consisting of collected readings from the journals and reports of some of Africa's most famous explorers. Well chosen and edited.

Kimble, G. H. T., *Tropical Africa,* Vol. I *Land and Livelihood,* Vol. II *Society and Polity,* New York. Twentieth Century Foundation, 1960. A good, well-written general work by a geographer. The first volume is highly recommended.

Oliver, R., and Fage, J. D., *A History of Africa,* London: Cambridge University Press, 1960. An excellent introduction to the history of Africa by two historians who have specialized in different areas of the continent.

Wolfson, F., *A Pageant of Ghana,* London: Oxford University Press, 1957. A collection of short readings about Ghana from the time of discovery by the Portuguese at the end of the fifteenth century to the present day.

Young, R., and Fosbrooke, H., *Smoke in the Hills: Political Tensions in the Morogoro District of Tanganyika,* Evanston: Northwestern University Press, 1960. A case study for the specialist, but a fascinating book focusing upon the problem of maintaining a stable society in a period of political and economic transition.